ROUTLEDGE LIB
SOCIAL AND CULTUI

CW00747505

—

Volume 4

THE GIFT ECONOMY

THE GIFT ECONOMY

DAVID CHEAL

Routledge
Taylor & Francis Group

LONDON AND NEW YORK

First published in 1988 by Routledge

This edition first published in 2016
by Routledge
2 Park Square, Milton Park, Abingdon, Oxon OX14 4RN

and by Routledge
711 Third Avenue, New York, NY 10017

Routledge is an imprint of the Taylor & Francis Group, an informa business

British Library Cataloguing in Publication Data
A catalogue record for this book is available from the British Library

ISBN: 978-1-138-92596-0 (Set)
ISBN: 978-1-315-68041-5 (Set) (ebk)
ISBN: 978-1-138-92828-2 (Volume 4) (hbk)
ISBN: 978-1-138-92831-2 (Volume 4) (pbk)
ISBN: 978-1-315-68182-5 (Volume 4) (ebk)

Publisher's Note
The publisher has gone to great lengths to ensure the quality of this reprint but points out that some imperfections in the original copies may be apparent.

Disclaimer
The publisher has made every effort to trace copyright holders and would welcome correspondence from those they have been unable to trace.

The Gift
Economy

David Cheal

ROUTLEDGE

London and New York

First published in 1988 by
Routledge
11 New Fetter Lane, London EC4P 4EE

Published in the USA by
Routledge
in association with Routledge, Chapman and Hall, Inc.
29 West 35th Street, New York NY 10001

Typeset in Linotron Bembo 10/11½pt
by Input Typesetting Ltd, London
Printed in Great Britain at the University Press, Cambridge

British Library Cataloguing in Publication Data
Cheal, David, 1945–
    The gift economy.
    1. Man. Social interactions. Role of gifts
    1. Title
    302

Library of Congress Cataloging in Publication Data
Cheal, David J.
    The gift economy.
    Bibliography: p.
    Includes indexes.
    1. Gifts.   2. Ceremonial exchange.   I. Title.
    GT3040.C48   1988   394   87–37643

ISBN 0–415–00641–4

The author gratefully acknowledges permission to use material from the following
sources: From Max Weber, H. H. Gerth and C. Wright-Mills, Oxford University Press; Symbolic Interactionism: Perspective and Method, H. Blumer,
Prentice-Hall, Inc., © H. Blumer 1969; Prisms, pp. 19–20, T. Adrono (trans.
S. and S. Weber), MIT Press, © Theodor W. Adorno 1967; Emile Durkheim
on Institutional Analysis, p. 234, M. Traugott, University of Chicago Press,
1978; 'The female world of love and ritual', C. Smith-Rosenberg, Signs 1 (1),
p. 11; 'Reference groups as perspectives', T. Shibutani, American Journal of
Sociology 60, pp. 562–9.

For Chris
1948–1983

Contents

Preface

Everyone has given a gift at some time, and for many people gift giving is a frequent activity from which they derive a great deal of pleasure. As an economic activity gift giving plays an important part in our lives and in the consumer goods industries. It therefore deserves to be better understood. Of course, gift transactions are not responsible for the great problems of our age, about which we hear so much. Social scientists studying modern societies have tended to pass over the gift economy as a subject for investigation, preferring to address economic issues that have more serious consequences. But in case gift giving appears to be an unserious subject, it is important to realize that in it are reflected many of the important issues of modern times. How people act in their gift transactions is a result of how they think about relations between the sexes and between the generations. Also, gift practices can be powerfully affected by economic and demographic change, and by the hopes and fears of ordinary people faced with personal crises, including the threat of nuclear war. In short, gift giving is as much a part of the struggle for existence in the modern world as is any other form of social behavior. At the very least, studying gift behavior gives us a window through which we can look into people's lives and see for ourselves what it is that moves modern men and women.

In this book a number of case studies of individuals have been presented, beginning in chapter 3, in which the connections between gift giving and everyday life have been described in some detail. Readers who are most interested in those materials may wish to skip the first two chapters, which deal with matters that are of special interest to the professional social scientist.

For social scientists the most challenging parts of this book are likely to be those that deal with the relative neglect of the gift economy by students of modern society. In addition to the pressures to make research relevant to social problems, there are two additional reasons why the modern gift economy has received little attention. One of them is that contemporary gift giving is normally a private activity, which is often carried out by women. Along with many similar topics it has therefore suffered from the benign neglect of a male-dominated discipline that has been more concerned with public issues and political solutions. In the research reported in these pages it is mostly women's voices that we will hear, because women are more active gift givers than men. The gender distribution of involvement in gift transactions is not coincidental, and its social significance should not be ghettoized within women's studies. Rather, it deserves to be taken seriously by sociology as part of a broader picture of how the modern gift economy works.

Arriving at that conclusion has been easy at the empirical level, but it has not been at all easy at the theoretical level. That brings us on to the third major reason why gift giving has been so little understood (and, I would argue, so often misunderstood) in the social sciences. We have not had an adequate conceptual framework with which to think about gift giving as a type of economic activity in modern society. That does not mean that we have had no theories of gift behavior. In actual fact there has never been any shortage of people willing to theorize about modern gift practices, often in grandiose terms. But there has been a great shortage of research related to theory. Most research on gift giving has been oriented towards data collection (that is, it has been empiricist). On the rare occasions when important theoretical issues have been raised in a research context, sociologists have tended to waver between structural functionalism and exchange theory. The difficulties involved in choosing one or the other approach suggest that neither is adequate to the task. In this book a deliberate effort has been made to integrate theory and research, and we shall move backwards and forwards between them. In the first two chapters we take up preliminary theoretical and methodological issues, drawn from several disciplines, in order to establish the perspective employed here. In those two chapters, and in subsequent chapters, I have tried to show where I think the views of others are wrong, and why I think they have been wrong.

The conclusions presented in the following pages have been arrived at from reflection upon the results of three years of field research, conducted in the period 1981 to 1984. During that time a number of investigations were carried out, ranging from small-scale participant observation to a random sample survey of the city of Winnipeg. A variety of materials is therefore presented below, but most of the information in this book is drawn from one study

– the Winnipeg Ritual Cycle Study – which is described in chapter 2. Wherever direct comparison has been possible, the patterns of gift behavior recorded in that study have been found to be consistent in most important respects with the findings from Theodore Caplow's Middletown USA study, and with findings from both national and local surveys in Canada. It is therefore reasonable to hope that a cumulative body of data is emerging that will soon enable us to place the sociology of the gift economy upon a firm footing.

During the years in which I have been engaged in research on gift giving I have received assistance from a number of individuals and organizations. Financially, the work could not have been conducted without generous support from the Social Sciences and Humanities Research Council of Canada. Supplementary support was provided by the Research and Travel Committee of the University of Winnipeg, and by a Government of Canada Work/ Study grant, administered through the University of Winnipeg Students Association. I have also benefited from the knowledge and skills of a large number of people. The following individuals deserve special recognition: Raymond F. Currie (1984 Winnipeg Area Study), Mary Gummeson, Meryth Suderman, Wylma Mitchell, Patty Rennick and Pat Cook (interviewing), Leslie Bowen and Ruth Anderson (coding), Maria Skoulas and Ian Lark (graphics), John Hilton and Holly Hardmann (programing), Glen Koroluk (data entry, programing), and Judy Shalay, Erin Rowe and Sandra Murphy (typing). These individuals are not responsible for the uses that I have made of their contributions. Finally, I wish to thank all those people who so generously gave their time to be interviewed.

1

Moral economy

In recent years, many of the most interesting developments in the scientific study of society have occurred at the boundaries between economics and the other social sciences. New approaches to economic life have reshaped the ways in which we think about familiar economic processes, such as labor markets. At the same time, there has been an upswing of interest in forms of economic life that were previously ignored. One of them is gift giving.

It is surprising that we know so very little about the reasons why we give things to others, for we do know that a great many people derive a great deal of pleasure from the act of giving. Yet, as social scientists, we do not possess ways of talking about this that make sense of everyday gift transactions in industrial societies. Researchers interested in social policy issues have drawn increasing attention to the many forms that giving, altruism, and self sacrifice take. As a result, it is now recognized that existing social theories have been inadequate, and that new ideas are needed. Further, it has sometimes been suggested that these alternative approaches must break with influential theoretical traditions in sociology and related disciplines (Stacey 1981).

In this book we will explore some of the limits to existing sociological traditions, as well as the possibilities that they contain. It will be suggested that the concepts of mainstream social theory are not as deficient as has sometimes been claimed, and that they can still throw new light upon important questions. At the same time, it is clear that many of the old answers no longer serve us well. In this chapter we are going to examine why it is that gift giving has not been seen as a significant social phenomenon in the study of modern societies, and we will consider what might be done to recover it as a topic for sociological theory. In addition, claims about gift practices that are not supported by the available evidence deserve to be exposed and, where they cannot be improved, discarded.

Sociological studies of gift behavior have been uncommon. In anthropology the situation has been quite different. Gift transactions in primitive societies have been intensively studied, and a great deal is known about them. From time to time anthropologists have pointed to the need for similar investigations to be conducted in modern societies (Belshaw 1965: 49–51; Firth 1967: 17; Munn 1973: 607–8). Despite that encouragement, sustained work on modern gift practices has been undertaken only very recently. The reasons for this neglect can be traced to the considerable influence among the social sciences of two theoretical approaches. They are *anthropological elementarism* and *political economy*.

The major barrier to the development of a sociology of gift practices has been the tendency to see them as archaic customs, whose influence on social life has been in decline for a long time. Marcel Mauss, for example, felt that in modern times gift morality must depend upon "people and classes who uphold past customs" (Mauss 1954: 63). He claimed that giving to others reappears in our own society "like the resurrection of a dominant motif long forgotten" (1954: 66). The conclusions that Mauss drew from this antiquarian approach to gift transactions have had such an enormous influence upon the social sciences (e.g. Lévi-Strauss 1969; Bourdieu 1977) that they deserve our close attention.

Beyond elementary structures

Mauss maintained that the study of the gift involved a "return to the old and elemental" (Mauss 1954: 67). That point of view, which Ekeh refers to as *elementarism* (1982: 128–32), Mauss derived from his mentor Emile Durkheim. Durkheim (1947: 4–7) believed that sociology would sometimes have to ignore things that are "secondary" in order to concentrate on the "essential" features of phenomena, as they appear in primitive societies. Mauss applied Durkheim's method to an analysis of the gift (Mauss 1954). He concluded that the essential features of gift transactions are the obligation to give, the obligation to receive, and the obligation to make a return for gifts received. Mauss's discussion of the latter has been particularly influential, and others have subsequently claimed that the norm of reciprocity is a cultural universal (Gouldner 1960). That point of view remains strong in the French sociological tradition (Maffesoli 1979).

The reputation of the French tradition of elementarism has owed a great deal to the claims made by Claude Lévi-Strauss (see especially Lévi-Strauss 1969: 268), who argued that universal structures of reciprocity are the foundations for all social life. Lévi-Strauss was fascinated by the potlatching of certain groups of North American Indians, and he believed that direct parallels could be drawn between it and gift practices in modern societies. He claimed that Christmas gift giving in contemporary North America "is nothing other than a gigantic potlatch" (1969: 56) conducted in the pursuit of prestige. That conclusion, which has been echoed in other anthropological commentaries (for example, Shurmer 1971), holds that gift practices in modern western societies are merely exaggerated versions of the competitive struggles for power and status that are to be found in certain primitive forms of exchange.

From the elementarist point of view, the cultural significance of gift transactions lies in their being the building blocks for human society, in which they are "first and foremost a means of controlling others" (Mauss 1954: 73). It must therefore be emphasized, in opposition to this point of view, that achieving control over others by overwhelming them with gifts is likely to be found on a large scale only where more effective forms of domination do not exist. In modern societies there exist a variety of means of domination in which gifts play little part. Large scale gift giving today is therefore not easily explained by drawing an analogy with the potlatch.

The major difficulty with the elementarist approach to the study of social relations is that it ignores the situated character of social practices (Habermas 1970: 363–5). It overlooks the fact, described by Simmel (Wolff 1950), that the same form of behavior may have many different meanings according to the local context, and it may therefore appear in a wide range of interaction episodes with different social effects. The unfortunate consequence of the elementarist approach has been that the diversity of gift giving in modern societies has been ignored. As Ekeh has pointed out, from the perspective of cultural elementarism ways of life that are peculiar to modern societies have been disregarded as "nonessential accretions" (Ekeh 1982: 128). This neglect of the present has meant that we have only just begun to comprehend the dynamic nature of the gift economies of contemporary western societies.

Gift practices are, as Mauss suggested, rooted in custom and tradition. But gift customs are not fixed, for they have been affected by changes in the larger society, as Theodore Caplow has concluded (Caplow 1982, 1984; Caplow et al. 1982). Caplow claims that in the USA there has been an increase in the ritualization of family life, as a means of stabilizing relationships that are both important and insecure. In his opinion it is the vulnerability of family life in modern society that is responsible for the great importance attached to gift giving (Caplow 1982: 391–2). Among the threats to family relationships, it is thought, are temptations for wives and mothers to reduce the amount of nurturing they provide for family members so that they can take up paid employment (Caplow *et al.* 1982: 243). Caplow and his colleagues have suggested that the material rewards from participation in the labor market are countered by symbolic rewards for caring for others, which are produced in the rituals of the festival cycle (Caplow *et al.* 1982: 244).

The tension between market relationships and personal relationships is a distinctive characteristic of social life in capitalist societies. Clearly, that tension is not found in the simplest societies, where an institutionalized market economy does not exist. Knowledge of the elementary structures of primitive societies is therefore likely to be of dubious value in interpreting the gift practices of modern societies. For this reason it is necessary to abandon elementarism, and instead to approach the study of social life in a different manner.

Many sociologists who are interested in economic life in capitalist societies have followed a broad interdisciplinary approach that is sometimes referred to as the political economy paradigm (Marchak 1985). According to this approach, social relationships are believed to be determined by power structures whose origins lie in systems of property rights. It is claimed, following Marx, that the most important rights are those over the means by which the goods used in daily life are produced. Historical changes in modes of production, including the shift towards capital intensive manufacturing, are therefore believed to have had profound effects upon social organization. The theory of political economy provides particular accounts of those effects, which have been discussed extensively elsewhere (see for example Baudrillard 1975).

The position taken here is that gift transactions cannot be adequately understood from the perspective of political economy, since its assumptions include three theses which trivialize gift behavior. They are: the thesis of capitalist transformation; the thesis of emotional sequestration; and the thesis of economic rationalization. I shall argue here that the effects of each of these processes have been overstated. Gift giving in fact makes a vital contribution to contemporary social life. The nature of that contribution will be outlined in general terms in the following pages. In later chapters it will be described in greater detail, with illustrations from empirical case studies.

Capitalist transformations

The theory of political economy shares with cultural elementarism the assumption that gift giving was a uniquely important type of economic relationship in pre-capitalist societies, but that to all intents and purposes it was destroyed by the expansion of the system of market exchange. This point of view is evident in a number of influential histories, such as Karl Polanyi's (1957) description of "the great transformation" by which capitalism came into existence. It is generally assumed that the emergence of capitalist society meant that morals were replaced by markets (Thompson 1971; Zelizer 1979), and that gift transactions therefore became of lesser importance. Viviana Zelizer, for instance, has shown that in nineteenth-century America support for the bereaved shifted from a gift-type of mutual aid to an impersonal market system served by insurance companies. She reports that family and neighborhood transactions were replaced by transactions with organizations, and that the management of death therefore became rationalized and formalized. This change had some fundamental consequences for beliefs about life and death. According to Zelizer, it broke "a powerful normative pattern: the division between the marketable and the nonmarketable, or the sacred and the profane" (Zelizer 1979: 43).

It is possible to accept Zelizer's observations, as I think we must, without necessarily implying that the social significance of gift transactions has been drastically diminished. In the first place, people in the western societies continue to spend large amounts of money on gifts, particularly during the Christmas season (Caron and Ward 1975; Cramer 1977). It is therefore most likely that what has happened is a process of the differentiation of gift transactions within a changing moral order of economic relationships. As a result, gifts are no longer used principally as practical means for mutual aid, but instead they are symbolic media for managing the emotional aspects of relationships (Cheal 1986, 1987a).

The sequestration of sentiments

The theory of the political economy of capitalism has not entirely ignored emotions and symbolic processes. It has described them as being consigned to a private sphere of family ties, which are thought to be segregated from the public world of industry and politics. The theory of public and private spheres has been very influential, especially because it provides a way of accounting for the different social characteristics of women and men (Gamarnikow and Purvis 1983). Women, in the middle classes at least, have often been confined to the private sphere, and so their lives have revolved around care giving in ways that men's lives have not. A large amount of work has been conducted on this topic in recent years, including studies on gift giving.

According to the theory of privatized family life in capitalist society, family commitments are thought to be separated from public involvements and to be limited to a narrow range of relationships (Barrett and McIntosh 1982). These relationships are grounded in the reproduction of life itself, and in the reproduction of daily existence within domestic groups. In the sexual division of work most domestic labor has traditionally been performed by women, and so the maintenance of this private sphere has normally been defined as women's special responsibility.

In many ways the theory of segregated private and public spheres of action is a useful vantage point from which to explore the social dimensions of gift behavior. It has been able to explain a wide range of findings which no previous theory could have encompassed. Thus, it has been shown that generosity in private giving and generosity in public giving are predicted by different factors (Cheal 1987b); that the most valuable Christmas gifts are given to close family members, especially spouses (Cheal 1986); and that women are more active in all forms of gift giving than are men (Cheal 1987a). In addition, it has been possible to extend the theory of contradictory consciousness (Cheal 1979) to show how gift transactions are shaped by the unstable boundary between market exchange and family solidarity (Cheal 1987a).

The strongest argument for the distinction between public and private worlds is that it casts new light upon those activities of women which were rendered invisible by the public biases of mainstream social science (Reiter 1975; Yeatman 1984). Nevertheless, this approach has been criticized by some feminists as being oversimplified and deterministic (Eichler 1980). It is argued that upon close inspection the distinction between private action and public action dissolves into a multitude of overlapping and interdependent contexts for interactions between individuals.

The difficulties involved in dichotomizing social life into private and public domains can be illustrated with reference to the North American custom of women's gifts to brides at pre-wedding "showers" (Cheal 1988b). In many ways these occasions are intensely private events. At a bridal shower everyone is there by virtue of a personal relationship, either to the bride herself or to one of her relatives or friends. The location of a bridal shower in the private sphere is further affirmed by the exclusion of men, and by the fact that only those women who have been invited are expected to attend. Nevertheless, bridal showers are not entirely privatized. In Canada they are sometimes organized as large gatherings, in which some of the guests may be unrelated to the bride and may never have met her before. Clearly, under such circumstances a close relationship between a bride and her benefactors cannot be assumed, and private knowledge is replaced by formal organization. The public nature of these occasions is demonstrated by the fact that they are held in public places, such as community halls, and by the fact that the interaction rituals include formal introductions made as public announcements. Are hall showers, then, to be identified as private encounters or as public events? In truth they are both, or neither. They are ambiguous occasions with their own logic that defies any neat division of the world into watertight compartments (Cheal 1988a).

In later chapters we shall see that bridal showers raise other interesting questions for the sociology of contemporary gift behavior. Here we will simply note that bridal showers dramatically confirm the importance that many women have traditionally attached to giving to other women. The gendered value of giving has often been overlooked in theories of the political economy of gift transactions.

Economic rationalization

Gift giving is often described by sociological theorists as a process of exchange through which individuals rationally pursue their self interests. This point of view, known as social exchange theory (Emerson 1976, 1981), is evidently modelled upon the political economy of market transactions. According to the exchange theorists, such as Peter Blau (1964), the generosity that we observe in gift giving is only an apparent altruism. In reality, Blau maintains, giving to others is motivated by the expectation of some reward, whether direct (such as power over others) or indirect (such as social approval). Blau's arguments have not gone unchallenged

(Bochner 1984: 578–80; Cheal 1984), and they have recently been criticized from a feminist standpoint by Nancy Hartsock (1983b, 1985).

Hartsock (1983a) has pointed out that grand theories derived from the political economy of market relations have not paid sufficient attention to the experiences of women within the sexual division of labor. Exchange theory, for example, has a male bias towards competitive interaction and cannot describe the relations between mothers and growing children. Hartsock has therefore suggested that, "one could begin to see the outline of a very different kind of community if one took the mother/infant relation rather than market exchange as the prototypic human interaction" (Hartsock 1983b: 41–2).

Hartsock has argued that the institutionalization of motherhood "results in the construction of female existence as centered within a complex relational nexus" (Hartsock 1985: 64). The social construction of femininity has three aspects which, Hartsock claims (1985: 65–6), are incompatible with exchange theory. Firstly, the importance of empathy in women's self-definition contradicts the assumption in exchange theory that individuals are fundamentally separate and purely concerned with their own interests. Secondly, women's experiences do not support the view that all social relations conform to the market model of voluntary transactions. Those who are responsible for small children typically have little choice over whether or not to interact with them. And thirdly, unlike market relations, which necessarily involve an opposition of interests, conflict is not at the core of the relationships between mothers and their children.

The generosity of most parents towards their children, even adult children, has been remarked upon in a number of studies (Caplow 1982; Cheal 1983). This well-known pattern of behavior raises questions about the relevance of exchange theory for understanding intergenerational transfers, which have not been satisfactorily answered (Cheal 1988c). Some of those questions will be taken up in later chapters, and further discussion of social exchange will be postponed until then. For now it is sufficient to acknowledge that not all social life in a capitalist society is dominated by the rational acquisition of goods and influence.

From the fetishism of the gift to the management of interpersonal relations

It would seem that sociological inquiries into gift giving have been impeded by the combined effects of two influential approaches. In the first place, anthropological elementarism implies that the only significant forms of gift behavior are those that are presumed to have once existed in primitive societies. From this perspective, modern gift practices are deemed to be of little consequence for the development of social scientific knowledge. Theories of political economy have also ignored contemporary gift giving, which is considered to be a minor appendage to life in a capitalist society. Gifts are economically trivial, it is thought, because the capitalist mode of production has replaced gift transactions with market transactions (the thesis of capitalist transformation). The remnants of gift morality are further assumed to be confined to privatized family ties (the thesis of emotional sequestration), and it is suspected that beneath their sentimentality all gift exchanges are really conducted for personal gain (the thesis of economic rationalization). Clearly, if gift giving is to be recovered as a topic for sociological theory there is much work to be done.

To begin with, it is possible to show that when the perspectives of anthropological elementarism and political economy are applied to the study of gift giving, they lead to systematic errors that render them incapable of explaining everyday life in industrial societies. Several difficulties have already been noted above. It will help to bring these issues into focus more clearly if we consider the weaknesses in an account which combines the principles of both anthropological elementarism and political economy.

Gregory (1982) has theorized that there is a distinction to be drawn between the commodity economy of a class society and the non-commodity (or gift) economy of a clan-based society. The former, he argues, is to be explained by theories of political economy derived from the work of Marx, and the latter is to be explained by the anthropological theory of gifts derived from the work of Mauss (Gregory 1982: 18–19 especially). In an essay entitled "The Spirit of the Thing Given", Mauss observed that in certain societies the nature of the bond created by the transfer of a possession is due to the fact that "the thing itself is a person or pertains to a person" (Mauss 1954: 10). He concluded that:

> It follows clearly from what we have seen that in this system of ideas one gives away what is in reality a part of one's nature and substance,

while to receive something is to receive a part of someone's spiritual
essence. To keep this thing is dangerous, not only because it is illicit to
do so, but also because it comes morally, physically and spiritually from
a person. Whatever it is, food, possessions, women, children or ritual,
it retains a magical and religious hold over the recipient.

(Mauss 1954: 10)

Gregory has interpreted Mauss's description of the fetishism of
gifts to mean that commodities and gifts are essentially different
forms of property. Commodities are alienable, that is to say all
rights in them are given up when they are exchanged for other
commodities. Gifts, on the other hand, are thought to be inalienable. Gregory maintains that the donor's rights in a gift are never
extinguished, and that it is this quality of the gift that creates the
obligation to give something in return. The defining characteristic
of gift exchange is therefore, for Gregory, that it is an exchange
of inalienable things between persons who are thereby united in a
state of reciprocal bondage.

The value of Gregory's model of gift exchange for understanding
traditional societies must be left to anthropologists to determine
(see for example Josephides 1985: 205–15). The important point
for present purposes is that this new version of elementarism has
ignored the fact that gift transactions are prevalent in capitalist
societies. Contrary to Gregory's definition of the gift, in the
modern western societies gifts are in fact alienable, and their alien-
ability is a precondition for their being gifts rather than loans or
shared possessions (Lowes et al. 1971: 87).

To be given as a gift an object must be alienable, in the dual
sense that the donor has the right to renounce ownership of it and
that the recipient has the right to possess it as his or her own
property. The most obvious confirmation of this fact can be found
in studies of communities where most goods are otherwise inalienable because they are held in common. An excellent illustration of
this can be found in Peter and Whitaker's (1981) observations on
gift giving among Hutterites in western Canada. The Hutterites
are a Christian sect whose members live communally, and who
collectively own the means of production and most subsistence
goods. One consequence of their distinctive way of life is that the
possibilities for converting communal property into gifts have been
very limited. Extensive gift giving is a recent phenomenon in the
Hutterite colonies, which has occurred because some individuals
have begun to acquire small private incomes. It is the slow but
steadily increasing privatization of Hutterite social life that is the

key factor in this change. The growth of a gift economy within Hutterite society both requires and reproduces an expanding domain of personal property.

Gift giving as we know it in the western societies has distinctive legal characteristics which distinguish it from other forms of non-commodity transactions. For a gift transaction to take place it is necessary for the donor to have the exclusive right to freely dispose of some object. Exclusive rights (i.e. rights of exclusion) are contrary to all communal forms of property holding. They are therefore a fundamental historical precondition for the emergence of differentiated gift economies. Goody has shown, for example, that the enormous increase in gifts to the Church in medieval Europe depended upon legal changes which made it possible for property, and in particular land, to be alienated from corporate kinship groups (Goody 1983: 91–125 especially).

Clearly, Gregory's model of gift economies has little value for the sociology of modern life, and it therefore fails as a general theory of the gift. The reasons for its failure go to the heart of the difference between the theory of political economy and the sociology of moral order. In an unduly neglected critique of the work of Karl Marx, Talcott Parsons (1967) pointed out that one of the major limitations of Marxism is that it does not have a sociology of institutionalization. It is this absence of a theory of the symbolic management of relationships which lies at the root of Gregory's unsuccessful attempt to distinguish a commodity economy from a gift economy. Lacking a conceptual framework with which to analyze reciprocity as *social interaction*, Gregory is forced to conclude that interdependence between persons is the result of psychological bonds between persons and things, and that it is therefore the circulation of things that binds individuals into systems of relations. We have seen that for western societies, at least, this simply will not do.

Interpersonal dependence is everywhere the result of socially constructed ties between human agents. The contents of those ties are defined by the participants' reciprocal expectations. It is these reciprocal expectations between persons that make social interaction possible, both in market exchange and in gift exchange (Cheal 1984). An adequate account of gift transactions therefore requires microstructural analyses of the communication processes by which expectations are formed and maintained.

The problem with Gregory's theory of gift exchange is that it conceives of social integration as the result of external constraints upon action, in the form of the powers of social objects. Whatever merits this model of deterministic social facts may have for the study of traditional societies, it can have little value for understanding the open texture of everyday life in modern societies (see for example, Douglas 1971). Accounts of social order in pluralistic societies must take into account individuals' choices between alternative lines of action. Concepts of subjectivity and individuality are therefore likely to be of some importance. This can be seen even in the unlikely setting of the Hutterite colonies, where a growing gift economy is associated with the expansion of individual freedoms and an enhanced subjective value attached to personal relationships. Within the moral economy of a Hutterite colony gifts have a special place, which is a result of their differentiation from the background of transactions upon which the well-being of colony members depends. The nature of that differentiation is central to understanding what a gift economy is, and why it takes the forms that it does.

The gift economy

Gift giving in capitalist societies has often been described as an extravagant waste of resources. Common-sense knowledge likewise maintains that extravagant giving is the result of "things getting out of hand". It is thought to be a regrettable, and hence avoidable, consequence of such modern institutions as the commercialization of Christmas. As a result, it is believed that the true spirit of giving that presumably prevailed in earlier times has been betrayed. This nostalgia for a "natural economy", which has been common among modern intellectuals, must be rejected (Denzin 1986). It has blinded us to the fact that excessive giving is not a contrived outcome of the capitalist mode of production. It is in fact constitutive of a differentiated gift economy. Following Riches (1981), it is claimed here that the defining characteristic of gifts is that they are *redundant transactions*.

Gifts are redundant transactions in several senses. A particular gift may not be redundant in every sense since it is the moral economy of gift giving, and not "the gift", that regulates gift behavior. It is, in other words, *the gift economy* as a system of action which is characterized by the principle of redundancy.

In the first place, gifts may be redundant transactions insofar as they are not due to conformity to norms. Many roles involve responsibilities to provide goods and services for others, which are simply taken for granted as inevitable consequences of the division of labor. It is only when the incumbents of roles go beyond their recognized obligations and perform gratuitous favors, that the situation ceases to be one of "mere" duty (Cheal 1984: 145). Arlie Hochschild (in press) has suggested that for a gift to be a gift it must be experienced as something extra – something beyond what we normally expect to receive. Thus, she argues, it is the culturally established baseline of conventional expectations that defines what will be viewed as a gift and what will not. Transactions which fall outside the range of legitimate expectation are redundant in a normative sense, and can be properly greeted with the ritual response of "Oh, you shouldn't have!"

Secondly, gifts may be redundant in the sense that they bring no advantage to their recipients, and thus add nothing to their well-being. Although this is rarely intentional (for an apparent exception see Befu 1967: 165), it is not uncommon. It frequently occurs when the recipients are not involved in choosing their own gifts. Gift givers do not always know others well enough to choose things that they will like (Cheal 1987a), and so it can happen that people receive gifts which are of no interest to them, or which they find offensive.

Thirdly, gifts may be redundant in the sense that they bring no *net* benefit to their recipients (Cheal 1986). This is the case where gift giving takes the form of symmetrical reciprocity. The value of the gift given to an exchange partner may be nicely calculated to balance the gift received (Lebra 1976: 98–9).[1] The inevitable result is that nobody is better off or worse off than they would have been if no transactions had taken place.

Fourthly, it is often the case that the objects received from others in gift exchanges are things which the recipients could have provided for themselves, if they had really wanted to. As Riches has explained, redundancy in transactions in this sense refers to "the rendering of goods and services which the recipient has both the ability and the entitlement to secure through his own immediate efforts" (Riches 1981: 216). In an affluent industrial society, this type of redundancy in gift transactions is likely to be widespread (Cheal 1987a).

Fifthly, and finally, redundancy in gift giving occurs as the result of a pragmatic tendency to make many ritual offerings where one might have sufficed for the purposes of interaction courtesy. One way of demonstrating the subjective importance of a significant other is to give that person a large quantity of things. This involves giving multiple gifts on a number of occasions (Cheal 1987a).

Giving to others beyond the levels required by immediate necessity would appear to be a general phenomenon, whether or not it is found in every primitive society, and whether or not it is ever found in a pure form. It has been argued here that the gift economy is in fact constituted by redundancy, and that it is this principle which distinguishes it from other economic systems. There is an important implication to be drawn from this point. If the giving of gifts to other individuals is not governed by an iron logic of necessity (whether understood in cultural or material terms) then the relative autonomy of gift transactions from structural determination must be high.[2] Interpersonal gift giving, that is to say, is not strongly determined, either by social roles or by the class system (Cheal 1986, 1987b). Rather, it is structured mainly by interaction processes and the requirements for effective social co-operation in moral economies.

Moral economy

The proposition that gifts are redundant transactions raises a fundamental question for sociology. If gifts are redundant, what social value could they possibly have which would account for the great importance which most people attach to them? The answer proposed here is that gifts are used to construct certain kinds of voluntary social relationships.

In the study of modern social life, sociologists have paid a great deal of attention to the networks of ties that link individuals in urban communities (for example, Litwak and Szelenyi 1969; Wellman 1979, 1981, 1982; Wellman and Hall 1986; Bulmer 1986). These networks are conventionally described as social support systems which have been designed to meet the needs of their members throughout the life cycle. However, concepts of life cycle needs have been unable to satisfactorily account for much relevant social behavior (Cheal 1987c; 1988a). It has therefore been suggested that transfers between individuals must be explained as outcomes of the rules and resources that actors draw upon in pursuing their goals (Cheal 1986; 1988c). What those goals are is open to debate, and the present work takes a particular point of view on this question. It will be argued here that transfers of gifts from one individual to another must be understood mainly as a feature of the institutionalization of social ties within a moral economy (Scott 1976).[3]

By a *moral economy* I mean a system of transactions which are defined as socially desirable (i.e. moral), because through them social ties are recognized, and balanced social relationships are maintained.[4] The maintenance of balanced relationships typically includes the provision of social supports. This occurs whenever externally derived imbalances in the relative distribution of well-being have exceeded tolerable limits. The theory of moral economy thus includes what I have elsewhere (Cheal 1988c) referred to as "rational transfers theory". Redistributing resources to others is an economically rational act whenever it is necessary to maintain, or to restore, a preferred balance in the quality of life between the members of a collectivity.

In the contemporary world system, moral economies exist alongside political economies.[5] The systems of relations within which moral economies are grounded are therefore only part-societies. These part-societies typically consist of small worlds of personal relationships that are the emotional core of every individual's social experiences (Sahlins 1972; Caplow 1982; Cheal 1986). In every society individuals have lived out their lives within small worlds of one kind or another. In primitive societies this was largely because the societies themselves were small. In modern societies it is because most people prefer to inhabit intimate life worlds. It is characteristic of any large, pluralistic society that the outcomes of action are always potentially affected by multiple interconnections between heterogeneous individuals. That is to say, everyday life today is enormously affected by the complexity of mass societies,[6] and by the adaptive practices of complexity reduction (see especially Luhmann 1976, 1979).

In mass societies it is often the case that difficulty in trusting others, or an absence of trust, is felt to be an acute problem. The responses of others are often unpredictable, because their motives are unknown, and thus the outcomes of lengthy chains of interaction are uncertain. Under such conditions the psychological demands of selecting appropriate lines of action are considerable, and practical solutions must be found to decision-making problems. Those solutions will include practices that achieve trust as a routine feature of everyday life. In a moral economy, trust is generated as a result of members sharing a common way of life. Individuals' commitments to fulfill their customary obligations to others make their actions predictable, and thus keep the complexity of the social environment at a low level. As Alvin Gouldner has argued (1973: 260–99), norms of beneficence resolve interaction ambiguities and thereby increase the stability of systems of relations.

A moral economy consists, in the first place, of a set of normative obligations to provide assistance to others so that they can carry out their projects. However, the vehemence of the reactions that occur when such norms are broken cannot be explained by the simple fact that they are social rules. The sense of betrayal that is provoked by the collapse of a moral economy (in families as well as in communities) is due to pre-normative beliefs that it is part of the natural order of things (Adorno 1978: 31–2). This tacit cognition of social order is often expressed in gift transactions, which comprise a differentiated gift economy. We have already established that gift transactions do not have as their principal purpose the redistribution of resources. They are, for the most part, redundant transactions that are used in the ritual construction of small social worlds.

Ritual in mass society

One of the most pervasive features of everyday life is that individuals routinely construct, and are selectively recruited into, specialized social worlds. In most cases social worlds are organized on a small scale, since small worlds are both comprehensible and manageable. These "micro-universes" (Luckmann 1978: 285), such as kinship networks, are the principal social contexts within which, and around which, ties to significant others are organized (Strathern 1981). Networks of significant others are important because through them individuals gain access to resources and opportunities for interaction (Craven and Wellman 1973). What is sometimes overlooked in accounts of these networks is that their component ties are social relationships that must be developed and maintained. They therefore depend upon a mutual recognition of interests that is derived from a shared knowledge of social identity (Turner 1982; Turner and Oakes 1986). How that social identification is produced and reproduced is a matter of great practical importance, since it is the basis for relations of trust within moral economies.

The social foundations of moral economies consist of three modes of the institutionalization of identity. They are: the standardization of forms of relationships; the continuity of members over time; and the routinization of availability. Together they produce a progressive, and pervasive, ritualization of interaction. We will describe each of these conditions in turn, in order to show why it is that gift rituals are often felt to be of such great importance.

Social interaction always requires the co-operation of at least two people. The fitting-together of the actions of two or more individuals can be achieved only if each is able to understand the other's purposes (Cheal 1984). Interpreting the actions of others with regard to the self is therefore a prerequisite for economic relations of any kind. The work of interpretation is much reduced if the others who are commonly encountered in everyday life can be assigned to a limited number of categories of actors, each of which is assumed to engage in certain typical patterns of behavior. The categorization of persons, and the attribution of dispositions to them, are therefore fundamental properties of the moral order of social life (Berger and Bradac 1982; Jayyusi 1984)[7] They are filters in the process of social selection by which access of one person to another is controlled. In modern societies, that process is used to create private social worlds within which individuals can maintain particular patterns of interaction without interference from outsiders (Benn and Gaus 1983; Cheal 1987b). Among the categories of actors that may be used in social selection are relational identities in *social relationships*, such as those of kinship and friendship. Associated with these categories are typifications of the different transactions that may occur between those who have relationships of various kinds (Argyle 1984; Argyle and Henderson 1985). As a result of cumulative social experiences, these typifications define normal practices, and interaction is stabilized by reciprocal role expectations (Berger and Luckmann 1966: 53–7).

Role incumbency entails broad limitations on the kinds of actions in which members can be expected to engage. Nevertheless, those limits are often broad indeed, and considerable behavioral variation is possible between different individuals following the same rules (Cheal 1980: 40). The amount of complexity with which social actors must deal can be further reduced, therefore, by interacting only with a limited number of known persons. As a result, the open texture of social life is constrained by the continuity of *personal relationships* (Duck and Perlman 1985). Personal relationships have the considerable advantage that the behavioral repertoire of the other becomes part of a shared stock of knowledge that is built up through repetitive interaction over long periods of time. In modern societies a great deal of importance is attached to these relationships because they provide a stable core of interactions in unstable social environments. Their stability, and hence the trust that members have in them, is achieved through the frameworks of mutual knowing that result from extensive interactions (Goffman 1971: 189).

The reduction of complexity achieved within frameworks of mutual knowing is often very impressive (Berger and Kellner 1964). Nevertheless, they do not remove the problem of uncertainty entirely, because personal relationships themselves may break down at any time. Individuals' feelings towards one another can change, and interpersonal constructs therefore have to be routinely confirmed in everyday interaction in order to retain their subjective validity as taken-for-granted facts of life (Blumer 1969). If the parties to a relationship are to be able to trust each other, therefore, it is necessary for them to communicate their continued *availability* to each other.

The reality of sentiments upon which relationships are thought to depend is articulated in a "vocabulary of motives" (Gerth and Mills 1953: 114–19) through which individuals account for their actions. That vocabulary, or idiom, defines for a particular linguistic community the various conventionalized emotions which are believed to bring about commitments to others and hence participation in their activities. Within contemporary western moral economies it is above all conventional sentiments of friendship, love, and gratitude that are thought to inspire giving. All three emotions involve the actor in identifying with others, so that for certain purposes the boundaries between self and other are denied, and a collective identity is defined *vis-à-vis* outsiders. The enclosure of persons within these supra-individual boundaries makes possible a characteristic mutuality of assistance between members, which may be achieved through the sharing of resources or through social exchange. As a result, the voluntary transfer of wealth is a social act which symbolizes the diffuse nature of a close relationship (Haas and Deseran 1981). It is for this reason that showing love to others by giving gifts to them is a highly valued ritual in intimate ties (Cheal 1987a).

Conclusion

Randall Collins (1985) has drawn attention to the fact that gift giving in ritual exchange networks is a key issue in one of the three great traditions in social theory. That tradition of enquiry, which Collins has identified as the science of social order, is descended from the work of Emile Durkheim. In anthropology it has been elaborated by Marcel Mauss and Claude Lévi-Strauss, and in sociology by Erving Goffman and by Collins himself. Despite the strength of this tradition of social thought, work on the gift economies of modern societies is remarkably undeveloped by comparison with other areas of research. The reasons for that neglect, and the possibilities of transcending it, have been set out in this chapter.

It has been suggested here that despite the enormous changes associated with capitalist modernization, gift transactions continue to have a vital importance in social life. The role that gifts play may be different in modern societies than in traditional societies, but it would be wrong to assume that they are therefore automatically of lesser significance. Unlike transactions such as the payment of wages or the unwaged preparation of food, gifts are not confined to a narrowly defined set of social relations. They can be carried out between a wide range of social actors (Lowes *et al.* 1971: 91). Gifts have a "free-floating" presence within the moral economy of interpersonal relations, and they therefore facilitate types of interaction that might otherwise be only weakly institutionalized (Cheal 1988a). We can therefore define the gift economy as *a system of redundant transactions within a moral economy, which makes possible the extended reproduction of social relations.*

2

Tie-signs

The contrasting theories of political economy and moral economy that were outlined in the previous chapter have provided the intellectual context for most social scientific work on gift giving. In the present chapter we will examine the different kinds of questions which are raised by those two approaches, and we will consider how they might be translated into research practices. As they have been stated here, ideal types of political economy and moral economy are abstract conceptual frameworks with very general implications for the study of human society. In order to clarify the implications that each has for studies of the gift economy it will be useful to identify exemplars for these two approaches, and to describe what they have had to say about gift transactions. Both of our exemplary social scientists have worked on the borders between anthropology and sociology. They are, for political economy, Bourdieu, and for moral economy, Goffman.

Bourdieu's observations on gift transactions have been widely read, and they may therefore be taken as defining the essential characteristics of the political economy of gift giving in the contemporary social sciences (Bourdieu 1977, 1979). The authority of his work rests in part upon its lineal descent from certain themes in the work of Mauss. As is well-known, the latter claimed that the appearance of voluntarism in gift transactions is an illusion, since in reality they are given and repaid out of a sense of obligation. Thus he concluded that: "The form usually taken is that of the gift generously offered; but the accompanying behaviour is formal pretence and social deception, while the transaction itself is based on obligation and economic self-interest" (Mauss 1954: 1).

Bourdieu has agreed with Mauss's conclusion that there is a contradiction between the intersubjective definition of a gift transaction, as a ritual act that is independent of all other acts, and the objective fact that it is one element in a succession of reciprocal transactions. He has further argued that this contradictory structure is a *necessary* feature of gift exchange, and that the defining characteristic of gift exchange is the temporal separation of gift and counter-gift in an indefinite cycle of reciprocity. It is because of the separation of gift and return gift that the actors can deny that there is in fact any obligation to make a return.

In Bourdieu's view the symbolic negation of economic calculation in gift exchange serves the requirements of strategic interaction. A deferred return obligates one individual to another, and therefore creates a social debt. In this way the giving of large gifts enables one person to gain control over another, while exchanges of little presents make it possible for both parties to a relationship to maintain continuous personal relations.

His concept of the gift is that it is a form of capital in which individuals invest in order to carry through their projects. Among the social purposes achieved in this way are mutual aid under conditions of economic and political insecurity. Gift exchanges, then, are to be viewed as rational adaptations to an "economy of insecurity", and as "symbolic taxes" by which conflict groups mobilize the loyalties of their members (Bourdieu 1977: 60, 95). The key to all this is seen as the deliberate pretence that gift giving is an act of public morality rather than an act of private calculation, so that:

> Gift exchange is an exchange in and by which the agents strive to conceal the objective truth of the exchange, i.e. the calculation which guarantees the equity of the exchange. If "fair exchange", the direct swapping of equivalent values, is the truth of gift exchange, gift exchange is a swapping which cannot acknowledge itself as such.
>
> (Bourdieu 1979: 22)

Bourdieu's description of the nature of gift giving raises three principal issues for social research. Firstly, it is important to know whether or not particular gifts are in fact elements in a system of reciprocal transactions. That means having quantitative data on the flows of gifts between social actors. Secondly, it is presumed that the process of social exchange takes place over an extended period of time. It is therefore necessary to know about the timing of gift transactions, and to have information about a number of gift giving occasions. Since many of these occasions are seasonal in nature, this would mean at a minimum collecting information about one complete annual cycle of gift exchanges.

Thirdly, Bourdieu has emphatically directed our attention to the relationship between the nature of gift transactions and actors' accounts of their behavior. His claims about the contradictory relationship between accounts and behavior can be evaluated only if information is collected about both *simultaneously*, so that comparisons can be drawn between them within the life histories of known individuals.

There has been no study of gift giving in the western societies which meets all three of these criteria. Nevertheless, limited information is available on the first two which does permit us to say something about the validity of Bourdieu's thesis. Surveys of Christmas gift giving in England (Lowes, Turner, and Wills 1971), the United States (Caplow 1984), and western Canada (Cheal 1986) have all shown that reciprocal giving is a marked feature of the Christmas festivities in these societies. It is also clear that the usual temporal ordering of gift transactions on that occasion is not one of separation, but one of simultaneity on Christmas Eve or Christmas Day. Furthermore, much of the giving at Christmas takes place in the face-to-face encounters of family gatherings (Caplow 1982, 1984). Not only is there little or no temporal separation of gift transactions, but there may be no spatial separation either, with the result that gift reciprocity takes the form of an immediate gift exchange. This might not be so damaging for Bourdieu's thesis if Christmas were a minor occasion for giving to others. But in the above-mentioned societies, at least, it is in fact the most important time for gift exchanges.

The pattern of Christmas giving in the Anglo-American societies appears to contradict Bourdieu's exchange thesis, and his elegant model of interpersonal transactions is not likely to provide the most useful basis for understanding modern gift economies. The alternative approach that was outlined in the first chapter conceives of the gift economy as a ritual order of presences and absences or, in other words, of approach and avoidance rituals. The most useful conceptual framework from that point of view is the one developed by Goffman, to which we will now turn.

Gifts are examples of that class of events which he referred to as "tie-signs" (Goffman 1971: 194–9). That is to say, they are transactions that contain evidence about the nature of the relationship between donor and recipient. An exchange of gifts usually confirms that a relationship is anchored in a framework of mutual recognition of the participants' social and personal identities. The nature of the evidence provided about these "anchored relations," as Goffman referred to them, and the means by which such evidence can be collected for social scientific purposes, are the key problems that must be addressed here. Among other things, we will be interested in the extent to which evidence from gift transactions is able to inform us about the structural arrangements of the small worlds of personal relationships.[1]

In Goffman's view evidence of the current character of a relationship is best obtained from studies of the interaction rituals performed by one individual to another (Goffman 1971: 195). He therefore concluded that ritual interchanges, such as exchanges of presents or visits, are concrete units of social activity that provide a natural empirical way to study interaction of all kinds (Goffman 1967: 20).[2] He pointed out that highly ritualized interactions,[3] such as christenings, graduation exercises, marriage ceremonies and funerals, have the great advantage for sociological purposes of being occasions when "a situated social fuss is made over what might ordinarily be hidden in extended courses of activity and the unformulated experience of their participants" (Goffman 1979: 1).

Ritualized occasions are relatively well-defined episodes of interaction which are the objects of explicit attention, and whose private significance is publicly acknowledged. They are, in other words, *rites* which express the social value attached to social objects. They therefore provide a window through which we may look into the social organization of the small worlds of personal relationships upon which the gift economy rests.

Goffman's principal concern was with the meanings conveyed by interaction rituals. Nevertheless, he maintained that most ritual actions are structured by two interrelated sets of rules. On the one hand, there are substantive or instrumental rules, and on the other hand there are ceremonial or expressive rules. The latter have "their primary importance – officially anyway – as a conventionalized means of communication by which the individual expresses his character or conveys his appreciation of the other participants in the situation" (Goffman 1967: 54).

According to Goffman all events that have a substantive significance also carry some ceremonial meaning. The ceremonial idiom employed by a given group will sometimes depend rather heavily upon the substantive values of transactions (Cheal 1987a), as he thought was generally the case with wedding gifts:

> While the substantive value of ceremonial acts is felt to be quite secondary it may yet be quite appreciable. Wedding gifts in American society provide an example. It is even possible to say in some cases that if a sentiment of a given kind is to be conveyed ceremonially it will be necessary to employ a sign-vehicle which has a given amount of substantive value. . . . In general, then, we can say that all ceremonial gestures differ in the degree to which they have substantive value, and that this

substantive value may be systematically used as part of the communication value of the act, but that still the ceremonial order is different
from the substantive one and is so understood.

(Goffman 1967: 54)

In Goffman's view the ceremonial order of material transactions
is worth distinguishing for analytical purposes, because it shows
how actors construct and control social situations through their
capacity to define them symbolically. Whatever the purposes are
that individuals pursue in their various interactions, all social life
depends upon such definitions (Goffman 1959: 3–4). Although the
ends of action may be quite varied, common means of achieving
agreement on situational definitions will be available so that cooperative action can take place (Goffman 1963: 8). His view of transactions is therefore compatible with the existence of an advanced
social system, in which there are extensive multiplex interactions
between individuals within a social environment that provides
considerable economic and political security for a variety of individual interests.

Goffman's view of social life clearly differs from that of Bourdieu
in several important respects. As a result he has directed our attention towards different aspects of the human experience. His work
has raised three main issues for research into the gift economy.

Firstly, it is important to explore the links between gift transactions and ceremonial processes, since gift giving is a common
accompaniment to many ceremonial occasions (Cheal 1988a).
Indeed, it may be such a prominent feature of some special
occasions that it is in fact constitutive of the occasion itself, as it
has been shown that it is at Christmas (Lüschen et al. 1972; Caplow
1984). It is not surprising, then, that detailed sociological analysis
of ritualized giving should have begun with Christmas (Cheal
1986). Other occasions for ritualized giving have received much
less attention, although some useful work has been done on
weddings (Leonard 1980). At this point in time one of the most
serious gaps in research into the gift economy is the lack of
comparative information about the variety of ceremonial occasions
on which gifts may be given.[4]

Secondly, the kinds of ties between individuals that are defined
by gifts need to be described in order to clarify how gift transactions are structured by social and personal identities. So far, the
most interesting field research on gift giving has been conducted
in conjunction with studies of family and kinship systems (Leonard
1980; Caplow 1982; Boholm 1983). There has been an obvious

logic to this choice of emphasis, since the most valuable gifts are given to close kin (Caplow 1982: 386; Cheal 1986: 432). Even so, it is clear that significant numbers of gifts are given to non-kin (Lowes, Turner, and Wills 1971: 91; Caplow 1982: 387). For this reason, and because of the difficulties that are inherent in using "the family" as a unit of analysis, it is necessary to look at all anchored relations as elements in *personal networks* that individuals construct as arenas for interaction (Wellman 1981).

Thirdly, Goffman has recommended that we should pay attention to both the instrumental and the expressive dimensions of gifts, and to the ways in which they are interrelated in everyday life. That means collecting information about the types of gifts that are transferred and their financial values, as Caplow did in his pioneering Middletown Christmas study.

From Goffman's point of view it is necessary to use data of this sort to illustrate the practical importance of symbolic interaction for social organization. In recent years the importance of studying gifts as symbolic objects has become clear (Caplow 1984; Cheal 1986), and ambiguities in the ceremonial idiom of gifts have been explored (Boholm 1983: 177–82; Cheal 1987a). The most widely discussed issue here has been the unacceptability of money as a gift (Webley, Lea, and Portalska 1983). Douglas and Isherwood have claimed that people draw a careful line between cash and gift in order to separate commercial relations from personal relations. They have also stated, somewhat contradictorily one might think, that "The right to give cash is reserved for family intimacy" (Douglas and Isherwood 1979: 59). Here it is only possible to agree with their disclaimer that "there are details that could be tidied up." It would obviously be most useful to have some concrete evidence from everyday life with which to clarify the points at issue here.

Clearly, more information about gift transactions is needed before we can expect to arrive at a satisfactory understanding of any modern gift economy. In the following chapters we are going to examine selected evidence from a detailed investigation into gift giving in Canada.[5] Most of the information is drawn from a study of ceremonial transactions in Winnipeg, known as the Winnipeg Ritual Cycle Study.[6]

Winnipeg Ritual Cycle Study

The purpose of the Winnipeg Ritual Cycle Study was to provide a comprehensive description of the gift economy considered as a differentiated ritual order. Like any other research project this one involved making a number of choices about the methods to be followed. Those choices, and the reasons for them, can be expected to have consequences for the results produced. They therefore deserve to be discussed so that the reader may judge the strengths and limitations of this work.

Sampling

In order to examine the various issues that were mentioned above it is necessary to have detailed information about gift transactions. Asking interviewees to describe an arbitrarily limited number of transactions, as Belk has done (Belk 1979), is likely to introduce biases that arise from either the investigators' or the interviewees' preferences. The most desirable solution, then, is to collect information about *all* gift transactions that occur within certain socially defined units of time, such as the Christmas season or the annual cycle. The Winnipeg Ritual Cycle Study was designed to obtain information about all gifts which the interviewees had given or received in connection with a ceremonial occasion over a twelve month period.

An intensive study of gift transactions such as this is very demanding, both for the researchers and for the interviewees, as we can see in one pioneering study of Christmas gifts and kin networks (Caplow 1982). The costs of such work, and the practical difficulties involved, mean that the sample will normally be small (Caplow's sample consisted of 110 adult Middletown residents). This in turn means that it is not possible to count upon having a representative sample of the population of a large urban center such as Winnipeg. That disadvantage, from the statistical point of view, can in fact be turned into an advantage from certain theoretical points of view.

In the Winnipeg Ritual Cycle Study eighty adults aged 18 or over were interviewed during the winter of 1982–3. As a check upon the validity of the results from this sample, a study of valuable Christmas gifts and wedding gifts was subsequently conducted using a random sample of 573 adult members of the population of Winnipeg. Some of the results from the latter survey, which was conducted as part of the 1984 Winnipeg Area Study, have been reported elsewhere (Cheal 1986, 1987b).[7]

The sample of interviewees selected for the Winnipeg Ritual Cycle Study was not designed to make representative statements about the population of Winnipeg. Rather, it was constructed in order to explore actors' concepts and their associated logics of action within socially organized frames of reference, such as ethnic subcultures (see chapter 1, note 6). The procedure followed was therefore that of theoretical (or purposive) sampling with a view to developing grounded theory, as that method has been described by Glaser and Strauss (1967). Some acquaintance with the method of grounded theory construction, and the manner in which it has been followed here, is necessary to appreciate the characteristics of the Ritual Cycle Study sample.

Developing a grounded theory is a systematic inductive strategy that consists of generating sociological concepts and propositions from successive encounters with data collected in field research. Exploratory field work inevitably reveals differences in behavior between individuals that are grounded in different cultural categories, or folk concepts. Research sites and subjects are subsequently selected in such a way as to extend the analysis of the interactional properties of those categories. That involves identifying *comparison groups* whose similarities and differences seem likely to generate theoretically useful insights.

The Winnipeg Ritual Cycle Study was the mid-point of a much larger project on gift behavior in Winnipeg. Exploratory work into wedding gift practices had already been conducted which made it desirable to investigate the interactional forms used in gift giving as instances of local cultural constructs. Although Winnipeggers' gift concepts have obvious similarities with those found elsewhere in North America, we should not assume that they are everywhere the same. In fact there are good reasons for suspecting that the opposite is the case (Cheal 1988a). Local gift practices must be studied, as they have evolved, in their local context. That means studying the actions and ideas of people who have lived most of their lives in Winnipeg, or who have become acculturated to some degree through lengthy residence in the city. It also means taking into account the ethnic subcultures that exist in a pluralistic city like Winnipeg.

The Winnipeg Ritual Cycle Study was designed so as to deepen understanding of the contemporary cultural contexts for a locally dominant contrast set of wedding gift categories, namely the *gift*

and the *presentation*. Winnipeg folklore attributes the origins of
these categories to the contrasting traditions of the two largest
ethnic "groups" in the city, those of British and Ukrainian descent.
Sampling procedures were therefore purposively developed to
produce a sample consisting of equal numbers of Anglo-Canadians
and Ukrainian Canadians.[8] The Winnipeg Ritual Cycle Study
sample in fact consists almost entirely of people who identify
themselves as belonging to one or other of those two ethnic
groups, or as non-ethnic Canadians (see Table 2.1). Most of them
had lived in Winnipeg for a number of years, and only 10 per cent
of the sample had lived in the city for less than ten years.

Table 2.1   *Winnipeg Ritual Cycle Study, Sample Characteristics*

	Anglo sample	Ukrainian sample	Total sample
Social identification			
Canadian only	28	22	50
Anglo-Canadian	10	0	10
Ukrainian Canadian	0	14	14
Other ethnic Canadian	0	1	1
Mixed ethnic Canadian	0	2	2
Non-Canadian	2	0	2
None	0	1	1
Church membership			
Non-member	12	12	24
United	20	2	22
Anglican	3	0	3
Roman Catholic	1	6	7
Ukrainian Catholic	0	12	12
Orthodox	0	2	2
Other	4	6	10
Years lived in Winnipeg			
0–9	2	6	8
10–19	8	10	18
20–29	9	13	22
30–39	7	7	14
40–49	2	2	4
50–59	7	1	8
60+	5	1	6
Totals	40	40	80

It is to be expected that age and gender will be related to variations in gift behavior (Cheal 1986), and quota sampling was therefore attempted in order to achieve a well-balanced sample. To be useful the sample should include representatives of all age groups, including the "old old" whose kinship ties may span several generations (Shanas 1980; Riley 1983). The coverage achieved in the Winnipeg Ritual Cycle Study in this respect is good, with the only lacuna occurring for men aged 40–49 (see Table 2.2).

The underrepresentation of middle-aged men is the extreme instance of the underrepresentation of men in general in the Ritual Cycle Study. Men were much more likely to decline to be interviewed than were women. Despite repeated efforts to interview men, the sample's sex distribution was heavily skewed, with women making up almost two-thirds of the interviewees (see Table 2.2). Regrettable as this imbalance is in one sense, it is not inappropriate for a study whose main purpose was to obtain detailed information about the universe of gifts given on special occasions. Whatever changes may have occurred in other areas of domestic sex roles, women in Winnipeg still assume the major responsibility for gift giving (Cheal 1987a: 153), as they do in Middletown (Caplow 1982: 387). Only 18 per cent of the gifts given by the male respondents in Winnipeg were given unaided, and a mere 1 per cent were given by two or more men acting together. The usual pattern of male giving consists of collaboration with a close female relative who does most of the gift work. It is not surprising, therefore, that women have a much more extensive knowledge of gift transactions than do men, and they are generally speaking the more reliable informants on this topic. In the inter-

Table 2.2   *Winnipeg Ritual Cycle Study, Age and Sex of Sample Members*

Age	Female	Male	Total
18–19	1	0	1
20–29	14	9	23
30–39	8	9	17
40–49	8	0	8
50–59	9	3	12
60–69	8	4	12
70+	4	3	7
Totals	52	28	80

views with men, husbands often relied heavily upon their wives
to fill in the details of "their" gift transactions.

Interviewing

The 80 informants selected in the manner described above were
contacted in late 1982 and interviewed on at least two occasions in
the period from November 1982 through Feburary 1983. The
interviewees were asked to describe all the gifts which they had
given and received on a special occasion during 1982, and they
were asked to provide limited biographical information about all
those who had been involved as donors or as receivers in their gift
transactions. A number of discursive questions about gift giving
were also asked in order to elicit the interviewees' interpretations
of their gift practices. In addition, biographical information was
collected on the interviewees themselves. This was kept to a
minimum because the uses of such data are severely limited for a
sample of only eighty persons and because the demands made
upon the interviewees' time by the other parts of the survey were
expected to be heavy.

The interviews were organized in two stages in order to reduce
the recall problems that might otherwise have been created by
fatigue and boredom due to the repetitive nature of the tasks. The
first stage of the interviewing was held before Christmas 1982 and
dealt with gift transactions on every special occasion from the
beginning of the year to that date. The second stage was held in
early 1983. In it data were collected about Christmas gifts and
other gift transactions that had occurred between the pre-Christmas interviews and the end of 1982.

Any project which involves repeat contacts with informants over
an extended period of time is likely to suffer some loss of cases,
especially where the subject matter is felt to be highly personal. Of
the 80 people who answered questions about their pre-Christmas
giving, 3 did not go on to answer the interpretative questions, and
another 5 did not respond to the request for information about
gifts given over the Christmas season. This attrition means that
there is a choice in the presentation of sample analyses, between
using all 80 of the cases, for some of whom the data are incomplete,
or using only those 72 cases for whom complete information about
transactions and transactors was obtained. Both choices have their
unique advantages and disadvantages, which have to be taken into
account when the data are analyzed. Most of the sample analyses

presented below will be based on the subsample for which there is complete information, since it is often desirable to avoid any bias that may arise from not having data on Christmas gifts for all of the respondents. At other times it may be preferable to use all of the available cases, in order to explore the scope of the universes of gift objects and significant others. In general, analyses of sample data have been kept to a minimum in this volume, in order to concentrate on individual cases and their relevance for issues in sociological theory.

Recording

The research instruments used in the Winnipeg Ritual Cycle Study were designed to generate a rich body of information that could be used for many purposes, only a few of which will be pursued in this volume. The different types of information gathered in the interviews were recorded in three ways. Firstly, the interviewees' biographical data were entered on the interview schedule itself. Secondly, information about gifts given and received, and about donors and recipients, could not be handled in this way due to the large volume of records. The data were therefore recorded on color-coded cards. This proved to be a flexible system which permitted the efficient collection of information from people with vastly different patterns of gift flows. The mean number of recorded gifts per sample member (giving and receiving combined) was 71. There was considerable variation around that figure. The lowest number of recorded gifts was 12, and the highest was 202. Thirdly, and finally, answers to the discursive questions were recorded on tape whenever possible, although written notes were made instead if the interviewee objected to the use of a tape recorder. The majority of the tape recordings were transcribed and, together with the field notes, were treated as qualitative materials from which a deeper understanding of the individual cases could be obtained.

One of the principal methodological concerns in developing the Winnipeg Ritual Cycle Study was that practical issues of questionnaire design should not be allowed to establish narrow limits to the numbers of transactions and transactors that could be recorded. In the past that has been a problem with studies of social networks as the number of ties about which information is collected has often been small (Wellman 1981; Alba 1982). The problem here is that when the number of network ties to be studied is limited in an arbitrary fashion there is no way of knowing how representative they are of the universe of ties in the respondents' social networks. Since the populations of personal networks are inherently unknown in most cases, sampling techniques cannot overcome this problem. The only satisfactory solution is complete enumeration of the universe of ties.

In the Winnipeg Ritual Cycle Study the interviewees were encouraged to provide precise information about the nature of the ties between themselves and all those with whom they were involved in gift transactions. That information can be used in a number of ways. In sociology the principal use for such materials in recent years has been in the mathematical modelling of the properties of social networks. That approach will not be followed here, since it is the properties of transactions with which we are most concerned.

In the following chapters we shall pay special attention to the significance of gift transactions in relation to individual life histories and situated contexts of interaction. This method of "case and situation analysis" (van Velsen 1967; Mitchell 1983) provides an important corrective to those models of gift behavior which assume an unrealistic uniformity in social action, and which therefore deserve to be re-evaluated in the light of new evidence. As has been pointed out:

> For the sociologist interested in social processes there are no right or wrong views; there are only differing views representing different interest groups, status, personality, and so forth. It follows from this, secondly, that as much as possible of the total context of the cases should be recorded – the cases should be presented situationally – and the actors should be specified.
>
> (van Velsen 1967: 147)

Case studies of individuals' actions over time have been infrequently employed in the social sciences, in part because of the lack of explicit techniques for the investigation of case materials, by comparison with the more highly developed methods for analyzing collective patterns of behavior. One useful tool in case studies is to be able to grasp the individual's personal network as a whole by means of a network graph. Unfortunately the available techniques for producing graphs of personal networks in mass societies are severely limited. As a result it has usually been impossible to provide visual representations of important features of networks of ties. New techniques are therefore needed with which to produce standardized graphic descriptions of personal networks. One such technique, developed especially for the Winnipeg Ritual Cycle Study, will be outlined here since it is consistent with the analysis of small worlds of interaction proposed in chapter 1.

Networks of ties

The social networks literature contains many references to graphs as the foundations for modern networks analysis. Nevertheless, there has been surprisingly little concern with how we might effectively use arrangements of lines and points for the purposes of ideographic description. In particular, sociologists who have taken an analytical approach to network studies have usually de-emphasized the graphic imagery of network charts in favor of algebraic graph theory. As a result little attention has been paid to the uses of graphs as visual materials in studies of personal networks. It is therefore worth considering what forms of ideo-graphic description are most likely to sensitize us to important variations in ego-centered networks. How can we, in fact, best display personal network data for the purposes of illustrating the relational properties of transactions?

Social anthropologists working with genealogical data have developed standard ideographic techniques for describing kinship networks, which seem to have suited their purposes rather well (Barnes 1967). For sociology, anthropological kinship charts have two great advantages, namely the specification of intergenerational relations and the precise description of the chains of ties by which those relations are ordered. However, they also have some notable limitations that are particularly disadvantageous for studies of mass societies. One of the most salient characteristics of personal networks in mass societies is that they invariably contain many different kinds of relationships. Within such networks, social circles consisting of kinship ties may be segregated from those composed of other ties, but that is not always the case. Emotionally significant relationships may be maintained with a friend's mother, or with the friend of a favorite aunt, and so on.

At present no effective technique exists for portraying networks in which family ties and other kinds of ties are intermixed.[9] The genealogical chart is clearly unsatisfactory in this respect, since it excludes non-kin. Other ideographic methods have therefore sometimes been recommended for use in networks analysis, such as the star graph (Barnes 1969: 58–60). Star graphs are diagrams consisting of points that are all joined, directly or indirectly, to a

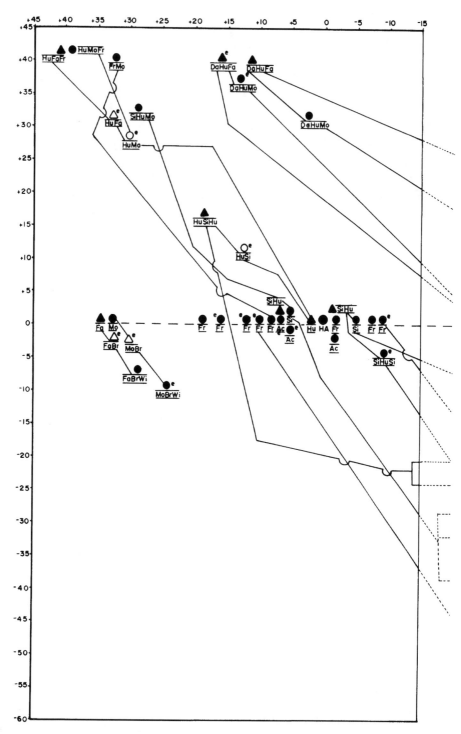

Figure 2.1a RANK graph, Hazel Anderson age 52

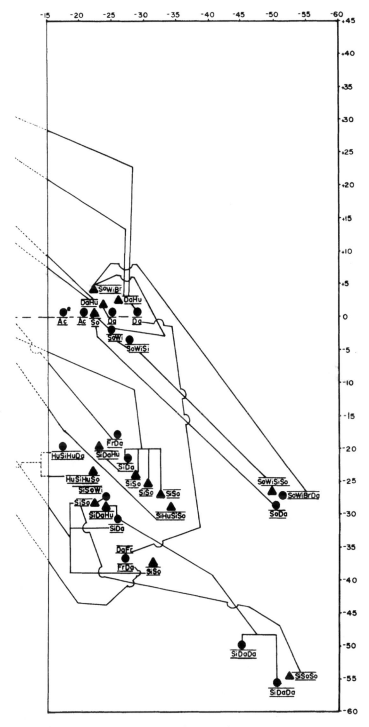

Figure 2.1b RANK graph, Hazel Anderson age 52 *cont'd*

focal person, or ego. The points closest to the center represent individuals directly related to ego, and they make up what is referred to as the first order zone of the graph. Points a little further out represent individuals related to ego through individuals in the first order zone (they are therefore in the second order zone), and so on.

Within a star graph a variety of types of ties can be entered as partial networks that occupy distinct segments of the graph. The only difficulty with this method is that since the ties in a star graph are ordered according to the number of links in the chain between ego and alter, it is not possible to preserve the pan-generational structure of kinship ties in large networks. Ego's mother's father and ego's mother's sister, for example, would be in adjacent positions in the second order zone despite the fact that they belong to different generations. That is a serious deficiency for present purposes, given the well-known influence of generational order upon the directions in which gifts flow (Caplow 1982: 387).

The ability to depict generational order is one of the great advantages of the traditional genealogical chart, which is unfortunately lost when star graphs are used. Clearly, it would be most useful to have an ideographic method that combined the advantages of the genealogical chart and the star graph. The solution that will be proposed here is the Relative Age Network Graph (or RANK graph).

The RANK graph is a rectangular coooordinate system (Cartesian plane) whose axes are defined as relative age variables. As in a star graph, ego is the focal point and therefore has a relative age of zero on both axes. The variable on the horizontal (X) axis is age relative to ego. The variable on the vertical (Y) axis is age relative to the person through whom alter is linked with ego. All alters who have a direct (i.e. unmediated) relation with ego naturally have a value of zero on the Y axis, and the first order zone of a star graph becomes a horizontal line passing through the origin (ego). All individuals whose relations to ego are not mediated by any other person are arrayed along this line according to their age relative to ego (plus or minus). Alters whose relations to ego are indirect (second order ties, etc.) are distributed as points throughout the rest of the graph according to their age relative to ego and relative to the first order intermediary. These points are joined by lines to produce a network which has the important property of illustrating the generational order of ties as a diagonal cluster (see Figures 2.1a and 2.1b).

Large networks, particularly those containing many unmediated ties, are often difficult to fit into dimensions that are convenient for storage and reproduction purposes. In those instances it is often desirable to make local alterations to the scales of the relative age variables. That may include expanding the zero on the X or Y axis, or both, into an open area within which a number of cases that have the same coordinates can be stacked.

It has been found useful in kinship studies to identify each person listed in a graph with symbols that convey certain basic information about their roles as social actors. The symbols used in RANK graphs consist of a series of geometric ideograms that convey information about the individuals' personal characteristics,[10] and a series of alphabetic abbreviations that convey information about their social ties (see Figure 2.2).[11] Together they make it possible to represent a set of transactions as a system of relationships involving a differentiated network of persons, each of whom stands in a distinctive relationship to ego.

Figure 2.2 RANK graph symbols

	Personal characteristics		*Social ties*
▲	Male (living)	Fa	Father
●	Female (living)	Mo	Mother
↑	Sex unknown (living)	Pa	Parent (sex unknown)
■	Animal (living)	Br	Brother
		Si	Sister
△	Male (deceased)	SB	Sibling (sex unknown)
○	Female (deceased)	So	Son
◇	Sex unknown (deceased)	Da	Daughter
		Ch	Child (sex unknown)
△	Male (vital status unknown)	DK	Distant kin (connection
⊖	Female (vital status		unknown)
	unknown)	Hu	Husband
⬙	Sex unknown (vital status	Wi	Wife
	unknown)	BF	Boyfriend
		GF	Girlfriend
e	Age estimated	Fr	Friend
		Ac	Acquaintance
		Pe	Pet

X   Before a symbol. Indicates that it refers to an earlier state of the relationship which has since been disrupted (e.g. X-Hu means ex-husband).

F   Before a symbol. Indicates that it refers to a foster relationship (e.g. F-Da means female foster-child).

Figure 2.1 demonstrates several distinctive features of the personal networks defined by gift transactions in Winnipeg. Those features are worth mentioning here since they show why it is that studies of the gift economy must be concerned with the forms of the institutionalization of ties. We can see, in the first place, that personal networks are composed of kinship ties, friendship ties, and other ties which have been designated in the RANK graphs as "acquaintanceships."[12] Kinship ties predominate, but Hazel Anderson's personal network is not a kindred one and cannot be explained by structural kinship models. Furthermore, the different kinds of ties, and in particular kinship and friendship ties, are intertwined in complex ways. Social networks like that of Hazel Anderson contain kin, friends, and friends of kin and kin of friends. These sets of kinship-friendship ties will be referred to here as *networks of love*.

Within networks of love the friends of ego tend to be clustered in age groups that are either the same as, or adjacent to, that of ego herself. Kinship ties, on the other hand, usually span a much wider range of age groups because they are the principal means by which the members of different generations are linked in emotionally significant relationships. It follows from this that most intergenerational gift transfers are in fact intergenerational family transfers. Despite all the changes that have occurred in intimate relationships in the last few decades, we have here an enduring aspect of personal networks. Family ties continue to be of enormous social and economic importance to many people mainly because they are believed to be more durable than other kinds of ties.

Conclusion

In this chapter the discussion of theories of political economy and moral economy has been extended to include consideration of the different kinds of research questions to which they give rise. It has been suggested that the perspective of political economy focuses upon questions that: are especially concerned with the material flows of gift transfers as forms of social capital; consider the timing of transactions to be of crucial importance; and direct attention to the possibility of contradictions between actors' accounts of their behavior and their real motives for giving gifts. Approaching gift giving from the perspective of moral economy, on the other hand, leads to an emphasis upon: the ritual dimensions of gift transactions as events that are performed on occasions set aside for ceremonial activity; the kinds of social and personal identities that are symbolically defined in interaction rituals; and the interdependence of instrumental and expressive interests in the social construction of systems of relationships.

The aspects of gift transactions that have been identified here will be discussed at various points throughout the following chapters, as we seek to clarify the sociologically important features of gift giving in a modern society. In those discussions two principal kinds of arguments will be presented. They are both intended to substantiate the thesis that what is most distinctive about a modern gift economy is the struggle to institutionalize feelings of solidarity as the basis for social interaction (Cheal 1987a, 1988a).

One line of argument insists that interpersonal gift transactions cannot be understood solely in terms of models of family and kinship networks, however valuable that approach may have been in the early stages of research into gift rituals. The principal reason for this should by now be clear. Kinship ties are sometimes only weakly differentiated from friendship ties, at least for certain purposes, with the result that they may be intermingled in personal networks of considerable complexity. A reconstituted concept of "the private" cannot easily handle this complexity. The thematic core of that concept is domesticity and the spatial seclusion of intimate ties, and it is therefore not much use for understanding those forms of "intimacy at a distance" that are often found in the geographically dispersed networks of the residents of mass societies. It is proposed here that gift transactions are best understood as outcomes of generalized structures of moral economy.

The other line of argument, to which we turn in the next chapter, claims that the moral order of personal and social relationships has been unduly neglected because of the pre-eminence of theories of political economy in recent years. It is therefore necessary to recover moral order as a topic for sociology by emphasizing the fact that moral relationships are prevalent within the gift economy. Gift morality takes many forms, but there can be little doubt that one of the most common is the desire to give to others as an expression of love for them. Social definitions of love are thus claimed to be of some importance.

3

Transactions and relations

Within a moral economy the social significance of individuals is defined by their obligations to others, with whom they maintain continuing relationships. It is the extended reproduction of these relationships that lies at the heart of a gift economy, just as it is the extended reproduction of financial capital which lies at the heart of a market economy. Between these two principles there is a fundamental opposition, as a result of which any attempt to combine them in the same social institution is likely to result in strain and conflict.[1] That is so because, insofar as individuals pursue their self-interests through economic exchange, the least profitable social relations are progressively broken off and replaced with more profitable ones (Blau 1964). Thus Sussman has claimed that when people do not receive "pay offs' for the benefits they give to kin, their motivation to maintain kinship ties breaks down and the kinship network ceases to be a viable social structure (Sussman 1970: 492).

In the ideal case an equilibrium should eventually be reached in the process of economic exchange, when there is no available relationship that could bring greater benefits to the individual than those in which he is already engaged (Homans 1961: 99). In practice, however, the multiple opportunities for interaction that exist under conditions of population mobility and dynamic density in mass societies must make this an unlikely outcome in most cases. If individuals practiced social exchange in every interaction in a modern society the general result would be a continuous turnover of social relationships. If, on the other hand, particular relationships are kept going, then it must be because the members have avoided more profitable exchanges that would otherwise have replaced the original relationships over time (see Eisenstadt and Roniger 1984: 34–7 especially).

In the social reproduction of relationships, individuals subordinate their interests in short-term profits from transactions to a long-term interest in sustaining the system of transactions generated by their relationship. As Bloch has shown, voluntary long-term relationships are possible only insofar as they are moral relationships, of which he says kinship is a prime example (Bloch 1973).[2] Moral relationships, that is to say relationships which are governed by rules that define the relationship itself as socially desirable, necessarily involve some limitation upon the pursuit of individual interests in the acquisition of valued objects and experiences (Askham 1984). It is therefore possible to say that within a moral economy relationships between persons and things are normally subordinated to relationships between persons. The important consequence of this is that whenever stability in relationships is highly valued, social ties will be institutionalized in the manner described earlier. That is to say, we will find that rules define transactions between categories of individuals who have personal relationships that are highly routinized. Where relationships of this kind are concerned, theories which claim that all social ties are composed of economic relations "in the last instance" can only obscure the nature of social practices. That point will now be demonstrated.

Accounting for gift flows

According to the exchange theorists, social life consists of a system of reciprocal transactions.[3] Since it is assumed that exchanges are conducted on the basis of a rational calculation of utilities given and received, repetitive interaction is thought to be characterized by balanced reciprocity. This arrangement has often been described as the dominant principle in gift transactions. Shurmer, for example, says that a gift sets up a debt relationship between donor and recipient, and therefore "all gifts demand reciprocation" (Shurmer 1971: 1242). In a similar vein, Belshaw has questioned "whether any gift is free of equivalence" (Belshaw 1965: 46), and Davis has claimed that the gift economy is constituted by rules of reciprocity (J. Davis 1972: 408).

There is much evidence to show that reciprocal giving is a prominent characteristic of ritual gifts at Christmas, although evidently not all gifts are reciprocated (Lowes, Turner, and Wills 1971; Caplow 1984; Cheal 1986). The Winnipeg Ritual Cycle Study data show that for all gifts given on ritual occasions in 1982, 53 per cent of those individuals who received a gift from an interviewee also gave a ritual gift to the donor during that year. Furthermore, the total number of gifts received from an interviewee during the year was highly correlated with the total number of gifts given to that person.

Pierre Bourdieu has proposed that strategies of social exchange require the denial of reciprocity through ideologies which affirm the disinterested nature of voluntary transactions. The Winnipeg Ritual Cycle Study respondents did, in fact, usually deny that they ever gave gifts in order to receive return gifts. Mrs Caruk, for example, claimed:

> I don't [give gifts] to get something back. I do it because I want to give. It's nice to get presents back – something from my kids on Mother's Day, or just because they were thinking of me – but I don't expect it. They don't have to give because their mother expects them to.

Mrs Caruk's remarks demonstrate all the ambiguity that we would expect to find in the ideological mystification of social exchange. She says that she does not give in order to receive, but she admits that it is nice to get presents back. In one breath she claims not to expect her children to give her presents, but in the next breath she recognizes that "their mother" expects them to do so. What should we make of such sincere confusion? Is Bourdieu correct after all?

In order to answer the above questions we shall have to probe the relationships between the behavior of social actors and their models (or notions) of their behavior in a more serious fashion than is done in most field research (Holy and Stuchlik 1983). To begin with, it is quite clear that Mrs Caruk's contradictory response is only one of several types of accounts that people give of the connections between their own gifts and those of their partners in gift exchanges. In some cases people claim that reciprocity is all there is to gift giving, which is not what we would expect from Bourdieu's law of social exchange. We shall begin by examining two such cases in some detail in order to see how this kind of situation works.

Case study: Melvin Fisher

Melvin Fisher (aged 75) and Mary Atamanchuk are both working-class people who are strong believers in the importance of mutual aid among those who are in a position to help each other. Neither of them is well-off. In Mr Fisher's case that is largely because he has been retired for a number of years. He reports that he and his wife can no longer do many of the things that they used to do, such as visiting relatives in Ontario and taking short trips to the United States.

Mr Fisher exchanges a lot of work and other favors with his sister's son, and with his neighbors. He thinks of these exchanges as gifts "of a sort." In the interviews he had very little to say, except when the opportunity arose to talk about his neighbors. With one of them he frequently exchanges minor services, such as repairs to domestic appliances. With the other neighbors it is mainly tools, and other pieces of equipment such as ladders, that are swapped "back and forth." This reciprocal aid is very important to Melvin Fisher because it is outside the market economy, and thus in most cases no money changes hands. As he put it:

> It saves a lot of money because [otherwise] – for instance, the vacuum cleaner, the stove, or I don't care what it is like that – you have to phone for somebody. As soon as he says he's coming, it could be anywhere from $10 to $30 right there.

Mr Fisher carried this practical attitude over into his views about gift giving on special occasions. He described himself as giving gifts to people who had done something for him, or to those who had given him gifts, because "if they give you a gift you're kind of obliged in a way to give them one." Returning a gift was the only reason Mr Fisher could think of for giving, in spite of the interviewer's attempts to probe for other reasons. We might therefore expect to find that the flows of gifts given and received by him are strictly symmetrical. In fact that is not always the case. Mr Fisher participated in 18 gift transactions on special occasions in 1982 (see Figure 3.1), in 12 of which he was the donor. Only one of his gifts (no. 11) is an unequivocal instance of social exchange, involving a small sum of money for the boy who delivered his newspapers. Five gifts (nos 6 through 10) are the reciprocals of gifts received from relatives (nos 13 through 16). In 1 gift transaction (no. 12) he and his wife were both the givers and the receivers. The remaining 7 of Mr Fisher's gift transactions consisted of unreciprocated gifts. In 5 of them (nos 1 through 5) he was a donor and in 2 (nos 17 and 18) he was a recipient.

More than half of Mr Fisher's ritual gifts involve reciprocity of some kind. However, his reciprocal transactions cannot be explained simply as a result of strategic considerations of social exchange, since they are also heavily influenced by other variables. Mr Fisher's gift transactions are in fact highly structured, and can be described by a few simple rules, even though he appears to be unable to articulate them himself.

Firstly, a systematic exchange of gifts occurs only at Christmas.

Figure 3.1 Melvin Fisher's gift transactions

Given by	*Given to*	*Occasion*
1. Self	Wife	Birthday
2. Self and wife	Wife's sister A	Birthday
3. Self and wife	Wife's sister B	Birthday
4. Self and wife	Wife's father's sister's son's wife	Illness
5. Self and wife	Wife's mother's sister's daughter	Christmas
6. Self and wife	Wife's father's sister's daughter	Christmas
7. Self and wife	Wife's sister A	Christmas
8. Self and wife	Wife's sister B	Christmas
9. Self and wife	Sister	Christmas
10. Self and wife	Sister's daughter	Christmas
11. Self and wife	Paper boy	Christmas
12. Self and wife	Self and wife	Christmas
13. Sister's daughter	Self and wife	Christmas
14. Sister	Self and wife	Christmas
15. Wife's sisters (A & B)	Self and wife	Christmas
16. Wife's father's sister's daughter	Self and wife	Christmas
17. Sister	Self and wife	Wife's birthday
18. Sister's son's wife	Self	Birthday

No gift given at any other occasion was reciprocated, whereas only one Christmas gift (no. 5) was not reciprocated (excluding the special case of gift no. 11).

Secondly, the ritual acts of women are more powerful than those of men. Women were recorded much more frequently than men as being the actors in Melvin Fisher's gift transactions. (Besides Mr Fisher himself, only one other male was involved – the paper boy, who was a gift recipient.) It would seem to follow from this that the strongest ritual ties are those between women.

Thirdly, in ritual matters husbands do not normally act independently of their wives. Except when he is giving to her, all of Mr Fisher's gift giving is done in conjunction with his wife (and so is most of his gift receiving).

Interestingly, these three rules combine to produce a fourth rule by derivation. On occasions other than Christmas, giving takes the principal form of unreciprocated transactions by women (sometimes with their husbands) to the wife's (principally female) kin. Melvin Fisher's unreciprocated giving is therefore mainly to his wife's female relatives, whereas his unreciprocated gift receiving is all from his own female relatives.

The gift rules employed in Mr Fisher's personal network are in themselves quite striking. What is even more striking is the fact that, although only a small number of gifts are involved in this case, they form a complex system of transactions which could not have been predicted from Mr Fisher's own representation of his gift practices. The flows of ritual gifts to and from Mr Fisher are not structured by a ubiquitous norm of reciprocity. It would seem that his own notions about gift giving are less important than the consequences of his membership in a kinship network based on female solidarity (see Figure 3.2).

Mr Fisher's set of annual gift transactions is unusual for its small size, which is why it makes such a useful illustrative example. Complex though it is, it is far less complex than those of individuals who are more active givers. One such person is Mary Atamanchuk, who was involved in a total of 85 transactions during 1982. Fortunately for us Mrs Atamanchuk was a much more articulate informant, and she was able to show how additional decision rules may enter into gift practices.

Case study: Mary Atamanchuk

Mary Atamanchuk is 56 years old and works in a cafeteria. She is a widow, living with her 76-year-old mother who needs constant attention. Mary is not well-off, and has to employ somebody to stay with her mother while she is at work. Without a spouse, with no children, tied to an ailing parent, and with little discretionary income, Mrs Atamanchuk is nevertheless a long way from being socially isolated. She maintains an extensive network of social ties, which are marked by gift giving (see Figures 3.4a and 3.4b).

Like Melvin Fisher, Mary Atamanchuk's thoughts on gift giving are conditioned by her limited resources. She, too, sees gifts as ways of repaying favors and as returns for gifts received earlier. She describes gift giving as being largely a matter of "showing appreciation." The ritual occasions at which gifts are customarily given in Winnipeg have no symbolic meaning for her, and she was unable to suggest a single reason why Christmas and birthdays should be considered important times for giving. Mrs Atamanchuk simply takes it for granted that "somehow everybody gets so excited around Christmastime." In her eyes the traditional

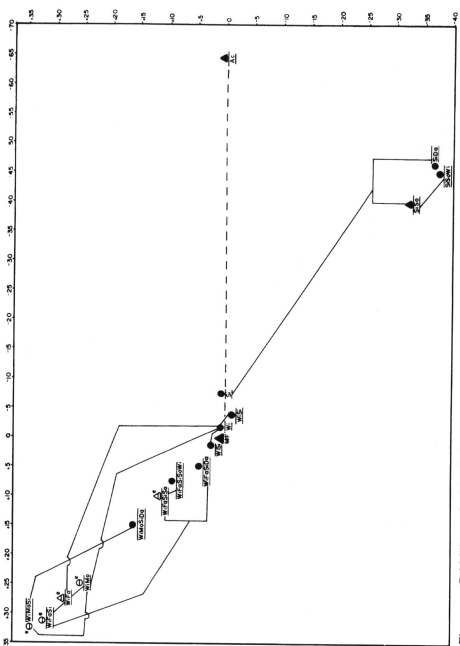

Figure 3.2 RANK graph, Melvin Fisher age 75

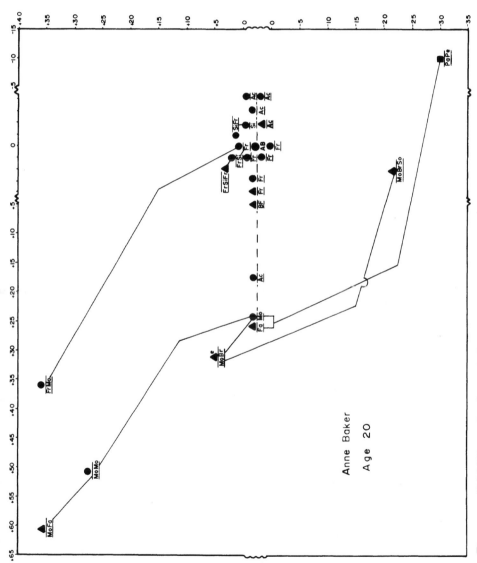

Figure 3.3 RANK graph, Anne Baker age 20

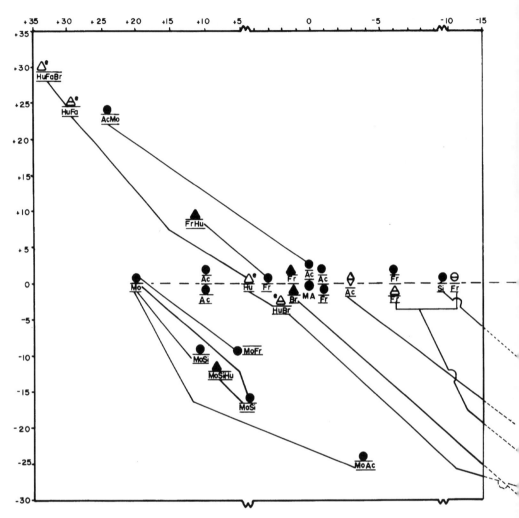

Figure 3.4a RANK graph, Mary Atamanchuk age 56

occasions for giving are times for returning gifts to those who
gave to her the previous year, and they are opportunities for
"paying back" those who do a lot of things to help her, but who
refuse to take direct payment in cash. In the latter category Mrs
Atamanchuk mentioned her sister as being especially important.

> My sister drives and I don't, and she does a lot of errands for me, you
> know, shopping, and anything that I want. I phone her up, and if she
> can do it she will. So it's little things like that that count, especially the
> last year or so. I can't get out much in the evening because I can't leave

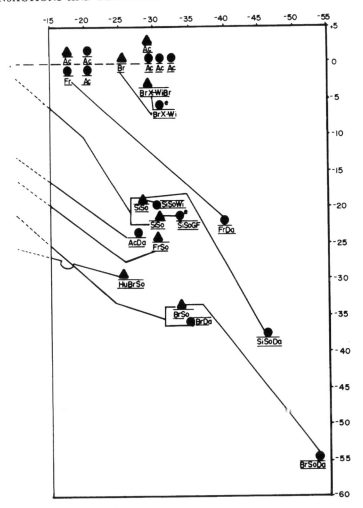

Figure 3.4b RANK graph, Mary Atamanchuk age 56 *cont'd*

my mother alone. So if [my sister] can do it, she does it, and then it saves me the trip.

Paying her sister back does not take the form of giving her more gifts than she receives from her. The numerical balance of gifts is in fact in Mrs Atamanchuk's favor, since her sister gave her an unreciprocated gift at Easter (see Figure 3.5, no. 25). Instead, Mrs Atamanchuk aims to spend more on each gift for her sister than she spends for other people. With Christmas coming up, she said that she had a pretty good idea of who would get what. "Who does more for me gets more; who does less gets less." As we would expect, she intended to favor her sister, with the result that a sexual division is drawn among her siblings. Mary Atamanchuk feels that, "My sister usually gets more than my brothers do because she does more for me. . . . She gets more than the others because actually she's got it coming almost."

Figure 3.5 Mary Atamanchuk's unreciprocated gift transactions

Given by	*Given to*	*Occasion*
1. Self	Priest	Christmas
2. Self	Ex-coworker A	Christmas
3. Self	Coworker A	Christmas
4. Self	Coworker B	Christmas
5. Self	Coworker C	Christmas
6. Self	Coworker D	Christmas
7. Self	Coworker E	Christmas
8. Self	Brother's daughter	Christmas
9. Self and sister	Sister's son's daughter	Christmas
10. Self	Brother's daughter	Birthday
11. Self	Brother's son	Birthday
12. Self	Brother's son's daughter	Birthday
13. Self	Sister's son's girlfriend	Birthday
14. Self	Sister's son's daughter	Birthday
15. Self	Mother's sister's husband	Birthday
16. Self	Ex-employee	Birthday
17. Self	Mother	Mother's Day
18. Self	Husband's father's brother	Funeral
19. Self & group of coworkers	Ex-coworker B	Birth
20. Self & group of coworkers	Employer's daughter	Birth
21. Self	Friend's son	Wedding
22. Self	Brother's ex-wife's brother	Wedding
23. Self	Husband's brother's son	Wedding
24. Self	Ex-employer	Anniversary
25. Sister	Self	Easter
26. Ex-coworker C	Self	Christmas

Mrs Atamanchuk is strongly committed to a view of gift trans-actions as founded upon exchange, a view which she had no hesi-tation in describing and which she reiterated throughout her inter-view. During the course of the interview, however, other themes gradually emerged to produce a more complex picture. Although most of Mrs Atamanchuk's gift giving in 1982 consisted of gift exchanges, she did give a number of unreciprocated gifts, which have been listed in Figure 3.5. Some of those gifts went to people who were unlikely to have done anything significant for her in the previous year.

A few of Mrs Atamanchuk's unreciprocated gift transactions can plausibly be accounted for as balancing exchange accounts with those who had assisted her in some way. Her gifts to her coworkers and to her priest are cases in point. However, not all of her unreciprocated gifts could have been returns for favors, since some of the recipients were in no position to help her. These were either people who Mrs Atamanchuk recognized for certain purposes on certain occasions, but with whom effective ties were not maintained, or they were people whose energies were devoted to coping with their own problems.

An example of the first type is Mary's brother's daughter, age 21 (no. 8). She no longer lives in the same province, and Mrs Atamanchuk sees her once a year or less. They are sufficiently out of touch that Mrs Atamanchuk was not sure at the time of the interview if her niece was still employed or had gone back to school. An example of the second type is Mrs Atamanchuk's mother's sister's husband (no. 15). At the time of the interview he had been out of work for the past year. He was currently in hospital fighting cancer, and at age 64 he would seem to have been a poor prospect as an exchange partner.

Contrary to the exchange model of behavior which Mary Atamanchuk herself espoused, she does not seem to have benefited from every transaction with her kin. Nevertheless, she did not see these one-way transfers of resources as being problematic. Deviations from her explicit exchange rule were aligned[4] with it through one or other of several culturally available accounts of extenuating circumstances.

In the first place, Mrs Atamanchuk expects to receive a gift from those to whom she has given only "if they can afford it." If they are short of money, on the other hand, she is prepared to believe that they would give to her if they could, and so she reports that such a failure to reciprocate does not bother her. Also, she recognizes that there are always those who need assistance. In this connection wedding gifts are seen as exceptions to the exchange rule, and Mrs Atamanchuk says that "you don't expect anything in return for that." When a couple are "starting out" in married life they "need so many things," she says, and therefore they have "no reason" (that is, no obligation) to give a gift back.

Young people in general are often excused from the obligation to reciprocate, and Mrs Atamanchuk appears to expect recurring losses in her transactions with her young kinsmen. Asked to think about individuals with whom she does not expect balanced giving to take place, she said:

> My nephews. I usually don't get too much from them. But they always get a fair amount from me, not only on occasions but even in between. I do a lot of canning and gardening and . . . I give them stuff like that in between, too, especially if I feel they need it.

Finally, Mrs Atamanchuk accepts net losses in certain exchanges because she *prefers* that outcome to making a net gain. Her main concern in comparing gifts and counter-gifts is that she does not want to feel "like I owe them something." If people do spend more on her than she spends on them she tries to make up for it in some other way. Not to do so would make her feel "kind of guilty," she says. The best way to avoid that state of affairs is to end up with a slight balance in the other person's favor, and so she says that "I like to give more than I receive."

Reciprocity reconsidered

Despite her insistence upon the connection between giving and getting, Mrs Atamanchuk's gift giving cannot be accounted for by a simple model of profit-seeking exchange. Her rule of symmetrical giving and receiving is combined with other rules for loss-making in asymmetrical transactions, which are allowed to override the norm of reciprocity in certain situations.[5] Further-more, the principal exchange rule that Mary Atamanchuk applied to her gift transactions is not one of utility maximization, as we should expect from exchange theory, but one of debt avoidance. In this she was not alone. Although very few people in Winnipeg speak of giving in order to get things in return, a number of them do report feeling obliged to make return gifts for ones they have received. They also often feel that it is necessary to ensure there is a rough equivalence in the value of presents given and received. The reasons for the strength of that feeling have to do with the more general desire to maintain balanced relationships with significant others.

Blau has argued that there is a tendency towards imbalance in social exchange, as individuals seek to impress others by providing them with superior benefits (Blau 1964: 26–7). Thus, he claims, the mutual attraction in most intimate relationships is the result of an imbalance of contributions that compensates for inequalities in spontaneous affection. Mrs Atamanchuk's preference for giving more than she receives might be explained in these terms, and the plausibility of exchange theory could thereby be preserved.[6] However, most individuals are not the judgmental dopes that exchange theorists have sometimes assumed.

Most people actively interpret the social significance and potential consequences of others' transactions with them, including any exchange imbalances that may arise. Transactions are therefore evaluated not only for the rewards that they are perceived to bring, but also for what may be learned from them about the motives of actors. In a study of weddings conducted as part of a wider program of research on gift behavior (the Hotel Chateau Study, reported below pp. 125ff.), one young couple were completely unconcerned about an extraordinarily expensive gift which they had received from some old friends of the bridegroom's parents. They interpreted the value of the gift as an attempt to re-establish close relationships with their parents, and thus as having no social consequences for themselves. Ascriptions of motives of this sort are made all the time about gift transactions, and they are consciously incorporated into gift culture.

The attribution of dispositions to others is a social process of great importance,[7] since actors use this knowledge in forming their own lines of action. In turn, competent actors are well aware of the battery of interpretative considerations to which any action is inevitably exposed. They therefore shape their gift behavior so as to control its communicative effects (Cheal 1987a). "Buying" friendship is a manipulative stratagem which is part of the common stock of knowledge, and for which counterstratagems have been devised. Defensive practices consist mainly of ways of talking about extravagant gifts so that the gifts themselves, and the donors' ascribed motives, are devalued. In order to avoid "looking stupid," therefore, it may be necessary to calculate very carefully what is given so that the financial values of gifts given and received are carefully balanced.

Imbalanced exchange is often deliberately avoided in order not to create the wrong impression of an individual's orientation towards another. Here we see very clearly that gift giving is not just a process of exchanging utilities. It is also a process of impression management,[8] through which individuals seek to sustain certain definitions of their gifts, and thereby of themselves. Among the many problems with exchange theory is that it fails to take into account the fact that a gift (or any other type of transaction) will have its intended effect only if its meaning as defined by the donor is allowed to go unchallenged. Costly gifts which are defensively labelled by their recipients as "unnecessary" or "ridiculous" (both responses were recorded in the Hotel Chateau Study) do not produce very much in the way of social returns. Far from gaining any prestige from such gifts, the donors are likely to forfeit the respect that might otherwise have been accorded to them. This point can be illustrated from Leonard White's remarks about his brother-in-law.

Leonard White is a 53-year-old university professor. His prejudices about expensive gifts are rooted in an academic subculture that often disparages the money-making business ethic in capitalist society. Dr White's brother-in-law Michael is a businessman who owns his own company. From time to time Michael has embarrassed them by coming up with some very expensive gifts which they have felt unable to match in their own giving. For example, when Leonard married Michael's sister he gave them an expensive picture as a wedding present. Mrs White said that they would have liked to reciprocate, but when Michael was married they gave him a place setting of sterling silver which was worth only about one quarter of the cost of the picture. Leonard White elaborated on this point by saying that:

> He, like some people, values a person by the dollar value, which I don't. He would make a big palaver of giving something like that. I think he paid $400 for the picture, which I think is silly, quite frankly. I mean, I like the picture and everything, but he tends to value a thing by the dollar value, not by the sentiment.

Dr White thought of his brother-in-law's attitude as being different from that held in their social circle, and he described Michael as "the odd man out." His wife, who participated in the interview, added:

> He's always been like that. It hasn't changed in all the years. He sees gift giving as an occasion to make a flamboyant gesture. I can remember twenty years ago, he would rather not give anything unless it was *something*. If he was pressed for money, he would rather not give anything unless he could afford something that was [splashy].

Leonard reiterated this point in a soliloquy that his wife attempted to steer away from troubled waters.

> It's an attitude. As you say, there's a flamboyance about money. A nasty business [attitude] – administration and all this sort of thing. He's hyped up on this business executive type of thing, and the big splash

is giving. I think it's really doing something for his ego, as he gives out a big present. (It has never created any difficulties, though.) We just accept him for . . . [wife's interjection – "what he is"] . . . the ass that he is.

Dr White is not alone in his views about people who give presents that are so valuable they are "silly." It is reasonable to suppose that most adult actors are aware of the possibility that their gifts – and they themselves – may be labelled in this way. Some people see this as a highly undesirable outcome which should be avoided if possible. Anne Baker certainly saw things that way.

Case study: Anne Baker

Anne Baker is 20 years old and is in her second year at university. She attends a local university, but she values her independence from parental scrutiny and has moved away from her parents' home to live with a group of girlfriends. When I visited on a Sunday afternoon I was told with great amusement that one of them was still "missing in action" after a party the night before.

Anne partially supports herself by working as a waitress in a fast foods establishment, but she still receives financial and other assistance from her parents, upon which she depends. Money is in short supply, and Anne and her room-mate are frequently broke. Thanks to her parents' generosity, Anne is slightly better off than her girlfriends and so she is often the one who buys the wine and liquor which they take to parties. Many of her gifts on special occasions are also alcoholic drinks, or other means of entertaining friends such as restaurant meals.

Having fun with a vital circle of friends and acquaintances is the center of Anne's life, and much of her gift giving is an extension of this (see Figure 3.3). Gifts to her friends are mainly things that either create an occasion for interaction, such as taking them out for dinner, or that add to the enjoyment from interaction, such as a bottle of wine. Anne's gifts to her family members, on the other hand, consist of things for personal use, such as a sweater or a bracelet. Here there is a much stronger sense of obligation to give, as Anne feels that she must give presents to her sister, her parents, and her grandparents, even though it is often hard to know what they will like.

Anne Baker gives gifts either because doing so makes her feel good, or out of a sense of family duty. Nevertheless, she was concerned that there should be a rough balance in most of her gift transactions. This was partly due to her belief in a rule of distributive justice, similar to that proposed by Homans (1961), since she said that she did not want to feel "ripped off." But it was also because giving less or more than others give to her would have contradicted the image of herself which she wanted to hold, and which she wanted others to hold. Unlike Mary Atamanchuk, Anne Baker does not like to give more than she receives, because it "doesn't look good." She says that "If you buy someone say a $50 present or something, and they buy you a $10 present, that kind of makes you look sort of stupid, like you're maybe trying to buy their friendship or whatever." On the other hand, Anne does not like to receive more than she gives, because to do so is to fail to be an equal partner in a relationship. If someone has spent more on a gift for her than she has spent on them, she says "I feel really cheap, because you're not measuring up to what they might . . . you know they don't expect it of you, but you sort of expect it of yourself, that you should not be spending less than they're spending on you."

In actual fact Anne Baker's emphasis upon balanced reciprocity only applies in her relations with her peers. Profiting from gift exchanges with her close friends was unacceptable, she claimed, because they were in the same, or similar, financial situation that she was in. Anne was quite prepared to benefit from other transactions, however, as "In the case of my parents and my grandparents they're making so far above what I'm making that it doesn't bother me." Anne readily confirmed what the data on her gift transactions show, that she spends less on gifts for her parents and grandparents than they spend on her. That is most obvious in the case of her grandparents, for although she spends less on them than she does on her parents they are most generous to her. At Christmas, for example, she bought her grandfather an aftershave kit and her grandmother some slippers, at a cost of approximately $10 each. Her grandparents, on the other hand, gave her $200 to get whatever she wanted. Anne believes that this imbalance in her favor is acceptable, because of the greater resources of those who have accumulated financial capital over a lifetime of earnings.

> It's basically finances. I don't think age has a lot to do with it. Although the older you are, usually the more money you have that you've saved. You're more established in a career. A lot of people I know are students, or they've gone into working out of high school, and they might not have a really well-paying job or anything like that. My Grandpa used to own a store, and they've saved quite a bit of money.

Conclusion

The modern theory of gift transactions began with Marcel Mauss's description of autonomous systems of prestations, whose principal internal dynamic is the obligation to provide a return gift for one that has been received. Our initial empirical description of a modern gift economy has therefore focused upon the reciprocity of gifts as a fundamental condition of social interaction.

Not everybody in Winnipeg is prepared to recognize that there may be an exchange process in the gift economy. Some people deny that they, or others who they know, ever expect to receive a gift. Nevertheless, it is not hard to find people who are quite open about the personal importance of reciprocity, even though they often find it hard to articulate a vocabulary of motive for it, or to relate that vocabulary to their observed practices. On these people Bourdieu's unsympathetic thesis of a socially necessary mystification of gift exchange must founder. An illusion that is shared by some, but not by others, is not derived from a universal logic of interaction. Equally serious, 2 of the respondents discussed in this chapter have little education, and they do not belong to that privileged intelligentsia which prides itself on being able to uncover the illusions of others. Whatever the wisdom of ordinary people may turn out to be, it would seem to be worth listening to.

The calculations that actors make about their gift transactions are complex, and there is no simple formula that can account for them. We have seen that in some instances (with some alters, and on some occasions) gifts are carefully balanced, and symmetric reciprocity is the rule. In other instances asymmetric reciprocity is preferred, or there may be no gift reciprocity at all. A more extensive analysis of cases, including the statistical analysis of gift flows, is necessary in order to establish the precise relationship between these two patterns of behavior (for a preliminary investigation, see Cheal 1986). Nevertheless, we have seen enough here to permit two conclusions that are of general significance.

The first point to make is that imbalances in gift transactions seem to be most likely to occur whenever an individual assumes personal responsibility for nurturing another. Thus we have seen that Mary Atamanchuk expects to give more to her nephews than she receives from them. Furthermore, she continues to supply them with home-made foods even though they are now adult men (their ages range from 22 to 30). Similarly, we have seen that Anne Baker's grandparents give generously to their 20-year-old granddaughter, and that she accepts her dependent status as a perfectly natural state of affairs, in that particular relationship though not in others.

Relationships of nurturant dependence such as those reported here (see also Figure 3.4) are most often intergenerational relationships, in which transfers of resources typically move in a serial flow from each generation to its successors (Cheal 1988c). In addition, they are often relationships in which women play an extremely active role, as we saw in the case of Melvin Fisher (see also Cheal 1987a). Both of Mr Fisher's unreciprocated gift receipts consisted of food provided by female relatives – a Chinese take-home dinner from his sister and a birthday cake from his sister's daughter-in-law.

The second important point to make is that a deeper understanding is needed of the norm of reciprocity. In one of his most astute observations Herbert Blumer (1969) pointed out that the subjective validity of any norm depends upon the meanings that are assigned to it. It is therefore always necessary to explore what particular norms mean to particular persons, and how their conformity to a norm makes sense to them within a particular point of view on social interaction and their place in it.

We have seen here that reciprocity may be desired in order to benefit from rewarding exchanges (Melvin Fisher), and out of an interest in distributive justice among those who are engaged in practical and symbolic interchanges (Mary Atamanchuk and Anne Baker). Reciprocity may also be preferred, as we saw in Anne Baker's case, because symmetric reciprocity denotes a preferred equality of standing within a peer relationship. More generally, reciprocity of any kind (whether symmetric or asymmetric) denotes standing as an active participant in a relationship, as someone who has the capacity to contribute to it. From this point of view, "buying friendship" is to be avoided precisely because it signifies the social inferiority of the more generous donor. Few people want to be thought of as so lacking in social skills and attractions for others that they must resort to that kind of stratagem – at least not somebody like Anne Baker. Anne's physical attractions and lively spirit mean that even a Sunday afternoon interview is disrupted by a casual male acquaintance dropping by to enquire about taking her "out for a ride." It is, of course, true that not everybody can afford to be so relaxed about their value to others. Mary Atamanchuk may well have had occasional self-doubts on that score.

At the beginning of this chapter it was suggested that in a moral economy relationships between persons and things are typically subordinated to relationships between persons, and that the social significance of the gift economy lies in the reproduction of relationships. Perhaps the most interesting evidence for this has been the irrelevance of Melvin Fisher's notions of exchange for his gift practices on ritual occasions. Rules for the maintenance of certain kinds of social ties, and not calculations of economic advantage, in fact had the greatest influence upon his gift behavior. Insofar as this principle applies more generally, it has a noteworthy consequence for the incidence of unreciprocated gift giving. Complete failure to reciprocate is rare, and its incidence is notable only where social ties are breaking down.

Social relationships may disintegrate for a variety of reasons, but in a mass society one of the most common is surely the fact that people have "drifted apart." The pursuit of individual goals, and organizational decisions over which individuals have no control, constantly pull people apart by causing them to relocate in new areas and to take on new jobs with new sets of colleagues. As a result, they see much less of each other than before, and their social interests become oriented toward those who are closer at hand. This was the only reason Anne Baker could think of for why she might ever stop giving gifts to somebody with whom she had once had a close relationship.

> When you stop giving gifts to someone, maybe it will be a friend that you've grown apart from who lives in another part of the country now. Because I have girlfriends that when they lived in the city we would always exchange gifts for birthdays, but now that they don't live in the city anymore, and I rarely hear from them, we just don't do it anymore.

Not all relationships with those who have moved away are allowed to wither in this fashion. Although it frequently happens to friendships that were formed in high school, and to other ties formed on the basis of shared experiences within formal organizations, it does not happen as often to kinship ties. Relations of intimacy at a distance are often maintained with absent family members, particularly where a relationship of nurturant dependence had previously existed, or could be claimed to exist under altered circumstances. The consequences of this inequality in the strength of ties show up in the differences between Mary Atamanchuk's reciprocal and non-reciprocal gift transactions.

Mrs Atamanchuk's personal network included several people

with whom she had once been closely associated, but who she now saw infrequently due to the original connection having been broken. Although gift giving took a reciprocal form in the majority of her personal relationships, this was not true of her transactions with these "ex" associates. Mary's "ex" relationships were marked by only one instance of reciprocity, whereas she had given to five of them and received nothing in return, and had received a present from one to whom she had not given anything (see Figure 3.4). All but one of these "ex" ties had been formed through an employment relationship (three ex-coworkers, an ex-employer and an ex-employee who had provided home daycare for her mother).

People who have "grown apart," as Anne Baker put it, are less likely to engage in reciprocal transactions, because they lack the reciprocity of perspectives which makes them equally desirous and confident of continuing the relationship. Certain categories of ties, such as those with people once known through work, seem to be more vulnerable than others to losing this reciprocity of perspectives, presumably because they depend heavily upon continuous, frequent contact. The reciprocal recognition of family and kinship ties, on the other hand, is comparatively unaffected by shifting patterns of interaction. This suggests that there is a certain rigidity, or stereotypical quality, to social definitions of these relationships, which makes them both more compulsory and compulsive. In recent years some feminists have suggested that heterosexuality is compulsory. It is also compulsory for children to love their mothers. When they do not, there is bound to be trouble. We shall want to consider the reification of family life, and the problem of ungrateful sons, in more detail in the next chapter.

Like many other Canadians, the three people whose case studies have been examined in this chapter did not live in a "conventional" nuclear family composed of husband and wife with children. Only one of them (Melvin Fisher) lived with a spouse, and none of them had ever had a child. Even so, the family life world was very real to them, and the majority of their gifts were given to kin rather than to friends. If school friends and coworkers are often people who grow apart, then family members, it is thought, are people who should grow together.

4

Love culture

Emotions of love, affection, and caring have not received a great deal of attention in the social sciences, due to the common belief that they are ideological phenomena which conceal the real (i.e. material) structures of social life. Structural network analysts, for example, have claimed that ideas and feelings are simply effects of structural constraints acting upon rational individuals who are in competition for scarce resources (Wellman 1983; Richardson and Wellman 1985). The weakness in this approach is that it is based upon rational choice theory, and therefore fails to take account of the intersubjective meanings on which social interaction depends (Aguilar 1984; Cheal 1984). Those meanings include "feeling rules," which define the legitimate emotions that are held to be consistent with particular kinds of social situations (Hochschild 1979).

In structures of interaction the structural significance of feeling rules lies in the ways in which they sustain actors' commitments to situations. Voluntary commitments to repetitive situations involving considerable personal sacrifice are likely to be sustained only when they are defined in terms of diffuse feeling states that are not tied to particular events. The social construction of long-term patterns of interaction is thus made possible by culturally recognized orientations towards social objects, such as feelings of love towards family members. How those feelings are produced, and reproduced in rituals such as Mother's Day (Hausen 1984), is therefore of some importance.

From the perspective of political economy, social interaction is merely "the overlay of social relations on what may begin in purely economic transactions" (Granovetter 1985: 498). It will be necessary to turn this approach on its head. In the gift economy long-term relationships are inscribed in an overlay of transactions on what begin as purely social relations. The most obvious evidence for this point is the fact that biological reproduction is a social event which has enormous consequences for the individuals involved, as Emile Durkheim pointed out.

In his critique of utilitarian reductionism, Durkheim stated that association with others is the most imperative determinant of behavior, "for it is the source of all other compulsions." He went on to observe that we cannot avoid associating with particular others whom we do not choose, since, "As a consequence of my birth, I am obliged to associate with a given group" (Durkheim 1964b: 104). It may be true, he concluded, that we later acquiesce to the requirements of the groups into which we are born, but this does not change the fact that it is the accident of our birth, and not a free choice of exchange partners, that has given us one set of kinship ties rather than another.

Durkheim's sociology was overly deterministic, as we shall see later, but it did unambiguously identify one way in which systems of relationships give rise to sentiments between individuals. In this chapter we shall see that there is much to be gained from looking at gifts as expressions of the management of emotions within long-term relationships of nurturant dependence (see also Hochschild, in press). That also happens to be the way in which most natural actors explain their own gift behavior. Hazel Anderson, whose network of ties was illustrated in chapter 2, thought about her gift giving in this way.

Case study: Hazel Anderson

Hazel Anderson is comfortably middle-aged and middle-class. She is 52 years old, works as a teacher, and is married to a pharmacist. Mrs Anderson acknowledges that at her present stage of life she has no financial worries, and she can therefore afford to enjoy the pleasures of giving to others, which she does extensively. Her views on gift giving are relaxed and largely unproblematic. It is, she thinks, "really a form of communication" that is about "the whole expression of feeling."

Mrs Anderson says that she gives gifts to people for a variety of reasons: "to help them celebrate, to let them know that I'm thinking of them, to share in their feelings or whatever it may be, sympathy or excitement or happiness or to let them know they're special people." Gifts are therefore given on the *big occasions* that come once in a lifetime, in which she includes marriage, the birth of a first child, or a sixtieth wedding anniversary. They are also given on the *regular occasions*, such as birthdays, in order to let people know that she is thinking about them. The nature of the occasion, and the nature of the gift, are not the most important considerations, Mrs Anderson believes. It is the person (of the recipient) and how they receive the gift that is really important. Her gifts tend to be practical things, she says, but:

It's basically the message thing. And also thinking of that person as someone special and making that person feel special at that time. I think that's the essence of a lot of giving, what it's doing for that person's feeling of themself – especially for somebody who's alone. It's really important that they know they're being thought about and this is a way of showing it, not just going, but going with something, because you're giving of yourself.

It is the expressive functions of gifts, and not their instrumental functions, that were emphasized by Mrs Anderson. That is not only because she herself does not need material assistance, but it is largely because the redistribution of resources to those in need is not the main effect of the gift economy. Rather, gifts serve to connect individuals to one another, insofar as people are willing to participate in the process of social exchange. Several reasons for this emerged in Mrs Anderson's account of her gift practices.

In the first place, those who are in need of social support often suffer more from lack of social contact than they do from physical want. Mrs Anderson feels that this is particularly true of the elderly. Depending on the needs of the person, she considers that it might be appropriate to give money to someone with children, because "maybe that dollar would be really, really important." But otherwise, giving money would show a lack of sensitivity to the individual's situation:

Because there's lots of people that don't need money. That's not the thing they need. They need sort of personal thought. I'm thinking of all these older people. I mean, they don't have a lot of money, but I never give them money because it's the thought of me choosing something for them and me thinking of them that is significant to them. And even if it's little, if it's cookies I bake, that's way more important to them than giving them the money. Or even [than] going out and buying the cookies actually.

A further reason why material circumstances are rarely the predominant consideration in gift transactions is that those who do have pressing financial needs may indicate that they are not willing to receive the things that others would like to give them. That is usually because they are not prepared to accept a particular relationship (or perhaps any relationship) of nurturant dependence. The desire not to feel indebted to others is often sufficiently strong that some people prefer to break off gift exchanges rather than feel obliged to make a return which they cannot afford. Mrs Anderson reported that this was the case with her husband's brother's wife, who had subsequently been widowed, and who was now raising four children on her own without any assistance from them.

> Early in her marriage she established the fact with us that she really didn't care to exchange gifts, that she thought it was a waste of money and time and that she would [just] send us a Christmas card at Christmastime. And that's fine. That's what we do. Because this is her feeling about gifts, and I don't want to impose mine on her. She would feel beholden, or she would feel just plain stupid to be spending money this way. . . . And so we don't respond to each other in that way.

Finally, Mrs Anderson feels that although gifts are never the decisive factor in a relationship they can help to cement it by adding to the flow of messages between two people. She therefore regrets that she and her husband's brother's widow have not exchanged gifts.

> Basically, the relationship wasn't that close to start with, so I don't know that [the absence of gift exchanges] changed it. It might have made the relationship better if we had had more communication and response to each other's feelings for each other. I'm sure some form of communication back and forth – any form of communication, it didn't have to be a gift – but it would have helped that situation. The occasional card and the rare letter certainly doesn't keep the warmth open that the regular communication does. I'm not sure that gifts would have made a difference though.

Hazel Anderson's remarks show that maintaining family ties – and what is effective and what is not – are important practical concerns for many people. That is true especially (but not exclusively) for women, whose kinship work has received increasing recognition in recent years (Caplow et al. 1982: 230; di Leonardo 1984: 194–218).[1] Studies of informal social organization have shown that the central ties in personal networks are often enduring family relationships (Wellman 1979; Fischer 1982; Bulmer 1986), which are maintained largely through the kin-keeping activities of women (Rosenthal 1985).

Much recent sociological work on gender has claimed that the position of women within the family is an inferior one, and that family ties are therefore significant obstacles to women's happiness and fulfillment. Why women have continued to put up with this situation has been an urgent political question for many feminists. Not surprisingly, this has led to a renewed scholarly interest in the question of what might account for the perpetuation of family systems (for example, Smith 1973; Chodorow 1978). The question, "what keeps the family going?" (Bruegel 1978), may seem naive from a commonsensical point of view, but it has some force in the social sciences, since at various times it has been argued that urbanism, industrialism, and capitalism must eventually lead to the dissolution of family life as we know it. The failure of those predictions has been strikingly demonstrated in a number of studies (Salaff 1981; Williams 1981, 1983), and the reproduction of family ties has therefore become something of a sociological puzzle. We shall explore the nature of that puzzle in order to clarify the theoretical issues that are involved in the relationship between the family and the gift economy.

Family theory and the logic of necessity

The continued existence of family structures has been one of the principal battlegrounds in "the war over the family" in contemporary social thought (B. Berger and P. Berger 1983). Four main types of sociological explanation have been advanced to account for the family's remarkable persistence. All of them have employed some form of functionalist logic, according to which social practices are explained by the needs which they are thought to fulfill. Where those four approaches have differed is in their identification of whose needs are in fact met by family life.

The classical functionalist explanation for the persistence of families is that of structural functionalism. As is well known, this theoretical approach assumes that the parts of any society are adapted to perform certain functions that help ensure the survival of the whole society. Kingsley Davis has argued that the existence of family groups is to be accounted for by the ways in which they meet society's need for the continued replacement of its members (K. Davis 1948: 394–6). In his view the four main social functions of the family are therefore the reproduction, maintenance, placement, and socialization of the young. Subsequent discussions narrowed the definition of familial functionality, but throughout the 1950s and early 1960s the structural functionalist argument remained much the same. The family was considered to be a universal institution because it fulfilled universal functional prerequisites for the survival of human societies (Reiss 1965).

The fundamental flaw in the structural functional theory of the family was that a variety of structures, some "familial" and some not, might conceivably fulfill a given functional prerequisite

(Weigert and Thomas 1971).[2] And if that were so, then it became clear that *the family* might not be a universal institution after all (Collier, Rosaldo, and Yanagisako 1982). As a result of this realization, attention shifted in the 1970s to studying the functioning of particular types of family structures in particular types of societies, such as the isolated nuclear (i.e. private) family in industrial capitalist societies.

Recent work on co-resident nuclear families from a Marxist perspective has tended to conclude that the persistence of family life in capitalist societies is a result of the need for women's unpaid domestic labor, by means of which (male) labor power is reproduced as an instrument of capitalist production (Fox 1980). The family is therefore believed to serve the needs of capital by providing an abundant labor force that can be employed at low wages. The critical weakness in this argument has been the same as that of structural functionalism, namely its failure to account for the uneven social distribution of functionally equivalent practices.[3] The practical necessity for *some* social division of labor does not account for the particular form of the patriarchal family, nor does it provide a sufficient explanation for the existence of the nuclear family in any form whatsoever (Bruegel 1978; Barrett 1980; Miles 1985). The reason for this is that in a modern capitalist society social needs could be met through a variety of institutional arrangements, and it is therefore necessary to explain why specific individuals use one functional alternative rather than another.

A more useful form of the functionalist account of the family has been to argue that while needs may be met in a variety of ways, the strength of the family lies in the fact that it is a source of aid when other social institutions have failed. From this point of view, the family is held to exist mainly because it provides supplementary resources to disadvantaged sections of the population when other means of need fulfillment have proven to be inadequate (Humphries 1977). The family is conceived of, as it were, as a back-up institution that fills in the gaps created by failures elsewhere in the system. Propositions of this sort are most commonly encountered in connection with models of extended family, or kinship, networks (Litwak and Szelenyi 1969).

Sussman has claimed that kinship networks are constituted by the reciprocation of assistance, and that they are therefore organized as systems of mutual aid (Sussman 1970). Recent research into social networks has cast considerable doubt upon the validity of this claim, since it is apparent that the provision of aid is not always mutual (Wellman 1982). Furthermore, the maintenance of meaningful relationships with kin and other intimates does not depend upon those relationships being supportive (Wellman and Hall 1986). Non-supportive ties to significant others can apparently be maintained over considerable periods of time, and it seems that not everybody benefits from family relationships (Wellman 1981).

If, as seems likely, some people benefit more from familial transactions than others, then it may be that there are systematic differences in privileges within the family that are related to inequalities in power. That has been the argument presented by a number of feminist theorists, who have maintained that the family is a locus of struggle between men and women as they pursue their different interests (Hartmann 1981). The fact that men generally have access to more resources through their participation in the market economy means, from this perspective, that men must have the preponderance of power within the family, and that family life must serve the interests of men (Land 1983). The family is therefore thought to have been maintained as an essentially patriarchal structure, despite minor changes, due to the capacity of men to impose upon women those social forms that benefit males (Smart and Smart 1978; Burstyn 1985).

The most serious problem with the theory of patriarchy as an account of the persistence of the family is undoubtedly that women themselves have frequently been enthusiastic advocates of family life, and that they have actively joined in its reproduction (Wearing 1984). Bridal showers, which are organized by women for women and from which men are usually excluded, illustrate this point in an acute manner. On these ritual occasions for transferring items of domestic capital to future brides, some women define other women as adult females. In the process they define domesticity within marriage as a part of their feminine identity (Cheal 1988b). These impressive bursts of collective female activity could no doubt be claimed as manifestations of illusory communal interests, propagated by a male power structure. But before we dismiss them as "mere" false consciousness, we should be aware that that act itself is of dubious origin. It is but one more step in a succession of questionable revisions that have occurred in the debate over the family during the last four decades.

There are, it would seem, many kinds of needs that functionalist theories can point to, any or all of which the family may be thought to serve. There are the needs of society, as set out in the structural functional model of the nuclear family; there are the

needs of capital, as stated in marxism; there are the needs of individuals facing personal crises, as claimed in the theory of the
modified extended family; and then there are the needs of men, as
they have been described by radical feminism. This overdeter-
minism of "necessary" conditions is open to unlimited extension,
and we may well wonder if the functionalist logic of necessity is
capable of providing a sound description of family interaction.
That it is not in fact capable of doing so can be illustrated by one
of the case studies from the Winnipeg Ritual Cycle Study.

Case study: Margaret Rose

Margaret Rose's gift behavior cannot easily be explained by any
of the models described above. What compulsion to give of herself
can there possibly be for a woman who lives alone, who is unmarried, who is financially independent, and who has nobody who
really needs her support? What does "family" mean in a situation
like this, where there is no objective necessity for it? In Margaret
Rose's case it means a great deal indeed.

Mrs Rose is no longer married, but she belongs to that generation of Christian women for whom the respectability of the
married form of address is important in any context where her
children are likely to be discussed. She attends services of worship
regularly and participates enthusiastically in other activities of her
church. Nevertheless, it is not Christian duty that is her principal
concern when she talks about giving to others. It is, rather, her
ties with friends and family members that she thinks about more
than anything else.

Mrs Rose is in her early 60s and has recently retired from a
professional position in a hospital in order to spend more time
with her friends. She owns her own home, and since she has only
herself to support she does not expect to have any difficulty in
managing on her retirement income. Her two children live independently now, and earn above average incomes. Margaret Rose's
unmarried daughter has needed financial help from time to time,
but her married son's success in business has enabled him to
provide well for himself and his family without any assistance
from her. The fact that she can no longer find things to give to
him that he really needs is in fact a source of some anxiety to her,
since she worries that her gifts may not be completely convincing
tokens of her love (described in Cheal 1987a).

Mrs Rose believes that gifts are often valued for very selfish, practical reasons. On the one hand, there are people who "expect a lot" and who are "always looking for handouts" (see also Lux 1972). On the other hand there are:

> these people who give gifts to buy affection or to buy attention. I think often people give gifts to cover up their own feelings of guilt. If they've done something to hurt you, maybe they think that they can buy your affection back again by giving a gift.

Margaret Rose believes that these are not the true principles of gift giving, but that they are corruptions of an underlying moral order of social relations. She thinks that, "The basic idea of gift giving [is] to sort of show your love and concern and interest in that person, whoever they might be. To help tie a family together. And give them something to remember you by."

These interlocking themes of love, family, and remembrance recurred throughout her discussion of gift giving. Struggling to put her feelings into words, Mrs Rose summarized her perception of her gift practices by saying:

> [I think I'm] sort of giving something of myself, so that people will have something to remember me [by], and thus with family to enrich the bonds in the family. Not necessarily that I want to be remembered, but I want them to remember me because I hope that I'm important to them. I think sometimes having something there to look at that came from my mother or my sister or my son or daughter makes me think of them when I see it, and therefore the more you think of a person the richer that relationship should be. And I think that things they've given me help me to think of them, and the things I give them help them to think of me. It's just sort of to enrich the relationship.

Unfortunately there are times when gifts do not enrich relationships. That happens, Mrs Rose feels, when the recipients do not value what they have been given. Nevertheless, it is essential to keep on giving to them on future occasions because not to do so would be to risk jeopardizing the relationship. If the relationship is already somewhat strained, which is more likely than not in such cases, then extra care is called for. Thus, when questioned about the reasons why she felt that she had to continue giving to people who had not shown any appreciation for her past gifts, Mrs Rose replied:

> Oh, I don't know. Well, you just feel because they're going to be at the Christmas outing or gathering, or because it's their birthday and you've always given them a gift, you just feel as if you have to continue with this tradition. It's expected of you. You carry on and do it [so as] not to create any waves. If you didn't give the gift to somebody, say,

in the family that you've always given to, then [they think]: "Oh!
Mother's mad," or this type of thing. So you don't want to create
waves. You want to try to consolidate the relationship. And maybe
with a gift you can show your concern and try to bridge the gap [in
the relationship] that you might subconsciously feel isn't as strong as it
should be.

In western Canada the social-psychological gap between two
people is often accentuated by enormous geographical distances
that separate individuals who have moved from the place in which
they were born. Margaret Rose was born in southern Ontario,
where most of her kin remain, but she moved to Winnipeg, in the
province of Manitoba, during the early years of her marriage. Her
son, in turn, has moved further west to British Columbia. With
her kinship network strung out across the country it is difficult
for Mrs Rose to keep in touch with everyone. And so it often
happens that she does not know what to get them for their birthdays or Christmas, and they do not know what to send her either.
As a result, the ideal of giving a tangible object by which a person
can be remembered is sometimes lost.

At the time she was first interviewed, Mrs Rose was wrestling
with the problem of what to do about her great-nieces and great-
nephews in Ontario. She explained that she had not sent gifts to
her nieces and nephews for a long time, but she did still want to
send to their children "because they're kids" and "it's nice to
remember the children." At the same time, she wanted them to
know that they had an Auntie Margaret, "because I don't see them
that often." As a result, Mrs Rose said that she "would like really
[to give] a gift that they'll say – 'Auntie Margaret gave me that' –
and remember Auntie Margaret because of the gift." However, in
previous years Margaret Rose had sent her great-nieces and great-
nephews money, due to the fact that she did not know what they
wanted. Unhappy with this situation, Mrs Rose was uncertain
what to do at Christmas. In the end the problem was solved for
her, as she subsequently reported at the second interview. Her
nieces had asked her to stop giving to the children since they would
feel obliged to give Mrs Rose something in return, and they too
did not know what to get for someone whom they did not see
very often.

For Mrs Rose there is, it seems, something very basic about
family ties that makes them worth emphasizing even under unfav-
orable circumstances. She therefore spends more on gifts for her
children and grandchildren than she does on her friends, even

though she feels very close to her best friends and sees them more often. Asked to explain the reason for this difference in expenditure patterns, her answer rests uneasily between the taken for granted nature of descent ties and the emotional significance of continuing personal relationships.

> Well, it's family and they're important to me. And I hope I'm important to them. [Pause] I want to for one thing, and I want to maintain. . . . [Long pause] I don't know whether you need a gift to maintain a bond or not – I guess probably it's tradition again. But they are my kids. And yet friends are very important too. They say you can choose your friends but you can't choose your family.

Although family members may not be chosen, the attention paid to them is often selectively increased or decreased, as we have seen in Margaret Rose's relations with her nieces and their children. In Mrs Rose's case the atrophy of her extended family ties, and probably the divorce from her husband as well, have led her to build up a large network of friends in Winnipeg. These friends are women of the same or similar age, most of whom are either members of the church that Mrs Rose attends, or they are members of a group that regularly plays golf together in the summer. Her "golfing group" as she calls them, have got into the habit of exchanging token gifts at Christmas. There are other friends who, she says, are every bit as close but to whom she does not give anything at that time of year. Mrs Rose says that with "close, sincere, faithful friends, it doesn't really matter whether you give a gift or not." Nevertheless, she does bring back little things for them from her trips, and she thinks of them in other ways too.

In some cases Margaret Rose's friends have admitted her to their own family circles (see Figure 4.1). Where these kinship-friendship ties have been maintained over a number of years the categorical distinction between good friends and family members has started to break down. That has not resulted in a socially redefined myth of kinship of the kind that anthropologists have described in certain tribal societies. Rather, the result has been a conflation of terms within a discourse of relationships as a network of love (Cheal 1987a). The predominant term in that conflationary discourse is *family*.

> I think a lot of the reason [for giving gifts on special occasions] is because it's habit. It's always been done, and so you think it's almost a duty to give a gift. Also, because it's mainly family or friends who are sort of acting like family. We have celebrated a lot of these occasions with the family. The Crawfords, they'll have Christmas one year and

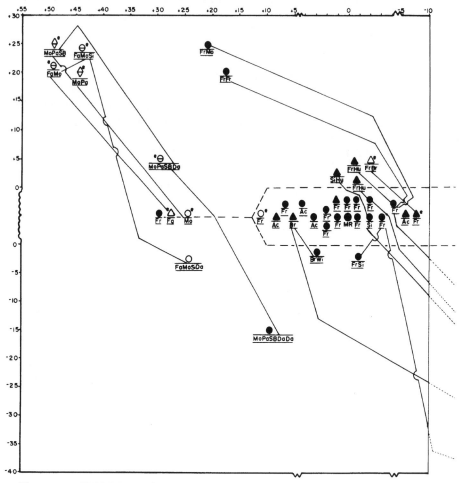

Figure 4.1a RANK graph, Margaret Rose age 61

we'll have it the next year, and the same with Easter and Thanksgiving
and so on, we'll share them too. So they are sort of my Winnipeg
family in some ways. So there again we usually give gifts to each one
of the family, as you like to remember everybody that's there.

Mrs Rose's experience of family life is not that of a structure
which has been programed to serve essential functions. Yet that
experience is clearly of vital importance to her. She has worked
hard to maintain it as a continuing reality in her life, despite
geographical separation from her kin, divorce from her husband,
and difficulties in her relationships with her son and his wife.
Family life is, in a very real sense, something that she has had to
construct for herself out of unpromising materials. Even those

basic descent ties with her children that she says we cannot choose have in fact been socially constructed. Her son was adopted, but nevertheless she refers to him as one of "my kids."

The social construction of family life

The extent to which Mrs Rose has clung to an ideal of the family as the foundation of her life is impressive. Hers is not the story of

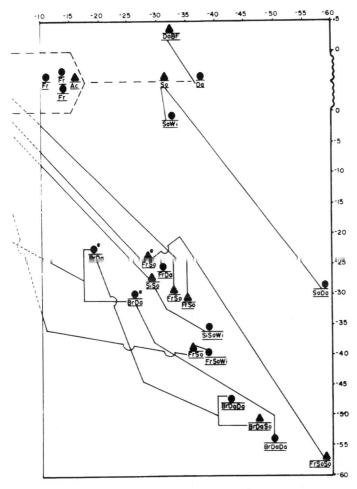

Figure 4.1b RANK graph, Margaret Rose age 61 *cont'd*

a woman who has been coerced into an oppressive structure that she resents, and which she has tried to resist. Rather, it is the story of a woman who has struggled to achieve certain ideals of family living, and who is sometimes afraid that she has not been as successful as she would have liked. Margaret Rose's efforts show in an unusually clear way that "the family" is not an objective necessity at all. It is a social form that has been constructed piece by piece, often in painstaking fashion.

One of the most important achievements of the feminist critique of the concept of the family has been to emphasize that "the family" is an ideological construct (Barrett 1980). Although the implications of this approach have been potentially revolutionary for the sociology of the family (Thorne 1982; Beechey 1985; Bernardes 1985), it is not an idea that is unique to feminism. Its intellectual origins lie in the constructionist, or constructivist, tradition (Berg 1987) which has deep roots in the social sciences.[4] The nature of that approach will be briefly described below in order to show why the family is so highly valued by Mrs Rose, and by the many women like her who think of it as a uniquely important type of moral economy.

The enormous variability of human behavior (including the variety of forms of family living) has suggested to many observers that there is very little that is biologically fixed in social life. It is thought that the social practices found in particular places at particular points in time are therefore selections from among the many possibilities for social organization that might be compatible with local conditions. Once certain selections have been made, however, those who have an interest in seeing them continue may find it necessary to defend those practices by justifying them with reference to authoritative final causes. Berger and Luckmann have pointed out that the most authoritative attributions of causes are those which apprehend human phenomena as if they were things beyond human control – "such as facts of nature, results of cosmic laws, or manifestations of divine will" (P. Berger and Luckmann 1966: 89).

In everyday discourse, "the family" is a reified world of this sort. It is experienced as a social world which actors may, in certain specialized capacities (for example, as bride or groom), choose to enter or not. But once the game has begun (as, in other capacities, it does for most people at birth), then the course it takes is seen as being a scarcely avoidable outcome of "the nature of things." Unless challenged by alternative ways of thinking about human behavior, family ideology legitimates social practices in the most fundamental way possible – that is, by declaring them to be inevitable.

There is little in Margaret Rose's experience of family life that was inevitable. Her marriage did not last, she did not give birth to the man she calls her son, and her "Winnipeg family" is unrelated to her by ties of blood or marriage. It is perhaps not surprising, then, that she does not legitimate her social relations with reference to biology or theology,[5] although there are undoubtedly also important cultural reasons for those absences (Cheal 1987b). She does, however, claim in an indirect way that "you can choose your friends but you can't choose your family." Clearly Mrs Rose does have an interest in seeing certain relations continue – namely, those with her children, with her nieces and nephews and their children, and with the Crawford family. She therefore uses the label "it's family" to define those relationships as unquestionable and (hopefully) as permanent.

The dominant family ideology held by most Winnipeggers conceives of family members as people who are linked by "natural feelings" for one another. Those feeling states are thought to be grounded in the personalities of normal people, although it is recognized that in practice not everybody feels that way. It is assumed that anybody who has been socialized properly within a happy, loving family will in fact love past, present, and future family members, and that they can be counted upon to express their feelings in displays of affection.[6]

In contemporary love culture love is defined as a diffuse feeling state that is the basis for enduring ties between persons. Without love, it is thought, personal relationships are fragile and easily broken. Fortunately, conventional wisdom holds that family members are people who love each other, and that family ties are therefore ties that endure. In a mass society in which social relations are fluid the future of social life is uncertain. Under these conditions family ideology is powerful, and "the family" is an attractive ideal, because it holds out the promise that if all else fails there will remain an irreducible core of enduring personal relationships. Despite the many problems associated with family life, it does at least provide a basis for believing that the individual life-course will have a social future. That belief is buttressed by the "archival function" (Weigert and Hastings 1977) of gift objects as material pegs upon which individuals may hang their memories of one another until such time as they can be called into use in the present (see Figure 4.2).

Figure 4.2 Margaret Rose's gift transfers (1982)

1) Baby's high chair 2) Mittens 3) Pewter box 4) Baby's rattle 5) Loaf
of rye bread 6) Chinese dinner, brought in 7) Bottle of liqueur 8)
Pottery bowl 9) Wooden rabbit 10) Glass elephant ornament 11)
Miniature pictures 12) Tissue box holders 13) Weaving kit, for wall
hanging 14) Place mats, for table setting 15) Magazine subscription 16)
Money, to buy records 17) Salad bowl set 18) Coffee-maker 19) Carving
knife 20) Electric frying pan 21) Money, unspecified 22) Memorial gift
– charitable contribution 23) African Violet plants 24) Money, to buy
books 25) Chocolate mints 26) Calendar for purse 27) Change purses
28) Make-up purse 29) Clothes brush 30) Ear-rings 31) Notepaper 32)
Coasters 33) Record 34) Ring holders 35) Stained glass apple ornament
36) Books 37) Place setting of china 38) Wheat hanging – ornament 39)
Plumbing utensil 40) Spaghetti measure 41) Christmas tree decoration
42) Crib toy 43) Play pen 44) Decorative candle

The family's promise of social continuity is not realized for
everyone, of course, and many more may fear its loss. The tragic
thing about Margaret Rose's situation is that since her son is not
her natural child, she is not convinced that he has the "natural"
feelings of devotion towards her that she believes a son should
have. Furthermore, his income is sufficiently high that he already
has many of the things that he wants and Mrs Rose does not know
what to get him that he does not already have. She has therefore
tried sending him money so that he can buy things that suit his
tastes and interests. In her opinion this was not successful because
"If they don't acknowledge and tell you what they've bought, you
don't know whether they've followed your instructions or not."
Mrs Rose therefore doubts that her son will continue to remember
her in the way in which she remembers her own mother. In the
middle of the interview she looked around the room and said:

> My mother just died a couple of years ago. When I look around my
> house, if it wasn't for gifts that my mother gave me I wouldn't have
> very much. I appreciate these [things], and they mean something to me
> because I remember the occasion they were given on, and that it was
> from my mother, and the relationship we've had. And this is why I
> think it's good to give gifts, because it does sort of cement a relationship
> and [it] gives you something to remember a person by. That's why I
> object to money. Money is kind of cold. It's spent usually on nothing
> in particular, and when it's gone the memory's gone.

Margaret Rose does occasionally give money, but only as a last
resort. Most of her gifts are carefully chosen items that she hopes
will appeal to the tastes and interests of the particular individuals

who will receive them. The result of this deliberate individuation of gifts is that within a span of twelve months she gave an incredible variety of things (see Figure 4.2). In this she is not unusual, since many other women (but not as many men) also put a lot of thought into selecting the objects that they give to others. The point is worth stressing, because it demonstrates one of several respects in which Lévi-Strauss's "gigantic potlatch" analogy for North American gift ceremonies falls wide of the mark.[7]

Lévi-Strauss has claimed that every year there is a vast destruction of wealth in North America as a result of the exchange of Christmas gifts. He asserted that this is due to "their frequent duplication because of the limited range of objects suitable as presents" (Lévi-Strauss 1969: 56). This would be an interesting point if it were true, but it is manifestly not the case. One of the most striking facts revealed by the Winnipeg Ritual Cycle Study was the enormous range of objects which are transformed into gifts for special occasions. Contrary to Lévi-Strauss, the diversity of the objects transferred is especially marked at Christmas.

Ritual gift giving in Winnipeg is not a meaningless exchange of purely conventional gifts. It is a vital custom whose social uses are expressed in the seriousness with which women like Margaret Rose try to attune their gift giving to the unique characters and contexts of their significant others. The reason that Mrs Rose goes to so much trouble is because the time and thought put into the selection of a gift are symbolic of caring for the other. Mrs Rose believes that the basic idea behind gift giving is "to help tie a family together." That view of gift giving has also been held by some sociologists.

Invented traditions

Lüschen has presented an account of gift rituals in which they are seen as means of stabilizing family relationships that have been threatened by the strains and stresses of modern social change. Thus he has claimed that, "Families in modern societal settings will adjust to separation from relatives by making more use of such means of communication as mailing, phoning and gift exchange" (Lüschen 1972: 86). In this structural functional theory of gift exchange the focus is upon the family considered as a system which responds to changes in its environment. According to Lüschen and his colleagues, "High strain and demands, change, and increasing mobility in modern society may well encourage the family to look for means of stabilization for its structure, and emotional support for its members, through means of its own such as family-oriented ritual." In order to survive, they say, the family has to employ means to reinforce its existing structure, such as the transformation of religious rituals into familial rituals. Hence, "It was the family and its functional needs that made Christmas the most important festival and then transformed it since the beginning of industrialization into a familial structure of its own" (Lüschen et al, 1972: 520, 535).

Caplow seems to have been unaware of Lüschen's work, and he arrived independently at a similar point of view. He has concluded that "ritualized gift giving, in any society, is a method of dealing with relationships that are important but insecure. Gifts are typically offered to persons or collectivities whose goodwill is needed but cannot be taken for granted" (Caplow 1982: 391). He has suggested that the American festival cycle celebrates family matters because the family is the institution most at risk today (Caplow et al. 1982). He has stated that the two principal points of stress in the contemporary American family are the marriage relationship and relationships between the generations. The insecurity of relations between spouses is due to the relative ease of divorce which, he points out, has implications for others besides the husband and wife. In particular, their children continue to be related to both parents and through them to both maternal and paternal kin.

According to Caplow, every widely observed festival in Middletown now celebrates the family and the related ideas of home, mother and child, and feminine roles. Private occasions such as birthdays, weddings, anniversaries, and reunions are equally familial, he believes (Caplow et al. 1982: 226). In Middletown Christmas is by far the most important festival occasion, and it is accompanied by the most extensive gift giving because it celebrates the family in its social network. Maintaining social ties and nurturing children are the principal cultural themes which are dramatized at Christmas. Both are symbolically affirmed by the giving of Christmas presents.

Lüschen and Caplow have suggested that family rituals at Christmas have acquired an increased importance in industrial societies due to the growing threats to family life. Nevertheless, few people in Winnipeg define their ritual practices as responses to change. Instead, they see Christmas as a time for "tradition" based on the customs of the different ethnic groups within

Canadian society. In the Winnipeg Ritual Cycle Study the interviewees' most frequent initial response to questions about the
nature of gift giving was that "it's just tradition." That was particularly the case for remarks about giving at Christmas, which they
thought was mainly due to socialization. Presents at Christmas
were important, most people believed, because "that's just the way
we've been taught to think about it" or "that's the way we were
all brought up, as far as I know."

In fact tradition in Winnipeg is an ambiguous phenomenon.
Many people are very conscious of a need for tradition, but at the
same time they are aware of considerable change and variation
around them. They are therefore sometimes unsure about what
the "real" traditions are. Furthermore, even when authentic
customs can be identified (usually with reference to some knowledge of ethnic or national background) it is often not clear how
much importance should actually be attached to them in practice.
That has become a particularly serious problem for many people
at weddings, where gift giving (and other) practices have in fact
been changing rapidly. Following tradition is thought to be
important at weddings, but at the same time traditions are openly
revised and discarded with little opposition if they are perceived
to be no longer useful. In short, the ritual order in Winnipeg is in
a process of continuous social construction that is nevertheless
legitimated with reference to the observation that "it's all
tradition." Family rituals in Winnipeg are, in fact, invented
traditions.

The invention of tradition is to be found not only in modern
family rituals, but also in a number of other expressive forms
where claims for collective identity are made. Historians have
recently discovered that it is a very general process whose study
should be of interest to a number of disciplines (Hobsbawm and
Ranger 1983). As stated by one:

> "Invented tradition" is taken to mean a set of practices, normally
> governed by overtly or tacitly accepted rules and of a ritual or symbolic
> nature, which seek to inculcate certain values and norms of behaviour
> by repetition, which automatically implies continuity with the past. In
> fact, where possible, they normally attempt to establish continuity with
> a suitable historic past. . . . It is the contrast between the constant
> change and innovation of the modern world and the attempt to structure
> at least some parts of social life within it as unchanging and invariant,
> that makes the "invention of tradition" so interesting for historians of
> the past two centuries.
>
> (Hobsbawm 1983: 1–2)

Invented traditions are ideologies which define the present in relation to the past and which justify the present in terms of its presumed continuity with the past. In addition, they assert that the future will be like the present since it too will consist of traditional ways of doing things. Invented traditions are thus powerful tools in the social construction of a social future. Traditions, like facts of nature, can be taken for granted simply because they are there. In ritual the visual demonstration of continuity with the past speaks for itself as unquestionable evidence that things do go on in the same way. Invented traditions should therefore appeal particularly to those who would like to believe that some things do not change, but who also have good reason to fear the future.

Case study: Colleen Williams

Colleen Williams is 24 years old and is in her last year at university studying for a degree in social work. Like many other students in Winnipeg, her studies have been extended by the need to work at the same time in order to support herself. She lives alone, and is financially independent. Colleen's parents separated a number of years ago, and both are now remarried. She has two brothers, one of whom lives with their father while the other brother lives separately with his girlfriend.

For financial reasons Colleen does not give very many gifts, although she would like to do more, and says that:

> The people that I give gifts to and receive gifts from are people that are very special to me. That doesn't mean that I don't enjoy a lot of other people's company. But I give gifts to people that are close to my heart. . . . There are people who are just acquaintances that I don't feel the closeness to. I enjoy them as people and I enjoy their company and everything else, and I certainly care about them. But they just don't have that place in my heart. They're just not really special people that I like to keep in close contact with. They're people that you might meet one year and be friends with them for one year – like a friend from university who might be in your class all year, and you're terrific friends for the whole year, and then you never see them again. I think that you just get a feeling for relationships like that. You know. You can tell by how much you're able to share with that person how close you are to them.

Colleen says that her gifts are given out of a special feeling for the particular person, but this does not mean that all of her giving is simply an outpouring of the emotion of the moment. Rather, it seems that on ritual occasions everyday emotions are set aside so that deep feelings can be revived and strengthened. Colleen says that she gives gifts on special occasions because:

> I think that you can easily forget about people. . . . Special occasions that are set aside are times for me to remember a person. Like, through the year you tend to forget about people and get caught up with your own life. But those days are set out for me. If I've been neglecting them at all [then I have] those times to show them that I care. . . . It's sort of bringing them into your consciousness that you should be thinking about them. I think it's a good reminder.

Christmas is one of those times when Colleen gets "really involved in doing things for people and having a fun time." Having a good time includes following invented traditions that are symbolic of an earlier period of family solidarity and of endurance in the face of hardship. Among the many presents that Colleen gives and receives at Christmas are gifts of food between herself, her mother, and her brothers. They consist of canned foods, such as shrimps and olives, which are unusual Christmas gifts in Winnipeg. Colleen explained that when she and her brothers were young, and the family into which they were born was still intact, their parents did not have much money. Such foods were rare delicacies in those days, and they were therefore precious. As a treat at Christmas her parents used to give each of the children a favorite food as a "stocking stuffer." Colleen, her mother, and her brothers keep up this practice, she says, as "a family tradition." In this invented tradition we see that family networks which have been disrupted by divorce, and which are in danger of being divided by competing loyalties, may nevertheless be stabilized by the retention of pre-rupture rituals. Such rituals are continued long after they might otherwise have fallen into disuse, because they define important ties that cut across reconstituted nuclear family boundaries. Those interstitial ties lack the practical social supports that derive from material interdependence within the household economy. At Christmas they are brought back into consciousness and claims for their permanence are reasserted.

Conclusion

The structural functional theory of family rituals in industrial societies has been very fruitful (Cheal 1987a, 1987b), and it continues to provide useful insights. The Winnipeg Ritual Cycle Study confirms the observation made by Lüschen and Caplow that

Christmas is the single most important festival in the year (see Table 4.1). Almost half of all gifts given in 1982 were given during the Christmas season, and although the value of the average Christmas present is not high, more is spent on Christmas gifts than on gifts for any other occasion.

Table 4.1 *Volume of gifts and volume of gift expenditures by occasion*

Occasions	Gifts★ %	Expenditures★ %
Anniversary	3.1	9.6
Birth	2.8	2.2
Birthday	21.8	20.6
Pre-wedding	2.4	3.7
Christmas	49.3	38.1
Easter	2.3	0.7
Father's Day	1.4	1.0
Mother's Day	2.1	2.4
Reunion	2.5	1.1
Valentine's Day	1.3	0.4
Visiting	2.0	1.5
Wedding	2.5	11.5
Sympathy	1.5	0.7
Farewell	1.3	0.9
Party	0.9	0.8
Other	2.8	4.8
Totals	100.0	100.0

★ Homemade gifts have been excluded so that the volumes of gifts and the volumes of gift expenditures are directly comparable for each occasion.

The Winnipeg Ritual Cycle Study data also show something else. Contrary to what would have been expected from the structural functional theory of the family, the data show that the second most important occasion is not a family festival. If the ritualization of personal relationships in Canada was due principally to functional requirements for the stabilization of family life, then we should expect to find that after the primary occasion of Christmas (which celebrates the Holy Family) the secondary rituals would be those dealing with family roles. Mother's Day and Father's Day (and possible inventions such as Daughter's Day or Sibling Day) should be prominent occasions. As Table 4.1 shows, that is not the case. Mother's Day is recognized in Winnipeg, but it is far less important than birthdays, and it clearly belongs in the pack of events that make up the third tier of times for gift giving. The humble birthday celebration, which receives relatively little publicity either from organized religion or from the advertising industry, far surpasses in importance any occasion other than Christmas. The most distinctive characteristic about birthday celebrations, indeed their defining characteristic, is that they are occasions for honoring individuals. It is true that family members are usually heavily involved in birthday ceremonial, but it is not the family as such that is the focus of attention at a birthday party. It is the unique existence of a particular person that is celebrated, as Colleen Williams pointed out.

> Birthdays are always special because [they] mean that I'm thankful that they were born so that I can share in their being with me. If they weren't around and didn't have birthdays they wouldn't be there to be my friend or a member of my family.

It would be wrong to suppose that the celebration of the individual and the celebration of family ties are necessarily opposed values. However, the cult of the individual cannot be explained by a theory of family functioning, since individualism has often proved to be corrosive of loyalties to corporate groups. The structural functional theory of ritual giving in modern societies therefore needs to be revised in the light of contemporary critiques of models of family structure,[8] and especially in light of the developments in constructionist theory outlined earlier. There is no universal form of "the family," and although there is impressive evidence for the existence of a stable deep structure of nuclear family relations in Canada (Davids 1980; Cheal 1986), it is not obvious that this is best explained by a logic of functional necessity. It is clear, however, that women such as Hazel Anderson, Margaret Rose, and Colleen Williams do try to keep up intimate relationships with other individuals who are important to them, and that they see gift exchange as contributing to that end. In other words, individuals work to maintain relationships with a set of significant others which they label "my family," and which is so labelled because it is believed to involve enduring intimate relations.

Contrary to the structural functional view of human society, there is no essential family structure that must be maintained in family rituals, since family life as we know it is clearly not a necessary condition for existence.[9] Rather, the form of family relations in modern societies is constituted by the management of emotions which sustains a system of intimate ties that transcend the limits of time and space.[10] The social value of "the family" lies in its being a generalized social structure to which individuals can turn, and return, throughout the life-course. Family members are people who can be trusted to support one's interests, it is thought, because their feelings of love can be taken for granted. Gift giving throughout the annual cycle of regular occasions contributes to the constant renewal of those emotions. Considerable importance is therefore attached to gift behavior by people such as Colleen Williams, because "showing them you love them" provides concrete, visible evidence of invisible feeling states that might otherwise be suspected of having faded away.

There is an important point to be made about the social construction of gift giving that follows from these observations. It will be recalled that Pierre Bourdieu made the ideological misrecognition of exchange the basis for his political economy of interpersonal transactions. It is now possible to show that when misrecognition occurs it is just as likely to be a result of the moral economy of gift transfers. An explanation from the perspective of moral economy is to be preferred, simply because it is consistent with so many other observations about the Canadian gift economy.

Although some men and women interviewed in the Winnipeg Ritual Cycle Study openly acknowledged the desirability of reciprocity in their gift practices, many did not. Even some of those who stated a preference for balanced exchange were not prepared to see it as supplying the dominant motive in their gift transactions. Anne Baker is one of those who did not like to admit that other individuals might want to receive a gift from her, or that she herself might want to receive a gift from others. Her opposition to this idea was typically voluntaristic, and vague.

> [The people I give gifts to do] not necessarily expect it. I give them a gift because I want to. There might be people who didn't expect to get anything from me, but it's just that [when] a good friend has a birthday, if they're a good enough friend you'll get them a gift, if you want to and you feel you should. It's not that it's expected, it's just . . . [her voice trails off into silence]

Anne Baker's emphasis upon voluntarism is consistent with the resentment expressed by a number of people towards giving obligatory gifts when they have little freedom of choice. The views of Philip Walker on this issue may be a little unusual, but they are not extreme. He expressed a strong dislike of people collecting money for collective gifts (for example, for a member of a work group who is in hospital or who is about to leave for another job). The problem, he says, is that "they always tell you how much to give, and that's like a dictatorship to me." Other communal occasions when people often feel compelled to give, and sometimes dislike having to do so, are the ritual events associated with marriage. That happens quite frequently at those bridal showers where the nature of the gift, and in the case of a monetary contribution its value as well, is determined in advance by the organizers. Colleen Williams is one who objects to that sort of organized giving.

> I sometimes get peeved when I am invited to a shower and told that I don't have a choice in the gift, that I have to contribute $10. To me that's just too systematic. It doesn't allow a person any creativity in showing and expressing what they feel for the person. It's just – "we are buying this. Will you or will you not contribute?" And if you don't contribute, well, they prefer you didn't come to the shower, so you can't partake in any of it unless you are giving what they want you to give. I get a little upset at things like that because I just don't believe in giving gifts that way. I'm still thinking of them, but not in the way that I personally might have thought of them.

Interaction difficulties with giving that is involuntary are to be expected from the account of the gift economy as a system of redundant transfers that was outlined at the beginning of this volume. It was stated there that one of the senses in which gift giving may be seen as non-essential is that it is socially defined as non-normative (i.e. non-rule governed) behavior. Forms of gift giving which contradict that definition of the situation are likely to be seen as not quite right. They are ambiguous events which can be brought within the dominant folk model of gift transactions only with some difficulty.

In Winnipeg the vocabulary of motives for gift behavior is overwhelmingly detached from any notion of reciprocal expectations generated in interaction. People give gifts, they say, because they "want to," because it makes them "feel good," because not to do so would make them "feel guilty," and above all because "it's tradition." Actors' accounts of their gift behavior, in other words, are consistently opposed to sociological models of social action. The reasons for this lie in the profound folk belief that gift giving is the product of natural feelings that are inherent in individuals who have been raised in normal families. According to this *ideology of love* feelings of generosity are believed to spring directly from the individual's being, without social intervention. Gifts are therefore seen as the products of autochthonous emotions, that is as the spontaneous acts of people who have genuine feelings for each other. That is because gifts can be symbolic of interpersonal commitments only if they are understood to be the results of voluntary acts. If gifts were not socially defined in that way, then they could not be interpreted as evidence for the existence of subjective states, and they would no longer serve to symbolize enduring personal relationships. In other words, the most potent symbolic effects of gifts as tie-signs depend upon a systematic disavowal of reciprocal expectations of giving and receiving in balanced relationships.

In the next two chapters we shall explore some of the dimensions of, and limits to, the ideology of love and its effects upon the Canadian gift economy. We shall see there that the subjective plausibility of the ideology of love is achieved through the management of emotions within intimate structures of nurturant dependence. Like any other ideology, it is not easily sustained outside the plausibility structure within which it has been formed.[11] That does not mean, however, that gift giving is confined entirely to intimate familial relationships, or even to extended family kin. We have already seen that gifts are given to a variety of associates, and that some gifts are collective rather than personal.

5

Social reproduction

Meyer Fortes once pointed out that the extension of any social system into the future entails the reproduction of two kinds of resources upon which actors draw in constructing their ways of life: human capital, that is people, with the knowledge and skills to make them productive members of society; and social capital, that is the material facilities and social forms used in action. The latter includes not only the forms of property that are passed from one generation to the next, but also the cultural codes and social rules which make cooperative action possible (Fortes 1969).

Social reproduction, in this broad sense, is the reproduction of systems of relations. It is through the temporal extension of social relations that individuals construct their social futures. They do that not only for themselves, but also for others, since otherwise they could not plan for a *social* future. Social reproduction therefore necessarily includes altruistic behavior within moral economies, which is why no society has ever existed on the basis of a purely political economy.[1] In this chapter we are going to describe the part that the gift economy plays in the process of social reproduction.

Gift transactions occur on many kinds of occasions, only a few of which have been studied in any detail. Some of the most important occasions have in fact been almost entirely neglected, and as a result some fundamental mechanisms of social reproduction through gift giving have been overlooked. Contemporary sociology has been too preoccupied with issues in social stratification to pay much attention to the moral economy of social order. Gift transactions in capitalist societies have typically been described as aspects of the political economy of consumerism or the political economy of marriage. We shall see in the next chapter that neither of these approaches has much relevance for the explanation of gift practices.

Gifts are investments in human and social capital. They are redundant transactions employing resources which have been diverted from present obligations.[2] Diverting those resources may involve making difficult choices, if it means having to give up something else that is desired. The decision rules which are employed in making those choices reflect the different priorities which people attach to their various social interests (Cheal 1986). Making the decision to spend money for a gift is easier on some occasions, and on some people, than it is on others. In general, attitudes towards communal forms of giving are less favorable than they are towards more intimate transfers. Bernice Genyk explained why that is so.

Case study: Bernice Genyk

Bernice Genyk is 27 years old and is employed full-time as a secretarial services supervisor. She is not married, but is cohabiting with a man whom she described as her fiancé. Frank has two children (ages 6 and 8) from a previous relationship who live with them. The transition from carefree single woman to careful mother has been abrupt for Bernice. As a result, she has become much more selective about the money she spends on gifts.

> When I was single and lived by myself I used to give more – [there was a] larger value to it – whereas now I watch what I get. Because I do have a family to look after, and it's money [that has] to be spent wiser. Like, you don't really have to give a gift, but I want to give a gift. Whereas before it didn't matter to me whether I had to or what – I want – like I wanted to. I knew I could afford it, so it didn't matter. Now if I can't [afford it], then a card will have to be sufficient.

It is, perhaps, for financial reasons that Bernice Genyk is not always pleased to be invited to other women's bridal showers. As illustrated in the above quotation Bernice, like most other natural actors, sees "wanting to" and "having to" as incompatible motives which are not easily reconciled in accounts of her actions. Since gifts are assumed to be given voluntarily, she has some difficulty in describing the sources of her compulsion to give at times when she does not feel like it. The problem, apparently, is that you sometimes receive invitations which you wish had never been sent.

> [Not wanting to give a gift happens] in some cases, not very often. . . . You get an invitation in the mail and you really don't know the person, but you feel obligated to go. . . . It's usually people that I don't really know, people of my parents, like someone my Mom has known and we've gotten an invitation and I don't really know them. But you feel obligated to go because you've gotten an invitation. . . . Like, in my case, because I wasn't married, someday they assumed I would get

married, and this person would get invited [to my shower]. I think it would only be fair to go to their shower and give them a gift if I wanted them to come to my shower. Not only for the gift, but just for the fact of being there and sharing their occasion with them.

If Bernice sometimes attends bridal showers reluctantly, out of a combination of fear of incurring social sanctions and desire to participate in social exchange, that is not true of her giving on other occasions. Bernice's largest gift expenditures were for Frank and his children (now her children) at Christmas and on their birthdays, and birth and christening gifts for the child of a friend and the child of Frank's nephew. As she explained:

[I give to] the people that I feel most close to in my life, that I share my life with the most. Like, I mean I have a lot of relatives that I just send cards to but I don't see them that often. And I don't share as many things as with the people that I'm more closely involved with.

The people that Bernice is most closely involved with are the other members of the household in which she lives. They are the ones she has to look after now, as she says. In addition, Bernice likes to spend more than usual for the birth of a baby, since "a lot of people don't have anything to start with." We see in Bernice Genyk's preferred patterns of giving that it is in the process of nurturing life – in biological reproduction and in the reproduction of everyday life – that the deepest commitments to giving of oneself are located.

The social organization of social reproduction

Nurturing life is the most fundamental form of social reproduction in any society. It takes place in three ways. Firstly, there is the physical reproduction of persons in the production of new members and in the maintenance of daily existence. Gifts at birth, which customarily consist mainly of baby clothes, are typical investments in the biological sustenance of the next generation of members. Secondly, there is the psychological (i.e. affective-cognitive) development of personal relationships, that is to say of emotionally charged relationships between individuals who possess personal knowledge of each other's biographies and an intersubjective knowledge of shared experiences. Gifts that create memories through their facilitation of enjoyable occasions, or which are "mementos" that stimulate the recall of cherished memories, are familiar examples (Boholm 1983). The most literal form of memento is the photograph, which has become an important domestic symbol in the second half of the twentieth century (Csikszentmihalyi and Rochberg-Halton 1981: 66–9). Photographs are sometimes given as gifts on special occasions, particularly at Christmas. In the Winnipeg Ritual Cycle Study it was found that photographs amounted to a little over 1 per cent of all gifts given and received, and nearly 2 per cent of Christmas presents.

The two types of social reproduction described above both involve intimate relations. That is because one requires the close physical proximity and physical contact that is involved in serving another's biological needs, and because the other entails frequent interaction and mutual confidences out of which detailed knowledge of that person is accumulated. For most people, but especially for women like Bernice Genyk who "have a family to look after," those intimate relationships have an immediate relevance to everyday interests. They therefore remain constantly at the foreground of attention. It is the structure of the life world, that is the world of lived experience, that determines which social actors receive the most attention, and therefore about whom the most comes to be known. That point was expressed by one respondent, Kay Michaluk, in the following manner: "[I give gifts] mainly [to] the people that I keep in touch with on a regular basis. And who I feel I know well and who know me well."

Not all gifts are given to confidants, however. The third type of social reproduction does not necessarily involve intimate relations (although it may do), and is often conducted through forms of communal action. It consists of the reproduction of social, rather than personal, relations.[3] That is to say, the reproduction of social life includes the collective production of actors as members of particular social categories, or statuses, which are defined as having different capacities and responsibilities within the social division of labor. The production of adult men and women through displays of gender membership is one of the most widespread forms of communal construction, since it reproduces the genderized forms of intimate relations through which physical and psychological reproduction have traditionally been organized. Displays of gender membership are often most visible, and most dramatic, in the rites of passage arranged in connection with marriage (Westwood 1984; Cheal 1988b).

It was suggested in chapter 1 that from the perspective of moral economy transactions are to be seen as structured by relationships between socially defined categories of persons. As long as the discourse of relationships does not change, actors are motivated by a desire to maintain those categories and the relationships between them, since they are the conditions for their nomic security (P. Berger and Luckmann 1966). We should therefore expect to find that conventional constructions of categories and relationships are generally reproduced in gift transactions.

That view of economic relations is nowhere more applicable than it is to the "big occasions" that come once in a lifetime, which are known in the social sciences as rites of passage. In the lives of most people the most dramatic rites of passage are those associated with marriage, and in particular the wedding ceremony (Barker 1978). As described by van Gennep in his famous account of rites of passage, marriage ceremonies mark the transition from one socially defined stage of life to another that is different, but which is equally well-defined (van Gennep 1960). He had much to say about the place of gifts in the ritual process of marriage. In order to appreciate the nature of his argument it is necessary to outline the main points of his theory of ritual.

According to van Gennep, all ritualized passages consist of a sequence of three phases, beginning with separation from the old social position, followed by an in-between stage of social marginality, and ending with the phase of incorporation into the new social position. All three of these phases may be accompanied by gift giving, but the forms of giving can be expected to vary according to the nature of the rites with which they are associated. For example, in pre-industrial societies, where the labor power and reproductive capacity of women is of enormous importance, rites of separation are often accompanied by compensatory gifts from the bridegroom to the bride's family. Rites of incorporation, on the other hand, typically involve larger numbers of people because wider social groups are affected by them. He claimed that rites of incorporation are most prominent at marriage because "in the last analysis a marriage is the incorporation of a stranger into a group" (van Gennep 1960: 11, 141).

Sociologically speaking, the most important characteristic of marriage for van Gennep is that it is a "social disturbance" that involves a number of actors. Gift transactions at marriage are therefore, in his view, often rites of incorporation. The exchange of gifts (such as rings) between the marriage partners unites them as a couple, whereas other gifts "have a collective significance, either in joining one or the other of the individuals to new groups or in uniting two or more groups." Acceptance of the interactional adjustments that must be made by group members is symbolized by the transfer of gifts, and the obligation created by their acceptance binds the individual to his or her position in the group. In this way, he observed, the economic nature of marriage becomes "intertwined with the rites proper" (1960: 119, 132–3, 139).

Substance and ceremony

The economics of marriage is one of several economic systems that can be identified within the Canadian gift economy. The marriage system is in many ways the most distinctive system, and it will therefore be the focus of special attention later in this chapter and in chapter 7. Here it is necessary to begin by saying something about the internal differentiation of the gift economy, and about how it is related to the modes of reproduction described above.

In the previous chapter we saw that in the span of one year Margaret Rose gave a great variety of gifts. The variety of her giving was not particularly unusual, and an enormous range of types of gifts was recorded in the Winnipeg Ritual Cycle Study. After experimenting with a number of inductive coding systems, a set of twenty-one broad categories was produced for the purposes of the comparative analysis of occasions (see Table 5.1).[4]

Considered as economic events, ritual occasions in Winnipeg are not highly differentiated. That is particularly true of Christmas. The relative frequency of gift types at Christmas is practically the same as that for all occasions combined (see Table 5.1). As Caplow has observed, the range of possible Christmas gifts is "nearly infinite" (Caplow et al. 1982: 239). Other occasions involve more distinctive patterns of gift giving.

Weddings are unique gift occasions in Winnipeg, since that is the only time when a single gift type – money – accounts for the majority of giving. Gift giving on other occasions is broader, but some gifts are relatively more important than others. Altogether there are eight ritual occasions on which at least one gift type is sufficiently popular that it accounts for one-quarter or more of the gifts given. Those occasions (with the relative frequencies of these popular gifts) are: Easter (candy is 48 per cent of gifts given); Mother's Day (decorative vegetation is 33 per cent); a birth (day clothing is 34 per cent); pre-wedding events (food preparation equipment is 29 per cent, money is 26 per cent); a reunion (day clothing is 26 per cent); Valentine's Day (candy is 45 per cent);

Table 5.1 *Types of gifts given on ritual occasions*

Gift types	All occasions %	Christmas %
Food	3.6	3.3
Drink	3.1	2.4
Candy	4.4	3.4
Food and drink equipment	3.4	2.9
Food preparation equipment	3.3	3.1
Household essentials	4.4	4.6
Decorative household objects	4.7	4.9
Decorative vegetation	3.9	1.0
Day clothing	16.5	16.8
Night clothing	3.0	3.9
Other clothing	2.0	2.6
Play equipment	7.2	9.3
Reading equipment	4.7	5.0
Relaxation equipment and services	3.6	3.3
Activities equipment and services	3.3	4.0
Personal accessories	4.2	5.4
Body adornments	2.6	2.8
Body preparation equipment	5.3	8.1
Money	11.4	7.0
Personal relations media	1.7	1.7
Miscellaneous	3.9	4.4
Totals	100.2	99.9

weddings (money is 65 per cent); and times for expressing sympathy (decorative vegetation is 43 per cent).[5]

On ritual occasions the objects that are transferred as gifts have more than a substantive significance. They also have a ceremonial significance as symbols that are consistent with the social definition of the occasion. The particular meanings that particular occasions have for their participants are always framed by a wider set of cultural meanings within a subculture or society. In modern societies meanings are shaped by changing religious institutions, the mixing of cultures due to population movement, and commercial interests in ways that make it virtually impossible for any set of values to be both common and capable of defining a system of segregated ritual occasions. Nevertheless, some differentiation of occasions will be found, in local subcultures if not within larger social systems. As Colleen Williams has told us, people do use ritual to bring ideas into their consciousness. It is in fact the repetitive, habitual nature of the "traditional" occasions that makes it possible to think thoughts that have little place in the everyday life world of work and recuperation. If ritual occasions in general, and gift rituals in particular, are valued for this reason then we should expect to find that different occasions, and different gifts, are used to think different thoughts.

Although the range of gifts that may be given on special occasions in Winnipeg is very large, the range of gifts that are popular on particular occasions is much smaller. Five things account for one-quarter or more of the gifts given on the eight most distinctive occasions. They are: candy (Easter, Valentine's Day); decorative vegetation (Mother's Day, sympathy); day clothing (birth, reunion), money (pre-wedding, wedding) and food preparation equipment (pre-wedding events). Only one of them – gifts of food preparation equipment at engagements or bridal showers – is popular on one type of occasion only. Weddings, and the events that lead up to weddings, are the most substantively distinctive ceremonial occasions in Winnipeg.

It is immediately noticeable that the eight most distinctive gift occasions fall into four groups that are not random. One group is concerned with marriage (weddings and pre-wedding events), at which practical gifts of household resources (money and food preparation equipment) are conveyed. A second group is concerned with the physical experience of another person's presence within the individual's life world (birth and reunion) at which items for physical protection and comfort (day clothing) are given. The other two groups are more difficult to interpret, but one point is very clear. The things that are given at Easter, Valentine's Day, Mother's Day and at times of sympathy are luxury goods rather than things of practical utility. We may therefore suspect that their social significance is above all symbolic, and that they are intended to express emotions of certain kinds.

The evidence on types of transfers suggests that beneath the great variations in individual gift behavior there is an underlying system of meanings within which each ritual occasion has its place. However, we have so far mentioned only half of the types of occasions about which we have information. A truly cultural system of meanings should include all ritual occasions, and the interesting question is whether or not a semiotic analysis can be extended to the less distinctive times for giving. If there is such a system it is clearly a weak one, since on some occasions there is no gift type that is really popular. We have already seen that Christmas is an amorphous gift occasion (Table 5.1), and the 3 most frequent gift types account for only 34 per cent of all Christmas gifts. At anniversaries the 3 most frequent gift types account for only 31 per cent of gifts.

Things that are not especially popular as gifts may nevertheless be typical gifts for a particular occasion if they are given more frequently at that time than at other times. The typicality of gifts has been measured in this study as a relative frequency of giving 50 per cent or more above the average for all occasions. Using this measure a list of typical gifts was produced for all ritual occasions. The contents of those lists often overlap, and so the groups of

Figure 5.1 Typical gifts on ritual occasions

Co-operation
1) Wedding: money, food and drink equipment, decorative household objects, household essentials, food preparation equipment
2) Pre-wedding: food preparation equipment, money, food and drink equipment, household essentials

Sociability
1) Anniversary: relaxation equipment and services, drink, decorative household objects, food, personal relations media, decorative vegetation, food and drink equipment, household essentials
2) Visit: drink, food, decorative household objects, food preparation equipment, decorative vegetation
3) Party: activities equipment and services, drink, decorative household objects, household essentials, food and drink equipment, food
4) Father's Day: household essentials, drink, activities equipment and services, food, body adornments

Sentimentality
1) Mother's Day: decorative vegetation, personal accessories
2) Sympathy: decorative vegetation, miscellaneous, money, food

Attachment
1) Valentine's Day: candy, decorative vegetation, other clothing
2) Easter: candy, decorative vegetation
3) Farewell: money, personal accessories, candy

Presence-availability
1) Reunion: decorative household objects, day clothing, food and drink equipment, decorative vegetation
2) Birthday: day clothing, reading equipment, personal relations media.
3) Christmas: body preparation equipment
4) Birth: day clothing, night clothing, body preparation equipment, decorative vegetation

occasions discovered earlier become less distinct. At the same time, other occasions come into focus as being similar to one or other of the original four groups of occasions, and a fifth group appears (see Figure 5.1).

Earlier in this chapter it was suggested that gift giving is used for purposes of social reproduction. Three modes of social reproduction were identified, each of which reproduces one of the components of a system of social action. The three components of action are, the availability of actors, personal relationships, and social relationships. Each of these components of social action is reproduced by social bonds of certain kinds, and it is those bonds which are re-enacted on ritual occasions (see Figure 5.2). The annual ritual cycle contains times for dramatizing all of the bonds that are found in small social worlds. The ritual order of ceremonial occasions thus facilitates both the symbolic differentiation of specialized ties and the symbolic integration of multiplex ties through multiple giving.

In ritual giving the characteristics of different social bonds are expressed in the nature of the objects transferred. At reunions (such as returning from a trip), births, birthdays, and Christmas the central value of the occasion is the physical availability of significant others to each other as individuals who are co-present in space and time. Giddens has referred to this fundamental property of social action as "presence-availability" (Giddens 1979: 103). On occasions that celebrate the high presence-availability of significant others, the physical being of the other and the nurturing of that physical being are symbolized in the typical gifts of day clothing and body preparation equipment. With respect to the latter, the fact that body preparation equipment is the only typical gift at Christmas is remarkable, and quite unexpected. It confirms the extent to which Christian myths about Christmas, such as the story of the gifts of myrrh and frankincense for the infant Jesus, have been appropriated in the institutionalization of family ties. Secular symbols that are transformations of religious symbols still show the effects of their origins.

Valentine's Day, Easter, and times for bidding farewell (such as leaving for a trip or taking up employment elsewhere) are occasions for confirming attachments. The religious significance of Easter, in the crucifixion and ascent to heaven of Christ, would seem to be strongly related to the theme of demonstrating unbroken attachment in the face of separation that is the focus of farewell rituals. The typical gift that links all three occasions is candy, a non-

Figure 5.2 Ritual order of the social reproduction of small social worlds

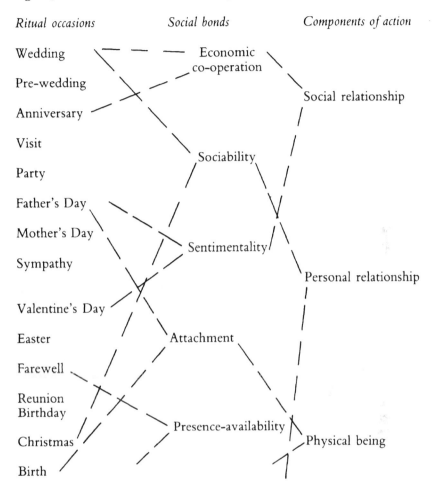

nurturing substance, whose prominence here is probably related to its sweetness. The sweetness of candies makes them very attractive, and they have the power to draw others close (particularly small children) and to hold their interest. As Barker has shown, giving candies is thus expressive of a desire to keep particular others close (Barker 1972: 580 especially).[6]

After candy, the second typical gift at Easter is decorative vegetation, which consists mainly of flowers and flowering plants. Flowers and plants are the most typical gifts on Mother's Day, and at times for expressing sympathy such as illness or death of a family member. They are given to others because they appeal to the senses and stimulate pleasant feelings. It is that emotion work which is the main theme on these occasions. Mother's Day and times of sympathy are occasions for sentimentality. That is to say, they involve a self-conscious attention to the feelings of respect and awe which individuals are expected to have for those who occupy certain statuses.

Anniversaries, visits, parties, and Father's Day are deliberate occasions of a different sort. Here there is a consciousness of interaction, and of the value of creating enjoyable relations within an encounter. They are, in other words, occasions for sociability. Sociability work includes providing things that help people to relax and to feel sufficiently at ease with one another that they actively join in lively intercourse. In Winnipeg alcohol is the most widely used substance for this purpose. Alcoholic drink is one of two typical gift objects that link all four of these occasions. The other typical gift common to these occasions is food. Eating food adds to the enjoyment of any celebration, and sharing food with others adds to the pleasure of being together.

In the last group of occasions being together takes a decidedly more practical and hard-headed turn. Weddings and pre-wedding events celebrate the setting up of a new domestic group through marriage. Married domestic life involves the economic cooperation of a man and a woman in a familial division of labor. That cooperative labor is celebrated at wedding anniversaries, but it is facilitated at weddings and bridal showers. On these occasions quantities of domestic capital in the form of household goods, and money, are transferred to the couple. On some occasions, such as the bridal showers held in community halls in the North End of Winnipeg, the quantities are large.

Signs of things to come

Weddings are important events in the lives of most people in Winnipeg because they are customarily followed by a substantial change in way of life, beginning with place of residence. The transfers of wealth that precede and accompany weddings serve to facilitate those changes in a practical sense, and to mark their achievement in a symbolic sense. In these ways wedding gifts contribute to the reproduction of a familial way of life, and to a sense of social order.

Despite the occasional reluctance of women like Bernice Genyk, bridal showers are popular occasions in Winnipeg. Among certain ethnic groups, such as the Ukrainians (to which Bernice belongs), these occasions have been elaborated into large, complex events with many interesting ritual features. Their economic dimensions are also most impressive.

In the spring of 1984 the author attended one such shower, a "Ukrainian" shower, held in a church hall. All the gifts transferred to the future bride at that time have been listed in Figure 5.3. Most of the gifts were physically brought into the hall and handed to the bride, who opened them in full view of the assembly. For the benefit of those guests who were not sitting close to the head table, the nature of each gift, and the name(s) of its donor(s), were broadcast over a public address system. In addition to the goods that were physically transferred in this way, two other forms of transfer were carried out symbolically at that time, although their physical completion came later. The first category consisted of large gifts that were not easily portable, and so had not been brought to the hall. They were a seven-cubic-foot freezer from the bride's mother (who was present) and a chesterfield from her father (who was not present). For these gifts, an announcement was made, and a photograph of the freezer was held up for the guests to see.

Figure 5.3 Bridal shower gifts given at a hall shower

1) Deep fryer 2) Electric can opener 3) Casserole dish 4) Four-piece china place setting 5) Set of crystal salt and pepper shakers 6) Bath towels 7) Tea kettle 8) Wine glasses 9) Electric mixer and dishcloth 10) Poultry shears and tea-towels 11) Kitchen tool set (small utensils) 12) Towels 13) Crystal goblets 14) Sheets 15) Tea-towels and a toaster 16) Onion soup bowls 17) Cake plate and name-plate 18) Set of glasses 19) Tupperware containers 20) Crystal bowl 21) Torte plate 22) Coffee mugs and tray 23) Towels 24) China dinner service 25) Portable mixer 26) Glasses 27) Silver cutlery place settings 28) Sheets and pillow cases 29) Silver cake server 30) Serving dish 31) Towels 32) Onion soup bowls 33) Oven mitts 34) Casserole dishes 35) Kitchen cutters and a kettle 36) Sheets 37) Saucepans 38) Gold bowl 39) Crystal decanter and glasses 40) Silver liqueur glasses 41) Pyrex roaster 42) Breakfast utensils 43) set of dishes – glassware and silverware 44) Quiche pan 45) Electric kettle 46) Place-mats and napkins 47) Breakfast utensils 48) Electric frying pan 49) Kitchen tool set 50) Onion soup bowls 51) Set of glasses and glass bowls 52) Crock pot 53) Cook books 54) Black lingerie (joke gift from male friends) 55) Towels 56) Onion soup bowls 57) Cookware set 58) Crystal vase 59) Towels 60) Place-mats, napkins, and napkin rings 61) Electric frying pan 62) Kitchen utensils and electric frying pan 63) Sheets and a comforter 64) Towels, pillows, and a chest freezer 65) Chesterfield

The second category of symbolic transfer consisted of money. Whether or not they bring a gift, most of the guests at a hall shower in Winnipeg contribute money, which may be done at the door as they enter. In addition, those who have received an invitation but who are unable to come may send a financial contribution instead. (An extensive network of kin is usually invited to attend a hall shower, which may include people living a day's drive or more from Winnipeg who are unlikely to attend.) The collective donation of money to the bride is thus an important part of the occasion, and the amount collected is announced after all the gifts have been opened. At the shower described here, it was announced that $350 had been collected "at the door."

Bridal showers are, above all else, occasions for helping a young bride to establish herself in her new home. More precisely, they are occasions when women join together to create a woman's place within the home. Most of the gifts are things that will assist a woman in the performance of domestic labor on behalf of her husband, which is assumed to be the inevitable and immediate consequence of marriage. Hall showers are also occasions for celebrating a girl's entry into the social world of adult women. Through elaborate ceremonial a young woman is incorporated into a homosocial support network (Cheal 1988a), and her femininity is displayed and openly confirmed (Cheal 1988b). Hall showers are thus occasions within which the fusion of substantive and ceremonial values is complete, and powerful.

The incorporation rites associated with marriage in Winnipeg illustrate very nicely the conjunction of family economics and public ceremony in the passage into adulthood that van Gennep described. In chapter 2 we saw that Goffman considered wedding gifts to be classic examples of ceremonial acts whose communicative efficacy depends rather heavily upon their substantive value. He does not seem to have questioned the harmony of substantive and ceremonial values in marriage rituals, but we shall have reason to do so. Difficulties in reconciling the social uses of different values sometimes arise at large communal rituals such as hall showers.

The substantive values of the gifts transferred at hall showers attract attention for several reasons. Among them is the fact that the financial value of the total redistribution of wealth is a measure of the success of the occasion, and of those who organized it and who attended it. A keen interest is therefore taken by all participants in the number of guests in attendance (approximately 115 at the shower described here),[7] and especially in the amount of money that has been raised. Since some people arrive late, tallying the money taken "at the door" is left till late in the proceedings, and so can delay the closing ceremonies. Nevertheless, it is considered essential to announce the results before the meeting is ended, and to applaud them.

The women who arrange successful hall showers are tremendously proud of their achievements, and rightly so, because they require considerable organizational skill and not a little influence. They can also expect to gain prestige from their success, as more than one guest confided to me. Those who give conspicuously generous gifts may also improve their social standing, if their motives are respected. While listening to the guests at a hall shower as they compare the present event with others they have recently attended, it is easy to believe that a spirit of rivalry – between kinship groups, if not between individuals – often enthuses those who throw themselves into hall showers. Veblen would have loved them.

At bridal showers women provide material support to other women in order to help them set up homes for themselves and their husbands. It is this kind of provision of social support that sociologists have generally found most interesting in research into the gift economy.[8] Transactions within social networks have usually been described as consisting of flows of resources (Richardson and Wellman 1985: 771), defined as "anything one individual family member can offer another to help that person satisfy needs or attain goals" (Hesse-Biber and Williamson 1984: 262).[9] The problem with this approach has been its one-sidedness. The substantive dimensions of transactions have been studied in great detail, but their symbolic dimensions have been ignored. Thus proximity in social networks has been seen as a question of availability to provide help, rather than of the ritual value assigned to presence-availability (see, for example, Litwak 1985).

The purpose of a hall shower is to redistribute resources that will be of practical use to their recipient. However, the objects transferred also have other qualities that serve other ends. A wife may need bowls and glasses with which to serve food and drink. But she does not have to have a gold bowl or crystal goblets. Nevertheless, these costly things are given at such times (see Figure 5.3). The fact that they are given shows us that in the gift economy transactions are always shaped by a dialectical relationship between practical and symbolic values.

Practical resources and symbolic media

When things are given for practical purposes it is said that the motive for giving is *instrumental*, whereas when they are given for symbolic purposes the action is described as being *expressive*. This distinction between instrumental and expressive interaction (Parsons and Shils 1962: 209) can help us to further understand the great behavioral diversity in the Winnipeg gift economy, since not all occasions have the same meanings. The distinction between instrumental and expressive interaction has not been used much in sociology, because of its location until very recently in a problematic theory of social differentiation.[10] It is therefore necessary to comment briefly on that theory, and on the contrasting approach that will be taken here.

In Parsonian sociology the specification of cultural values was thought to result in the evolution of functionally distinct (i.e. specialized) patterns of action. Parsons thought that as societies develop their constituent social units divide and an increasing number of functionally specific units emerge (Parsons 1966, 1977). The pressure for differentiation was seen as arising from the strains created when the same actors attempt to realize a variety of values in the same place at the same time. In small groups the result should be a range of qualitatively different types of behavior that occur at different points in time (Parsons and Bales 1955).

It is well known that Parsons' evolutionary model was not able to adequately account for situations of de-differentiation, in which social structures take on a wide range of functions (Tiryakian, 1985). Such situations occur regularly in radical religious and political movements (Cheal 1975; Tiryakian 1985: 119–20), but they can also occur in comparatively stable interaction patterns, such as rituals (Tiryakian 1985: 128). Special occasions for ritual are typically ordered over time in annual cycles, or longer. They should, according to the Parsonian model, be highly differentiated. At the level of gift behavior some occasions (such as weddings) are indeed very specialized, while others (such as Christmas and anniversaries) are not. More importantly, the difference in degree of differentiation are not random but are related to the social organization of social reproduction outlined above.

The degree of ritual specialization for an occasion can be measured from the frequency with which the 3 most common gifts are given on that occasion. The 3 most common, or principal, gifts have been listed for each occasion in Figure 5.4, and their combined relative frequency for each occasion is given in Figure 5.5. According to this measure, degrees of ritual specialization are highest for instrumental giving at weddings and pre-wedding events, and for expressive giving at times of sympathy and farewell and at Valentine's Day and Easter. All the other occasions show little evidence of ritual specialization. Clearly, there is no general pressure towards differentiation here, since the degree of compatibility of simultaneous instrumental and expressive interactions *depends upon the frame of meaning for the occasion.*

Figure 5.4 Principal gifts on ritual occasions

Instrumental (cooperation)
1) Wedding: money, food and drink equipment, decorative household objects
2) Pre-wedding: food preparation equipment, money, food and drink equipment

Instrumental and expressive (sociability)
1) Anniversary: relaxation equipment and services, money, drink
2) Visit: drink, day clothing, food
3) Party: activities equipment and services, drink, decorative household objects
4) Father's Day: day clothing, household essentials, drink
5) Mother's Day: decorative vegetation, money, body preparation equipment

Expressive (sentimentality and attachment)
1) Sympathy: decorative vegetation, miscellaneous, money
2) Valentine's Day: candy, decorative vegetation, other clothing
3) Easter: candy, decorative vegetation, day clothing
4) Farewell: money, personal accessories, candy

Expressive and instrumental (presence-availability)
1) Reunion: day clothing, decorative household objects, decorative vegetation
2) Birthday: day clothing, money, reading equipment
3) Christmas: day clothing, play equipment, body preparation equipment
4) Birth: day clothing, night clothing, money

All social events involve some combination of instrumental and expressive interactions, by virtue of the nature of social action as material practice. Resources, and the labor of preparing them, are necessary to set the scene for any occasion. At the same time cooperation in the social organization of an occasion as a sequence of interactions requires that people communicate to each other

Figure 5.5 Expressive and instrumental interactions on ritual occasions

Ritual occasions	Degree of gift specialization (%)	Interaction motives
Wedding	85.2	Instrumental
Pre-wedding	71.3	(cooperation)
Anniversary	31.1	
Visit	47.1	Instrumental and
Party	43.3	expressive
Father's Day	56.1	(sociability)
Mother's Day	52.4	
Sympathy	83.0	Expressive
Valentine's Day	72.5	(sentimentality
Easter	72.7	and attachment)
Farewell	68.9	
Reunion	50.6	Expressive and
Birthday	44.9	instrumental
Christmas	34.3	(presence-
Birth	60.0	availability)

their definitions of the situation and of their relations to it. The combination of instrumental and expressive interactions is most in evidence at times such as visiting. Gifts of food and drink help to make the occasion work as a scene for pleasurable interaction and gifts of things the recipients will enjoy having show that those present care for them and have a legitimate interest in their affairs.

On other occasions practical and symbolic values may be seen as mutually incompatible. That is not because of any functional requirement for the specification of values, but because some acts, it is thought, are more effective than others in achieving certain purposes. The clearest illustration of that point in Winnipeg is the giving of money at weddings. The social dynamics of that situation will be discussed in chapter 7.

Conclusion

In this chapter we have seen that there is much to be learned from looking at the gift economy as a ritual order of the social reproduction of small social worlds. Small social worlds are structured by an interlocking system of social bonds that have been identified here as presence-availability, attachment, sentimentality, sociability, and cooperation. In the moral economy of the gift these bonds are institutionalized through ritual transfers that provide the means with which to construct social ties, and the time and symbols with which to think about them.

The approach taken here has been to try to uncover the microstructures by which the gift economy has its social effects, and to describe how those microstructures work. We shall see in the next chapter that this approach provides a useful corrective to some of the generalizations that have been made about gifts and their uses. We have noted here that the moral order of gift giving does more than simply reproduce the social bonds that integrate small social worlds. It can also produce status rankings that are based on market incomes. In the next chapter we shall examine that possibility in some detail in order to see how well our characterization of the gift economy as a *moral* economy stands up by comparison with other approaches. The main conclusion at which we shall arrive is that the gift economy, like any other social system, is not a totality. It consists, in other words, of more than one principle of social organization whose ecology must be described.

Among several comparative points of interest, we will find it necessary to pursue the distinction between practical and symbolic values that was raised in this chapter. The relation between instrumental and expressive interactions, and therefore between practical and symbolic values, is a dialectical one. Put differently, they are both in harmony and in opposition. As a result, the gift economy is a dynamic economic system in a process of continuous change.

6

Intimacy and community

The ideology of love described in chapter 4 holds that gifts are given spontaneously, as a result of the natural affections of one person for another. In this chapter we are going to explore some of the limits to that notion.[1] The ideology of love is a product of the modern world, and especially of the modern middle class. It is the cement that binds personal relationships in those social groups where the constraints of material necessity and social control have long since ceased to have much force. This does not mean that material wants and social sanctions no longer have any relevance for people's lives. What it does mean is that in a modern mass society most people have available to them a large number of actors with whom they could enter into social relations, and between whom they must choose.

Under such conditions the chances of individual exit from any particular relationship are considerable, and personal relationships in general are more difficult to keep going. Insofar as certain relationships do endure, it is because some or all of their internal bonds of presence-availability, attachment, sentimentality, sociability, and economic cooperation have been tightened. One of the principal means of achieving that in the western societies has been to intensify the management of emotions, such as love, in those relationships which are planned to last.[2] The intensification of emotion management has taken the form of the privatization of personal relationships, initiated by the late eighteenth- and early nineteenth-century urban middle classes. As stated by Hareven, the invention of a well-defined sphere of private life "was related to the retreat of the family into domesticity, the segregation of the work place from the home, the redefinition of the mother's role as the major custodian of the domestic sphere and the emergence of sentiment as the basis of familial relationships" (Hareven 1980: 16).

In the modern urban milieu networks of personal relationships vary enormously in size and in the kinds of ties of which they are composed. Nevertheless, there is always some evidence of the structuring of interaction according to the duration of relations.

Long-term relationships with family members and with old friends are more intimate than the short-term, disposable relationships usually found among new friends, coworkers, and neighbors. Short-term relationships, however, can be more numerous and more varied, because less has been invested in them and the costs of breaking them are correspondingly smaller. The combination of these complementary structures of relations within one personal network provides important strategic advantages. Strong ties (that is, long-term relationships) permit a synchronization of action over time that encourages rational life planning (P. Berger, B. Berger, and Kellner 1973: 69–73).[3] On the other hand, as Granovetter has claimed, weak ties (that is, short-term relationships) may provide access to a greater variety of opportunities for acquiring resources and for engaging in shared activities (Granovetter 1973). Outside of the core sets of interlocking life-courses, then, personal relationships in the modern Canadian city are characteristically organized as sparsely knit, loosely bounded networks of ties (Wellman 1979).

The distinction between strong ties and weak ties has been found to be useful by sociologists interested in the structural analysis of networks (Wellman 1981). It is not only of interest to social scientists, however. Actors, too, are aware of the different effects of different kinds of relationships, which they define in contrasting ways. Strong personal relationships are defined as being "close," and motives of love and affection are ascribed to members. Weak personal relationships, by comparison, are less likely to be thought of as involving positive emotion states. Instead they are typified as consisting of shared beliefs or interests. At the limit, what is shared may be very narrow indeed. It may be confined to sanctioned conformity to normative exchanges of valued objects, and to the enjoyment of the social occasions at which they are transferred.

Long-term "strong" relationships and short-term "weak" relationships are both employed in social reproduction. For analytical purposes the social organization of social reproduction can therefore be described as taking two divergent forms. On the one hand there is the reproduction of life and of personal relationships that takes place between those who are closely involved in each other's affairs. On the other hand there is the collective reproduction of actors as members of particular social statuses in social relationships. We shall refer to these two types of social organization here as *intimacy* and *community*.

Intimate relations are those in which each actor knows a great

deal about the other, as a result of extensive contact in the present
and in the past, and as a result of having an interest in the other's
activities. Interest and contact cannot be sustained at high levels
with everyone, and so each person specializes in cultivating a
limited number of intimate ties. At the limit, perhaps only one
person is selected for intimacy, and the structure of intimacy then
takes the form of dyadic relations within a couple. At the opposite
extreme, communal relations may involve very large numbers of
people. Such ties are inevitably specialized in content and limited
in emotional involvement. Communal relations involve actors
who share specific interests and whose knowledge about each other
may be limited to what is necessary in order to get things done.
It is, in fact, possible for communal events such as hall showers
to be efficiently organized even though there is no one who has
a personal knowledge of everybody present. What is necessary,
however, is a sense of affinity and interest that makes people
available for mobilization into altruistic activities. In other words,
communal relations are constructed out of pre-existing social identities, such as kinship, identification with the same ethnic group,
neighborliness, etc.

Intimate relations and communal relations are both found within
moral economies. For financial reasons they may be experienced
as competing arenas for giving, between which individuals must
choose. Thus we saw in chapter 5 that Bernice Genyk has been
trying to cut back on bridal gifts to the daughters of her mother's
friends, in order to keep more of her scarce resources for her
"family" (that is, her fiancé and his children). Bernice's reluctance
to spend as heavily on things for bridal showers as she used to do
only makes sense in the context of her commitment to a set of
intimate relations to which she assigns a higher priority. That
simple point has some major implications. It means that structures
of intimacy and structures of community can only be understood
in relation to each other (Cheal 1987b, 1988b).

Too often studies of giving have looked at either the organization
of intimacy or the organization of community, but not both.
Focusing on one or the other leads to an inadequate sociology of
the gift, not only because it produces an incomplete picture of the
gift economy, but also because it must result in a failure to
adequately comprehend the parts. We begin this chapter with two
illustrations of that point which have some relevance for the history
of modern social thought.

Marriage and patriarchy

Marriage and the family are prominent themes in the Winnipeg gift economy, as they are in Middletown (Caplow 1982; Caplow *et al.* 1982). After Christmas and birthdays, the spousal relationship is the third most prominent focus for ritual giving. Pre-wedding celebrations, wedding festivities and wedding anniversaries together account for 8 per cent of all gifts and almost 25 per cent of all gift expenditures. Furthermore, at Christmas more valuable gifts are exchanged between spouses than in any other relationship (Cheal 1986: 432).

If one of the more important effects of the gift economy is to reproduce the institution of marriage then it may be that it also reproduces the inequality of women within marriage, an argument that has been advanced by Bell and Newby. They have claimed that men, as husbands, have stabilized their authority over women by manipulating a set of values that endorses the inferior position of wives within the patriarchal family. The key to this stability, they state, is the "deferential dialectic" where the tensions generated by hierarchical relations are overcome in family rituals, the best example of this being the benevolent gift. From the perspective of deference theory, asymmetrical giving in which husbands are more generous than wives is seen as a means of symbolic control; it reaffirms the system of sexual stratification in the family and the dependence of women upon men:

> We have been arguing that the relationship between husband and wife is a deferential one in that it is traditionally legitimated and hierarchical. It appears both natural and immutable. It also has become – because it has been in the interests of those in the superordinate position – a "moral" order. This "moral" order is expressed through and by ideological hegemony. We have also argued that the contradictions within the deferential dialectic of identification and differentiation need careful if not constant "tension management"; and that there are a number of social mechanisms by which this is done – most notably by the "gift".
> (Bell and Newby 1976: 164)

Bell and Newby's theory is fascinating for many reasons, and it is regrettable that no attempt has been made to follow it through. There has so far been no direct test of their claims, although an indirect test by the author demonstrated that women are net beneficiaries in exchanges of valuable Christmas gifts whereas men are net benefactors (Cheal 1986: 431, 434). Since that finding holds when personal income is controlled, it is surely a property of interaction between the sexes. The available evidence thus lends some support to Bell and Newby's thesis concerning benevolent gift exchanges between husbands and wives. However, it is not easy to see how their thesis could be extended into a *general* theory of the gift economy. Caplow has found that in Middletown women are more frequent givers at Christmas than men (Caplow 1982: 387), and that finding has been duplicated for the annual cycle of gift occasions in Winnipeg (Cheal 1987a: 153). Among married couples in England, wives are more likely to pay for presents than are their husbands (Pahl, in press). In the gift economy, at least, women are far from being passive receptors, as we see in the case of Mrs Chubey.

Case study: Pat Chubey

Pat Chubey is 40 years old and is married to a heavy-equipment operator in the construction industry. They have 3 boys and 2 girls. Pat describes herself as a housewife who works part-time as a library assistant. She also does freelance clerical work at home. Pat handles the family's bills, and has used her clerical skills to develop a detailed system of family accounts. Through it, she says, she keeps track of everything that comes into the house and everything that goes out. Pat is proud of her careful budgeting. She criticizes other families in their neighborhood who, she believes, live well now by running up credit card debts that they will never be able to repay. One of the ways in which the Chubeys live within their means is by spending as little as possible on gifts. Pat and her husband never give each other anything, and the children receive presents from them only on their birthdays.

In her interview Mrs Chubey became increasingly agitated as I began to collect data about all the gifts that she had given during the year, and their financial values. Finally she declared that the reason for her unhappiness was that she was afraid her husband might find out exactly how much she spent on gifts for her rela-tives. He expected her to manage on a tight budget, and that included paying for any gifts out of her own money (that is, her earnings). In practice she often found it necessary to use money intended for household needs for her gift purchases. She knew that her husband would be furious if he ever realized the extent of her subterfuge over the years, and it was therefore essential for her well-being that it should remain secret.

Mrs Chubey's concerns were clearly very much affected by the traditional patriarchal structure of her family life, in which she bore the responsibility for managing the family wage provided by her husband. But it was not patriarchy that she was reproducing in her illicit gifts. It was her network of female kin.

Mrs Chubey's pattern of giving cannot be explained simply as a result of her dyadic relations within marriage, however important that may be. To attempt to do so would be to ignore her frequent associations with her aunts, whose phone calls punctuated our interview. For Mrs Chubey there is a wider audience of significant others outside marriage whose good opinion is also desired. Thorstein Veblen (1918) made this point the basis for an entire theory of consumer behavior.

Conspicuous consumption

No social scientist has had a more long-lasting effect upon the sociology of gift giving than Veblen (see, for example, Schwartz 1967). His theory of the uses of wealth in status competition by members of the leisure class has been applied very widely (for example Blau 1964; Baudrillard 1981). It has, in fact, been applied so widely that it is commonly taken to apply to large sections of the population (Ewen 1976: 206; Leiss 1976: 57). That includes those who, like Mrs Chubey and the women who attend hall showers, are a very long way indeed from the leisure class. Veblen's influential theory has been the cornerstone for a conventional social science posture towards gift giving that may be characterized as "cynical realism." According to this point of view a gift is a challenge that must be answered since questions of status and wealth are immediately involved. Belshaw claims to have been convinced that "this is as true in our own society as in the aggressive potlatch" (Belshaw 1965: 47).

Critics of consumer societies have frequently described modern gift practices as forms of conspicuous waste. These critics include ordinary people (particularly those with relatively low incomes) who resent the social pressures to spend, and spend heavily, at Christmas. They also include social scientists whose alienation from the present is so complete that it can only be theorized by analogy with a mythologized past. Thus Lévi-Strauss has described the North American Christmas as seeking "the reintegration into modern society of the very general attitudes and procedures of primitive cultures" (Lévi-Strauss 1969: 50).

Lévi-Strauss's remark echoed the position taken some time

before by Veblen, who was one of the most forceful early critics
of the new American industrial society. According to Veblen the
more harmful features of industrial America were due to "the
predatory habit of life" which he thought had been "settled upon
the group by long habituation." He described the origins of this
"predatory culture" as lying in ancient "barbarian" societies that
had been founded on a warlike existence. Veblen claimed that
in societies with predatory cultures social life is dominated by a
competitive struggle for honor and esteem. Where the institution
of private property has been established, and especially as economic
productivity increases, that struggle manifests itself in invidious
displays of wealth. The principal forms of display are conspicuous
leisure and conspicuous consumption.

Veblen argued that conspicuous consumption became more
important than conspicuous leisure as a basis for social distinction
with the rise of cities. That is because consumer goods are more
easily visible to the large number of people with whom an individual has only transient relationships in urban life. (Veblen 1918:
86–91). He suggested that among those with relatively great wealth
personal consumption alone could not keep up with the requirements of status advancement. Vicarious consumption is also necessary. "The aid of friends and competitors is therefore brought in by
resorting to the giving of valuable presents and expensive feasts
and entertainments." Whatever the social origins of presents and
feasts may have been, Veblen felt that ostentation was their main
function, "so that their utility in this respect has now long been the
substantial ground on which these usages rest" (Veblen 1918: 75).

Veblen's cynical realism has had the effect of stunting sociological investigations into consumer behavior (McCracken 1985).
Those who have followed his lead have restricted themselves to
one narrow aspect of the communicative character of goods,
namely their ability to symbolize wealth within a system of status
competition. This approach has effectively excluded the consideration of other interpersonal uses to which consumer goods may
be put. Interestingly, the main opposition to his view of industrial
capitalism has come from within critical theory.[4] Adorno has
pointed out that in Veblen's debunking of modern consumerism
he had to reject culture in order to "get at the bottom of things"
(Adorno 1981). In so doing, the analysis of ceremonial values was
subordinated to the analysis of substantive values. Veblen therefore
failed to appreciate the dialectical relationships between culture and
action.[5] More recent critiques of capitalist society have pointed out

that expressive forms may, in fact, be acts of resistance through which individuals win a small personal space within a stratified society (Clarke *et al.* 1976).

Veblen's ideas on conspicuous giving have been influential for so long not because there is an overwhelming body of evidence for them (see Cheal 1986: 429–31) but because there has been little systematic work carried out on the gift economy. The design of the Winnipeg Ritual Cycle Study permits us to carry out a limited test of hypotheses derived from Veblen's model of status competition in predatory societies.

If Veblen's cynical realism is correct, and status competition is the main purpose of gift transactions, then we should expect to find that most giving consists of costly expenditures. The reason for this is that costly gifts are much more likely to attract attention to the donor, at the same time as they display his wealth.[6] We have already seen how this can happen in the case of Leonard White's brother-in-law (reported in chapter 3). According to Leonard's wife, Michael would rather give nothing at all than have to give an inexpensive item. If most people behaved like that then there would be fewer little gifts given than there are expensive gifts.

In the Winnipeg Ritual Cycle Study the interviewees were asked to state the financial value of each gift that they had given during 1982. They were not always pleased to do that, since many of them believe that it is really the thought behind the gift, and not its substantive value, that is most important. Nevertheless, once they had committed themselves to the interviews, almost all of the respondents provided financial data on their gift expenditures. Financial values were recorded for 96.5 per cent of all purchased gifts and money gifts which the interviewees had given, either by themselves or in conjunction with others.

Most gift giving in Winnipeg does not consist of valuable gifts. Half of the items recorded in the Winnipeg Ritual Cycle Study were worth less than $15, and only 4 per cent cost $100 or more. The gift economy in Winnipeg is made up of a large number of small gifts, whose social value is not directly related to their financial value. That is most evident in the case of stocking stuffers, illustrated in an earlier chapter (see p. 81), which are fun gifts given at Christmas and normally worth only a couple of dollars. Of course valuable gifts are also given at Christmas (Cheal 1986), but conspicuous giving of the kind that Leonard White's brother-in-law apparently engages in is in fact quite rare.[7] When donors do spend a large amount on one person they often divide it between a number of items, each of which is of only modest value.

Combination gifts, that is to say transfers consisting of more than one item on a given occasion, are not uncommon. It could conceivably be that this pattern of giving has become the predominant way of conveying an impression of personal affluence that does not openly reveal the donor's ulterior motive. In order to evaluate that possibility it is necessary to sum the values of the items in a combination gift so as to establish the total financial value of the resources transferred in one transaction. When that is done the economic dimensions of giving in Winnipeg are somewhat more substantial, but the difference is not dramatic. Almost half (47 per cent) of the gift transactions were worth less than $20 (see the column "total financial value transferred per transaction" in Table 6.1). Furthermore, the total financial value of the objects transferred in a transaction overstates the interpersonal impression created by gift giving. That is because few gifts are given by one person to one person. In the Winnipeg Ritual Cycle Study 60 per cent of the gifts that the interviewees gave were joint gifts (that is, were given by the interviewee and at least one other person) and 11 per cent were shared gifts (that is, were intended for two or more people to share). The interpersonal financial value of a transfer can be calculated as the proportion of the total financial value of a transaction that passes between two individuals.[8] When that calculation is made it is clear that the interpersonal impact of most gift giving is small indeed. Half of the interpersonal transfers

Table 6.1 *Financial value of gift transfers*

Financial value	Total financial value transferred per transaction %	Interpersonal financial value transferred per transaction %
$0.00–$4.99	11.2	31.6
$5.00–$9.99	14.5	18.5
$10.00–$19.99	21.1	18.9
$20.00–$39.99	19.4	15.2
$40.00–$79.99	17.6	8.0
$80.00 +	16.1	7.8
Totals	99.9	100.0
Mean ($)	$59.79	$30.05
Median ($)	$20.00	$9.99

were worth less than $10 (see the column "interpersonal financial value transferred per transaction" in Table 6.1).

There is very little evidence from our data on gift behavior in Winnipeg to support Veblen's predatory-giving hypothesis.[9] Insofar as conspicuous gift expenditure does occur, it would seem to be confined mainly to two types of occasions at which the average financial value of gifts is considerably higher than normal (see Table 6.2). Those occasions are weddings and anniversaries (the latter category consists almost entirely of wedding anniversaries). In Winnipeg weddings are times when most people spend heavily on individual gifts, and when some people spend very large sums indeed. Wedding gifts have the highest average financial value, and their standard deviation is huge.

Table 6.2 *Financial value of gifts by occasion*

	Value of Gifts*	
Occasion	Mean $	Standard deviation $
Anniversary	85.70	266.90
Birth	23.10	23.30
Birthday	27.00	40.20
Pre-wedding	44.10	114.90
Christmas	21.40	38.30
Easter	9.00	7.00
Father's Day	21.00	16.00
Mother's Day	34.20	100.20
Reunion	11.50	9.90
Valentine's Day	8.60	7.20
Visit	22.10	28.10
Wedding	117.10	394.40
Sympathy	14.80	10.80
Farewell	18.30	36.00
Party	29.00	69.90
Other	49.10	112.70

* Home-made gifts excluded (interviewees made 3.5 per cent of the gifts they gave on all special occasions in 1982)

Weddings, as van Gennep pointed out, are rites of incorporation that bring together many people. Whether or not wedding gifts are actually transferred in the presence of the large gatherings that take place at marriage, those attending can expect that the level of their gift expenditure will eventually become common knowledge.

They therefore provide unusual opportunities to impress large audiences through lavish expenditure. At the same time they create unusual pressures for emulation of conspicuous giving among those who fear the potential loss of respect from many of their significant others. It is the unique social organization of weddings that makes them such distinctive occasions for conspicuous giving.

Other occasions may have similar social dimensions to weddings as times for large ceremonial gatherings, although the combined effect of the number of ties and their emotional significance is never as strong. After weddings, the most expensive occasions for gift giving (in declining order) are anniversaries, "other", and pre-wedding events. As noted above, the category of anniversaries consists mainly of wedding anniversaries. "Other" is a residual category that includes high school and university graduation, and christenings. Pre-wedding celebrations include engagement parties, but the majority of these occasions are bridal showers. Some bridal showers are small events (that is, house showers) whereas others are very large events (that is, hall showers). It is at the latter events that the most expensive bridal gifts tend to be given.

Wedding anniversary feasts, graduation ceremonies and christenings, and community showers are times when gift giving is not entirely private but often takes on a semi-public or public character. That is because what is being reproduced on those occasions is not particular persons, or personal relationships, but social statuses. In particular, a wide interest is taken in each generation's preparation for adulthood through educational achievements and through the accumulation of resources with which to set up an independent household. Passages such as graduation and acquiring a dowry can therefore be elaborated into communal rituals with relatively little effort. Where they have taken that form they share with weddings the fact that levels of gift expenditure are heavily influenced by the comparisons that individuals make between themselves and their reference groups. It is this social-psychological process of presenting high standards of socially desirable behavior in front of large audiences that is most responsible for driving up gift expenditures on those occasions.[10]

The evidence is clear that conspicuous giving in Winnipeg does not occur very often, and then only in conjunction with a handful of occasions where gift giving takes on dimensions of public display. It should also be clear by now that that is not how most gifts are given in Winnipeg. By far the majority of gifts are transferred at intimate gatherings involving small groups of people,

such as groups of family and friends at birthdays and at Christmas
(see Table 4.1). At such times the audiences are small, and the
status benefits to be gained from lavish expenditure are not large
enough to justify incurring heavy costs. Status competition is
therefore a negligible factor in the major ritual occasions in
Winnipeg. Veblen's much touted political economy of consumerism is thus an unreliable guide to understanding most gift
behavior.

Although Veblen's theory of conspicuous consumption has
proven to be of lesser value than some social scientists might have
expected, we have nevertheless learned something very important
about giving as a result of our enquiries. Gift outlays have been
found to vary according to the nature of the occasion, in ways that
are evidently related to the distinction between communal and
intimate forms of social organization that was introduced at the
beginning of this chapter. It will be recalled that at the time the
point was made that theories which stressed either intimacy or
community to the exclusion of the other could not adequately
explain interaction in the gift economy. That point has now been
demonstrated with reference to the limitations of Bell and Newby's
theory of marriage and patriarchy and Veblen's theory of
conspicuous consumption. It is therefore time for us to pay more
explicit attention to the dialectic of intimacy and community.

Intimate and communal encounters and the spending of money

Bridal showers, weddings, and wedding anniversaries are occasions for celebrating entry into, and duration of, married status.
In Winnipeg considerable importance continues to be attached to
marriage, even when its practice is very different from traditional
Christian ideals, as we saw in the case of Bernice Genyk. Marriage
is a social relationship that is valued not only by the couples
themselves, but also by large numbers of other people who believe
that it is worth supporting. It is an institution whose social value
has less to do with romance and passion, or with domestic labor,
than it does with social placement in the community(ies) of adult
men and women (Cheal 1988a, 1988b).

Pre-wedding events, weddings, and anniversaries are of interest
to communities of several kinds. They therefore tend to be organized as communal events, attended by groups of varying sizes.
Furthermore, a number of events may be organized for one

occasion by different communities of interest, as is often the case with house showers. Within these gatherings, and in the communications about them within social networks, status ranking enters into the unofficial practice of the occasion. Collective pressures to give generously as a sign of respect for the marriage are reinforced by status competition, and conspicuous giving is common. Average gift outlays at these times are therefore the highest of all gift-occasion categories (see Figure 6.1).

Figure 6.1 Community and intimacy on ritual occasions

Ritual occasions	Range of average gift values ($)		Social organization
Wedding	117.10		
Pre-wedding	44.10	40–120	Communal
Anniversary	85.70		
Visit	22.10		
Party	29.00	20–35	Communal and intimate
Father's Day	21.00		
Mother's Day	34.20		
Sympathy	14.80		
Valentine's Day	8.60		
Easter	9.00	5–20	Intimate
Farewell	18.30		
Reunion	11.50		
Birthday	27.00		
Christmas	21.40	20–30	Intimate and communal
Birth	23.10		

At the other extreme there are the intimate occasions when social relationships and social statuses are largely irrelevant, and what is valued is the personal relationship between two individuals. Leave-takings and returns, and pain and grief, are things that can happen to anyone regardless of their social position. At times of sympathy, farewell, and reunion it is therefore the expression of personal interest and concern that is enacted in ritual. Easter and Valentine's Day, too, are times for acknowledging personal relationships that are independent of the normative expectations of social roles. At these times particular ties are identified as being especially close. That sometimes means that they are defined as spiritual ties. The clearest example of personal ties that go far beyond social roles concerns gifts to the spirits of those who are beyond life itself. Primitive societies are not the only ones in which people make gifts to the ancestors. Easter, as a few of our respondents reported, is a time for acknowledging dead parents by donating memorial gifts of flowers to their church.

On all of these occasions – sympathy, Valentine's Day, Easter, farewell, reunion – what is done and how it is done may be of no interest to anybody except the two people involved, and perhaps to only one person in the case of a memorial gift. Public display is not entirely irrelevant here, and in a culture that attached a social value to relations with the ancestors things might be quite different.[11] In Winnipeg, however, they are above all private matters. What counts on these occasions, therefore, is not monetary value but symbolic recognition. Financial outlays on gifts at these times are the smallest of all gift-occasion categories.

Between the low cost of the intimate occasions associated with personal relationships, and the expense of the communal occasions associated with marriage, lie the intermediate occasions that combine elements of both. These occasions are times for visiting, when people often gather together in small groups. Their social organization is therefore more communal than the intimate occasions described above. At the same time, the foci of these gatherings are individuals and the relationships between them, rather than social relationships between the occupants of social statuses. They therefore never approach the largest hall showers or weddings in size, and they are generally modest occasions. As a result, the possibility of intimacy is never in danger of being overwhelmed by the kind of formal organization that is typical of most communal events.

Conclusion

In this chapter we have seen that intimate relations and communal relations must both be taken into account in analyses of the gift economy. We have also seen that structures of intimacy and structures of community are not autonomous, but that they impinge directly upon each other through the decisions that individuals must make about the alternative uses for such common facilities as money. We shall have more to say about the uses of money in the next chapter.

In chapter 7 we shall see that community and intimacy are not only different principles. In a later chapter we will claim that intimacy and community can be effectively combined only under special conditions that have had an enormous influence upon the modern gift economy. Otherwise, it is generally the case that the mutual gaze of intimates separates them from the community and its collective activities, whereas the formal organization of communal occasions leaves little room for the unique interactions of a personal relationship. That is not to say that most occasions are either communal or intimate in nature. On the contrary, all social occasions have elements of both. The social forms of intimacy are derived from a collective system of meanings for which there is always a wider audience, and the social interactions of a community take place between individuals who must be able to get along with each other. Nevertheless, community and intimacy are often hard to reconcile. This can lead to tensions, conflicts, and to abrupt changes in practices whose social invention therefore becomes common knowledge. The most visible example of the latter in Winnipeg is the current preponderance of money gifts at weddings.

7

Gift games

It has sometimes been suggested that the social life of cities should be seen as an ecology of games (Long 1958). From that perspective the structured activities that co-exist in a particular territory are seen as comprising a set of interlocking games which together create the participants' sense of social order. These games provide people with goals, and therefore a sense of purpose, together with criteria for judging success or failure. Within the limits of a game the participants engage in rational decision-making which produces for each game a set of typical strategies. Most games involve the moving of pieces, and that is conspicuously true for a gift game. As in any other game the meanings of the pieces in a gift game are defined by a set of rules (Cheal 1980). One of the important social characteristics of games is that they can often be played according to several alternative sets of rules. The same pieces therefore come to have rather different meanings depending upon which rules are being followed. Those meanings are conveyed through the words that are used in the discourse of gift games.

The philosopher Wittgenstein observed that problems with the meanings of words can be cleared up only when they are put back into the contexts of the games from which they have been drawn (see Pitcher 1964). It is within what Wittgenstein referred to as language games that the connections between a name and the things named with it are established. Through language games words and things are interrelated within the stream of everyday life. It follows, Wittgenstein pointed out, that language games always grow out of particular forms of life. In this chapter we will take a look at two contrasting gift games and their languages, and their relations to communal and intimate forms of social life. Our first clue to the existence of these language games is that people like Bernice Genyk sometimes have problems with "incorrect" speech performances.

Bernice Genyk does not like giving money as a gift. She says:

> If I could [avoid it], I wouldn't [do it], because to me money is money,

it doesn't really symbolize a gift. I mean, you can say it's a gift of money, but you can get money from a bank, you can get money from any place, but you can't get a present [from just anywhere]. Say, if I'd forgotten a birthday or something, and I couldn't get a gift there on time, and I just send money, [then] I feel bad about sending money. I would rather have bought a gift and sent a gift than to give money. It's an easy way out. [I would never give money as a gift at] Christmas, or weddings – no – I started saying that but I forgot that presentation is part of a gift for a wedding. So . . . when I said wedding I was thinking of a wedding gift for like at a bridal shower.

Money is not a gift for Bernice, since a *gift* (meaning no. 1) is something that you choose for somebody with that particular person in mind. Nevertheless, she does give money as a "gift", that is as a ritual transfer (meaning no. 2), if the money is a *presentation* at a wedding. In Winnipeg the polysemous uses of the word gift, and specifically the problem of naming money gifts, is a philosophers' puzzle for ordinary people.

Gifts of money are thought to be uncommon on ceremonial occasions because money is regarded as an inferior means of communicating love for others (Cheal 1987a). Caplow found that in Middletown, USA only 9 per cent of Christmas gifts were gifts of money (Caplow 1982: 385). Similarly, Leonard's ethnography of weddings in Swansea has shown that in South Wales gifts of things as *presents* are much more common than gifts of money (Leonard 1980). At weddings in Winnipeg that is not the case.

Two-thirds of the gifts given at weddings in Winnipeg consist of money. However, things have not always been that way. Giving money at weddings is a minority tradition that has become a majority practice only in the last two decades. This is one aspect of interpersonal ritual where the majority of adults in Winnipeg are aware that a significant change has taken place in their lifetime. It therefore deserves our attention.[1]

There is a ready-made explanation for the expansion of money gifts, provided by Marxist political economy. In the "Manifesto of the Communist Party" Marx and Engels described how the bourgeoisie had revolutionized the means of production, and in so doing had wrought enormous changes in social traditions and ways of life. Among other things they claimed that wherever the bourgeoisie had got the upper hand it had put an end to all paternalistic social relations and had transformed personal worth into exchange value. As a result, there remains "no other nexus between man and man than naked self interest and callous cash payment."

In their view this expansion of egotistical calculation had reached right into the family. They concluded that: "The bourgeoisie has torn away from the family its sentimental veil, and has reduced the family relation to a mere money relation."

The expansion of money gifts in Winnipeg would seem to be consistent with this thesis. The absence of feudal social structures on the Canadian Prairies should have made the capitalist destruction of moral relations much easier and more rapid there than elsewhere. But that is not what has happened. In actual fact it is the presence of pre-capitalist social forms in contemporary Winnipeg that has facilitated a monetization of the gift economy in which the bourgeoisie has played no part. It is not the bourgeoisie that has transformed everyday life, but the interrelations between the political economy of the market and the moral economy of kinship-friendship networks.[2]

It will already be apparent from the evidence presented in earlier chapters that the giving of money at weddings in Winnipeg is related to its practical value in establishing the material basis for economic cooperation in marriage. The giving of money has been shown to be a form of instrumental giving, which in turn seems to be correlated with the communal organization of marriage rituals. Communal forms of giving have been particularly strong in traditions that have their origins in peasant cultures. Winnipeg is not the only place where that historical fact has contemporary relevance.

The ecology of wedding gifts

In parts of Spain the giving of money is a prominent feature of wedding festivities in the villages (Brandes 1973). The wedding offerings, which are presented openly in a public ritual, show several overt economic features, including the adjustment of the value of the *ofrecijo* to the costliness of the wedding dinner.[3] Although the offering is contrary to the usual urban practice in Spain, in which wedding guests privately present newlyweds with gift objects, Brandes reports that it has been strengthened, rather than dissolved, by increased urban contacts. Urban customs have been consciously rejected as less practical than the cash reserve produced by the *ofrecijo*, whose benefits have become more substantial due to the higher incomes of returning urban migrants.

A similar practice, known today as *presentation*, has also been retained in the Ukrainian farming communities of western Canada

(Klymasz 1970: 84–6).[4] At a pre-arranged time during the festivities which follow the wedding dinner the guests line up to present the bride and groom with cash gifts. Since the number of guests is "usually in the hundreds" the *presentation* is a major feature of the evening's activities. This custom has not disappeared as Ukrainian Canadians have moved into urban areas (although its scale may have been reduced somewhat). It is a well-established practice in the city of Winnipeg, which raises a number of interesting questions concerning the retention and expansion of rural European traditions under the very different conditions of urban residence in contemporary North America. Contrary to the claims of Lévi-Strauss and Veblen, the attitudes and procedures of primitive and barbarian cultures have not been reintegrated into modern society. But those of peasant cultures have been.

Ukrainians in Canada have undergone steady urbanization in this century and are now predominantly urban dwellers (Darcovich 1980: 10; Driedger 1980: 111–16). Of the three cities with the largest populations of Ukrainian origin (Winnipeg, Edmonton, and Toronto), Winnipeg has the longest history of significant Ukrainian settlement. In Winnipeg neither of Canada's "founding peoples" – the British and the French – comes close to being a majority of the population. In this pluralistic environment Ukrainian culture has been the second most important ethnic tradition. Ukrainian migration was originally focused on areas of Winnipeg close to manual employment in the railroad yards and machine shops, mainly in the North End. Although Ukrainians continue to be relatively more numerous there, they have since dispersed throughout the city and show a steady pattern of decreasing residential segregation since the end of the Second World War (Balakrishnan 1976: 493; Kuz 1979: 130–2; Balakrishnan 1982: 100).

According to Linton's theory of culture, we would expect this demographic dispersal to have given rise to a fluid situation of social change. As seen from the perspective of cultural anthropology, he argued that social change is the result of competition between cultural alternatives. In a pluralistic society such competition is most likely to occur when group boundaries break down and the subcultures begin to merge. In his view, "The first effect of this merging is that the distinctive features of the sub-cultures cease to be Specialties and become Alternatives, i.e., are thrown open to individual choice" (Linton 1936: 277).[5] The second effect is that some of the cultural forms that have been freed from their social origins by the merging of subcultures will be widely accepted, whereas others will fall into disuse. If one of two cultural forms is markedly more efficient than another in achieving specific goals, then it will be adopted by more and more people and the other form will gradually be forced out.

Most people of Ukrainian descent in Winnipeg today are well-integrated socially and economically, and as a result have experienced considerable acculturation. But so have their neighbors. The Ukrainian wedding complex has proven to be very attractive to people from other backgrounds. Ukrainian *presentation*, in particular, has appealed to people from just about every group in Winnipeg, including those of British descent and the middle class.[6]

In order to explore the changes that have occurred in wedding gift practices in Winnipeg eighteen recently married couples were interviewed in the fall of 1981, in the Hotel Chateau Study. Most of them were at the age when their friends were also getting married, and they therefore had current experience of wedding gifts both as recipients and as donors. All of them had hosted their wedding receptions in a large downtown hotel. The hotel had been built a number of years ago in the chateau style, and its managers advertised its historical presence and aesthetic grandeur as enhancing the drama of important occasions. At that time it was the second most expensive hotel in the city in which to hold a wedding reception. Most of the couples were very conscious of the costliness of their wedding arrangements, and of the careful financial management that had been necessary to bring them off successfully. Their prudence had, in some cases, included a careful appraisal of the relative merits of *gifts* versus *presentation* as different types of gift games.

Wedding gifts and the making of money

The *gift* is an object the nature of which is open, to be determined in principle by the donor. It may be given at any time convenient to the parties to the transaction, usually before the wedding. The transfer of a *gift* from donor to recipient is a private event (that is, the audience is restricted, usually to family and close friends) and takes place in a domestic setting. *Gifts* usually consist of goods that have been purchased. Their normal form, in other words, is a commodity that has been recycled from the market economy into the gift economy. *Gifts* can also be things that the donors have made themselves, or money if they feel that is appropriate, but neither is common. The most noteworthy ritual features of *gift* giving are the wrapping of *gifts* by their donors, and the conventional expressions of surprise, pleasure, and gratitude by their recipients.

A *presentation* is always money. It is given during the wedding festivities, normally late in the evening of the wedding day. The transfer is a public event which takes place in the hall or hotel where the wedding function is held. *Presentation* is organized as a collective ritual encounter, open to observation by all those attending the function. The wedding guests usually line up in front of the bride and groom, and they are entertained with music while waiting in line. The bride and groom receive each *presentation* in turn, and acknowledge it with a return gift, usually an appreciation scroll or a piece of wedding cake. Since the money is conveyed in an envelope together with a signed card the amount transferred is not publicized, but is later noted by the bride and groom who send the donors "thank you" cards.

Gifts and *presentations* are not mutually exclusive. However, few people give both for the same wedding, and most couples make known their preference for one or the other. Most wedding guests give only one gift, the major exceptions being close family members and friends. In the case of a *presentation* wedding, those who are close to the bride and groom often give them a *gift* in addition to the *presentation*. Since *presentation* is a collective ritual, which must be organized as a distinct episode in the wedding celebrations, it is normally considered essential for the bride and groom to decide upon, and to broadcast, the preferred form of gift giving for their wedding in advance. Those who are invited to attend the wedding typically feel a strong obligation not only to give something, but also to conform to the nature of the arrangements announced by the bride-to-be.

The diffusion of the custom of *presentation* weddings has not been without opposition. In some cases the opposition from one section of the wedding guests can be sufficiently strong (or the fear of causing offence sufficiently keen) that a compromise arrangement of *"presentation optional"* is announced. On these occasions some people give *presentations* (money) and others give *presents* or *gifts* (goods). Either is acceptable "if that is their custom." The division of opinion that is found on such occasions can be illustrated by the wedding of John and Carol Dugald.[7]

Case study: John and Carol Dugald

Carol and John Dugald are both from small towns in southern Manitoba, and have only recently moved to Winnipeg. John is 25 years old and works in construction. Carol is 23 and is a word processor operator. They had both lived with their parents until they got married, and therefore "needed everything" for their new home. The giving at their wedding was "split." Her side of the family, and most of his relatives, gave *gifts*, while John's friends gave money. John says the difference is because the (male) friends he invited are "more practical." He thought that *presentation* was better than *gifts* because, "You go out and shop all afternoon, and finally decide on a wedding present, and then you think, 'Will they really like it?' So why not give them money and then they can get what they want."

Carol disagreed with him, and said that, "It's nice to have something that you can look back and say 'I got that from whoever.' " She enjoyed receiving their wedding *gifts* because:

> We got some neat things that we would never have gone out and bought for ourselves. A lot of things that we aren't going to need right now. We probably won't use some of them for another fifteen years – silver trays, things like that. But they're nice – nice keepsakes if nothing else, remembrances of people.

John was not convinced by that line of reasoning, and argued that "a lot of young people" would probably "prefer to have the $50 than a silver tray that they will not use for another twenty years."

The gifts at John and Carol's wedding were split between money and goods because they themselves were divided. When, as is more often the case, the groom and bride state a shared preference for *presentation*, their wishes are usually respected – because it is "their wedding," and out of a desire to be supportive at a critical stage in their lives. People who feel strongly that money should never be given at such occasions do sometimes stick to their principles and give a *gift* at a *presentation* wedding, but that is unusual. More typical is the response of Mrs Black, who was interviewed in the Winnipeg Ritual Cycle Study. Mrs Black is a married woman in her late 60s who lives in an area of the city containing many middle-class Anglo-Canadians like herself. Not surprisingly, she prefers a gift "to be something of the person" with "some thought behind it." She dislikes giving and receiving money because "there's not the thought behind it," and she says: "I think that when you give money it's because you don't want to put the effort into doing something, you're just doing it the easy way. A money gift is just kind of an easy way out."

Despite these clear, strongly held sentiments, Mrs Black has given money at weddings where a *presentation* was asked for. Although she does not feel good about it, and complains that "they don't want my gift," she did it "because it was requested."

In the absence of *presentation*, or an equivalent social form, money gifts at weddings would probably exist as a penumbra of quasi-gifts, not quite legitimated but tolerated as unavoidable in certain circumstances. Under those conditions any expansion of money giving would have been slow, and would have involved various interaction difficulties. However, in Winnipeg the social form of *presentation* has been culturally available, and so the expansion of money giving there has been quite rapid. Those individuals who are opposed in principle to money gifts have neutralized the implications of their own contradictory behavior. They have done that by aligning their giving of money at weddings with the perception that *presentation* has been widely tolerated as a legitimate ethnic tradition. Anne Baker, whose case study appeared in an earlier chapter (see pp. 55ff.), had this to say:

> I rarely give money on special occasions. I'd rather buy a gift or say to the person: "I'll take you somewhere. I'll take you to a movie, or I'll take you to a bar or something," rather than give them an amount of money. I don't like [giving money] too much because it just shows you don't really have the time, either to celebrate the occasion with them, or the time to go out and buy them something. You just say: "Here's some money." Big deal. I don't consider money a good gift from me. . . . On a birthday I don't think I'd ever give money. Weddings are different. Giving money for weddings, that's okay, because that's presentation.

If the psychological process of neutralization explains the low level of opposition to *presentation* weddings among non-Ukrainians, their popularity is due to changing preferences among those who decide upon wedding arrangements. For some couples the choice between *gift* or *presentation* as the expected gift form at their wedding is simply the result of an unquestioning acceptance of family traditions. Other couples, however, clearly make a deliberate decision, which may conflict with the expectations of family members. In either case most young Winnipeggers these days cannot avoid being aware of alternative practices, and they describe their own wedding gift arrangements as having been conducted for certain kinds of reasons. From the interviews conducted in the Hotel Chateau Study it is possible to identify two developments associated with the diffusion of *presentation* that show how the political economy of consumerism has affected the moral economy of giving.

In the first place Canadian census data suggest that the number of young adults who left home to set up independent residence before marriage increased during the post-war period of economic affluence (Wargon 1979). One of the more common effects of independent residence before marriage is that domestic goods are acquired which couples would otherwise have to obtain when they got married. The need for domestic goods as wedding gifts is therefore likely to be reduced. Consequently money gifts may be seen as more useful than *gifts*, as the following example shows.

Case study: Graham and Janet McKenzie

Graham and Janet McKenzie are entrepreneurial business people in their mid- to late 20s. Graham is a self-employed sales representative and retailer of commercial and financial services, while Janet has a staff position in the mass communications industry. They grew up in Winnipeg and have lived there almost all their lives. Graham and Janet chose *presentation* rather than *gift* giving for their wedding because they had both lived apart from their families of origin for several years, and each of them had maintained an independent household. As a result, they said, they "didn't need a lot of things" when they got married. *Presentation* made sense to them because "you can always use money."

In addition to demographic change, wedding rituals in Winnipeg have been affected by an expansion of conspicuous consumption at marriage festivities. Although the evidence here is incomplete, this development is in all probability due to a high level of status competition at these communal occasions, as suggested earlier. From the perspective of the ecology of games, the important point to be noted here is that *presentation* weddings have a competitive advantage over *gift* weddings in raising capital for ceremonial display. That advantage is exceeded only by those young people whose weddings are paid for by wealthy parents. *Presentation* is therefore sometimes used by lower middle- and upper working-class couples to secure the financial basis for lavish celebrations, including some that are held at the Hotel Chateau.

Case study: Lisa and David Johansson

Lisa and David Johansson are in their mid-20s. Lisa has lived in
Winnipeg all her life and is now a laboratory technician. David is
a policeman. He grew up in Winnipeg but has spent four years in
other cities in the Prairie Provinces. He describes himself as having
no particular ethnic background. Lisa, on the other hand, strongly
identifies with her French Canadian background (she grew up
speaking French at home). In David's experience of weddings
presentation was the normal practice, which he does not seem to
have questioned. Lisa, on the other hand, prefers wedding *presents*,
but explains that "we chose presentation because we were paying
for the wedding" (that is, without calling on financial assistance
from their parents). She does not know if *presentation* has been the
custom among her kin, and she sees her choice as a personal
decision (influenced by her mother) that was made for good
reasons. Since Lisa was the first of her parents' children to get
married she thought that they were especially concerned about
"how things were looking." The arrangements for their wedding
reception were heavily influenced by Lisa's respect for her father's
wishes. He comes from a very large extended family and did not
want anybody's feelings to be hurt by their not being invited.
Furthermore, Lisa's cousins' weddings had been elaborate affairs
and her father wanted the same thing for her. According to Lisa,
"the Hotel Chateau, and the whole bit, was really for my Dad's
benefit." A number of his brothers' children had been married
earlier, and she says that "my Dad wanted a big show, and for
me to go out for them too, to reciprocate a bit. He just wanted
to gloat a little bit – this is my daughter – to make him feel good."

Choosing the right rite

Weddings are times when everybody wants to feel good about
themselves. For some people that means wanting to mount a lavish
display before a large extended family network, of which there are
many in Manitoba. For other people it means wanting to be close
to a few special individuals. In Winnipeg there is a choice to be
made. It is a choice which has a direct bearing upon the nature of
gift rituals, and most people are clear about their reasons for preferring one or the other. The choice between *gift* and *presentation* at
weddings· in Winnipeg is the visible outcome of a deep structure
of gift types about whose outlines most people are not quite so

clear. The structuration of giving is in fact a consequence of the difference between expressive and instrumental interactions that we encountered in an earlier chapter. I shall refer to the two types of gift rituals here as symbolic gifts and practical gifts, because that is how some of the interviewees themselves referred to them.

Symbolic gifts

Symbolic gifts are thought to express the quality of the relationship between donor and receiver, and the nature of the occasion on which they are given. The rules regulating their use include both prescriptions and proscriptions. Some objects, if given as wedding gifts, are felt to be "tacky" (that is, in bad taste). Gifts to the couple are symbolic of their wedding, and therefore anything which might reflect negatively upon that event is frowned upon. Baby things for a pregnant bride definitely fall into that category. Similarly, though less forcefully, personal items (such as clothing or jewellery) are not appropriate since they will be used by only one partner, and are "not for the marriage."

Money was not a preferred symbol because its capacity to symbolize personal relationships was considered to be too weak. The Hotel Chateau interviewees were normally more prepared to receive money than they were to give it, but in one woman's opinion it was the only thing that should never be given at a wedding. Money is regarded as an inferior symbolic gift because it does not require much thought or time to give, and thus cannot symbolize a caring relationship. With a *gift*, "There's a little bit more behind it than just taking money out of your wallet."

Objects that were most highly valued were those which will evoke the memory of the donor, and of the occasion, long after the event. *Gifts* were therefore preferred, rather than money, because "When you use a gift you think of the person who gave it to you." The most evocative *gifts* are objects not intended for daily use whose distinctiveness claims attention.

Expensive china and crystal ware, silver tea services, and costly ornaments and art objects are considered to be especially desirable. These objects have several qualities which make them particularly potent symbols. In the first place they are, of course, accoutrements of domestic life, and therefore symbolic of the marriage and the formation of a new domestic group. Secondly, they have a high conventional aesthetic value. They are "nice things" which "most people want." Thirdly, they are luxury goods, things whose utility in daily living is low compared with their expense. Most couples "starting out in life" would not normally buy them for themselves because they "cannot afford them." These goods therefore have a separate, and superior, status in the home. Fourthly, they are highly effective as mementos because they last a long time. They will not be used up, and because they are used infrequently they will wear out only slowly and are less likely than most domestic goods to get broken. Lastly, they are things that will be brought out for conspicuous consumption on special occasions in the future, when they will be the foci of attention and polite admiration. They are perfect symbolic gifts.

Symbolic gifts are used in expressive interactions. They are acts of communication which are valued mainly for the contribution they are presumed to make to strengthening personal relationships. The purpose of symbolic gifts, therefore, is to define personal relationships as elements in an enduring moral order that is quite separate from economic exchange. The main concern in giving symbolic gifts, therefore, is the moralization of interpersonal relations.

At weddings the moralization of interpersonal relations has a dual aspect. In the first place there are the bonds of sentimentality and attachment between the man and woman who are being united in marriage. It is the celebration of those bonds, and of their institutionalization within a social relationship, that constitutes the official definition of the occasion. As one young bride stated:

> It was nice that people showed that they cared, that they had an interest in our marriage. A lot of people were really wishing us well, and giving us their congratulations and best wishes, and the gift was sort of a symbol of that.

The accumulation of such symbols enhances the ritual confirmation that this is a "special day." The flood of gifts makes the wedding itself more special because most couples have never experienced anything like it before, and never expect to again ("Christmas will never be the same again" said one woman). Wedding gifts are therefore seen as important because of their dramatic effects. "It's a day that you'll remember for the rest of your life. If it wasn't special, if it was treated just like any other day, then you wouldn't remember."

The bonds that make a couple out of two individuals are the center of attention at a wedding. In addition, many of those attending the wedding also have their own bonds of sentimentality and attachment towards one or both of them. Symbolic gifts are therefore also used to define, and to redefine, the relationships between the guests and the bride and groom. The nature of a symbolic gift is expected to be related to the level of intimacy between donor and recipient, and it can therefore be used to help establish that level in relationships which might otherwise lack symbolic supports. One couple, for example, described their own experience with friends as follows: "You can see how much they care, and then you can show you care, and it goes from there."

Gifts were seen as particularly potent symbols and were often carefully chosen for their effects. For those who thought that *gifts* were important, the ideal object was one which demonstrated that thought and care had been taken in selecting something that the recipient would like, and which at the same time reflected salient characteristics of the donors. In this way the *gift* is symbolic of the donor as an interested person, and may become part of a reality defining order of objects within the home. In the Hotel Chateau Study interviews, several new brides expressed pleasure at being able to look around their homes and to identify particular things with the individuals who had given them. That is not how people think about practical gifts.

Practical gifts

Practical gifts are things which are considered to be useful for a couple starting out in married life. Most people in Winnipeg believe that it is important for young couples "starting off from scratch" (that is, without any domestic goods) to have financial support at that time. The custom of wedding gifts is seen as providing an opportunity for people to give that support.

According to this view people should give gifts that are useful. That means giving articles that are attuned to the couple's needs, or money. Useful gifts are principally domestic goods, such as kitchen utensils, serving ware, electrical appliances, household furnishings, etc. Money is useful because after the wedding the couple can buy exactly what they want with it, and because it can be used to defray the costs of the wedding.

From the latter perspective, *presentation* weddings were often described by participants in terms very similar to economic exchange. Money, goods, feasts, and entertainments were all seen as being exchanged in a series of related transactions. The young in particular seem inclined to feel that the size of a *presentation* should reflect the cost of the meal, drinks, and entertainment (normally music and dancing) that has been provided. For the guests to meet the expenses incurred on their behalf is seen as being "the least that they can do." It follows from this that guests should adjust the value of their *presentation* according to the quality, and therefore costliness, of the wedding arrangements. That point of view was expressed in such comments as: "You feel that you should at least pay for your meal." Or more forcefully: "The wedding party is put on for the guests, and if the guests don't put in enough to pay for that then they're not giving [the couple] anything."

Presentation is not the only form of practical assistance, however. Wedding *gifts*, too, may be defined as a real financial help, as long as they are articles that the couple would otherwise have had to buy on their own. Wedding guests are therefore expected to find out what the couple really need or want, and they are expected to avoid buying things that will never be used. *Gifts* that are not useful are a burden since they must be stored. They take up space in the home that could be used for other things, or they must be left with parents. It is therefore believed that *gift* givers should try to buy things according to the tastes of the recipients, as expressed in the intended decor of the new home. Careful choice of patterns and colors is required, and *gift* givers were not expected to buy things simply because they liked them themselves. Finally, if they are to be of any assistance *gifts* should be "practical" rather than ornate or decorative. Things of the latter sort were sometimes described as being essentially useless, since their main purpose is display.

Practical gifts are valued for the contribution they are expected to make to the economic cooperation of husband and wife within an independent household. For young people who have never been married before wedding gifts often provide much of the capital investment that goes into setting up a new home. The main concern in giving practical gifts, therefore, is the rationalization of capital accumulation. From that point of view *gifts* may be seen as more of a hindrance than a help because people don't always get what they need or can use. *Presentation* is the most efficient means for the rationalization of capital accumulation, because it is the only sure way "to eliminate the problem with gifts." As one new husband put it, "It makes it a lot easier for everybody. You don't know what to buy people, and don't know what they already have, and this way you get the things you really need."

Couples who thought about wedding gifts in this highly

instrumental fashion saw *gift* giving as a less efficient means of providing practical assistance than *presentation* in several respects. The problem most often referred to by the interviewees was that of duplication. The likelihood of duplication increases with the number of *gifts* the couple receive, which is principally a function of the number and size of bridal showers held before the wedding, and of the number of guests attending the wedding. On both counts marriages in Winnipeg are often supported by large numbers of donors. Secondly, it is often believed to be difficult for potential donors to find out what the bride and groom want. This difficulty may owe more to the differentiation of tastes in an affluent consumer society than to logistical difficulties, but communication problems were pointed to, especially in the case of relatives living outside of the city. Thirdly, the final choice of a *gift* almost always lies with the donor, and donors are unpredictable. More than one new bride remarked that even though people may ask for suggestions, and even though lists of desired items may be circulated, the expected *gifts* do not always materialize.

In Winnipeg the *presentation* wedding is a culturally available solution to the irrationalities involved in raising support in kind from weakly articulated collectivities. But it is more than that. It also offers certain advantages in the pooling of financial capital, and thus permits a higher level of economic management for household formation. The *presentations* of a large number of individuals may, for example, be pooled in order to make large purchases which are beyond most donors' notions of a *gift*. Large appliances and pieces of furniture are sometimes obtained in this way. Or the accumulated *presentations* may be used for the down payment on a house, or simply put into the bank as a conjugal fund which is available to meet future needs. *Presentation*, in other words, permits rational life-course planning.

In addition to efficiently meeting life-course management goals, *presentation* is often chosen in order "to pay for the wedding." Providing suitable festivities for the wedding guests was seen by many couples as an important, but risky, venture. If they were arranging everything themselves it could result in an overall financial loss, and avoiding a loss was sometimes seen as the major practical goal in the plans for a wedding. From the point of view of those couples who finance their weddings themselves, *gifts* are an inefficient means of covering the expenses incurred in hosting the festivities. Even if the wedding *gifts* received have the same total market value as the food and entertainment that the couple provide for their guests, there is no guarantee that it will in fact save them an amount of money equal to what they have spent. A *gift* may turn out to be something that the recipients would not have bought anyway, with the result that no saving is achieved. Furthermore, any saving which results from a *gift* might lie in the future rather than the present, if it is something that the couple do not consider to be an immediate necessity. With a monetary return those risks are avoided. The money can be used to defray the celebration costs directly by paying off debts incurred during the wedding preparations, or it can be used indirectly to purchase things that the couple would otherwise have bought with the money that was spent on the wedding. In either case the maximum utility possible is extracted from the gifts received. That point was summarized by several interviewees in the opinion that *presentation* is "more practical" than *gift* giving. Of course it is, if giving is only instrumental interaction.

Conclusion

Attitudes towards gift giving at *presentation* weddings seem to be far removed from the love culture that was discussed in chapter 4. Indeed it may be wondered if the two sets of ideas even belong in the same economic system. It is certain that our observations about money gifts do not accord with Douglas and Isherwood's description of the gift economy. They have claimed that gift transactions are hedged around by rules which maintain a boundary between the commercial exchanges of the market and the social exchanges of personal relationships (Douglas and Isherwood 1979: 58–9). It is for this reason, they suggest, that a careful line is drawn between cash and goods. In Winnipeg that is obviously not the case. The haphazard mixing of money and goods at Carol and John Dugald's wedding is unusual, but not unique. It is clearly inconsistent with any theory of the gift economy as a boundary maintaining system.[8] The position advanced in this study has been that, rather than maintaining the boundaries of preformed social units such as "the family," gifts are in fact used to construct a wide range of possible social worlds as stable arenas for social interaction. Gift giving is not simply a reflection of social structure, but it is a formative social process in its own right.

I have argued that the gift economy is an autonomous moral economy consisting of redundant transactions. Symbolic gifts and practical gifts both belong in that economy. In the first place, both symbolic gifts and practical gifts are elements in a moral economy of transactions. They are used to produce, and to reproduce, social worlds as systems of relations. Symbolic gifts and practical gifts are also both redundant transactions. References to this point have been made in several places, but they have not yet been drawn together, nor have we commented upon their general significance. It is therefore time to return to the theory of redundancy.

It will be recalled that there are five ways in which gifts may be redundant: when they are not produced by conformity to norms; when they bring no advantage to their recipients, and thus add nothing to their well-being; when they bring no *net* benefit to their recipients, as a result of symmetrical reciprocity; when they transfer resources which the recipients would otherwise have provided for themselves; and when they take the form of many ritual offerings where one would have sufficed for the purposes of interaction courtesy. The last of these types of redundancy is different from the first four, since it has to do with expressive redundancy. Redundancy here takes the form of a superfluity of messages within the ritual process (Cheal 1987a: 161). We will see in the next chapter that this form of redundancy has been of some importance in the internal expansion of the gift economy. But it is not a basis for the gift economy as such. The first four types of redundancy, on the other hand, are constitutive of the gift economy. They are truly fundamental because they establish the manner in which ritual transactions are superfluous to the requirements of other systems of action.

Figure 7.1 Types of gift redundancy

I *Instrumental redundancy*
  1) Surplus to normative requirements
  2) No addition to well-being

II *Substantive redundancy*
  3) No net gain
  4) Resource transfers unnecessary

III *Expressive redundancy*
  5) Superfluity of signals

The redundancy of gift transactions with respect to other systems of action takes two general forms, as illustrated in Figure 7.1. Adapting the usage of Weber, they will be described as instrumental redundancy and substantive redundancy (Weber 1968). In his view instrumentally rational action occurs when social objects are used as means for the achievement of rationally calculated ends or purposes. In this sense symbolic gifts are instrumentally irrational. They do not serve to meet the role obligations of the donor, nor do they add to the well-being of the recipient. In short, they are not integrated into either the normative or utility-seeking means–end chains of which daily life is made up.[9]

Symbolic gifts are redundant as a result of their sentimentality. That is to say, they are redundant because they are consciously thought of as the products of pure emotion. They are irrational transactions insofar as they are not believed to serve any end outside of the action itself. People give symbolic gifts, they say, because they "want to," because it makes them "feel good," because "it's tradition," and so on. Symbolic gifts are defined by an ideology of love, the consequence of which is that many people deny that they ever give gifts when they do not want to (that is, when they are socially obligated to do so).

In this chapter we have seen that one of the outcomes of sentimentality in gift giving is that symbolic gifts are often "useless." They are not attuned to the needs of the recipient, but to the sentiment of the occasion as a "special" time which is to be marked by signs of distinction. These signs of distinction include luxury goods, often of an ornamental nature. Several interviewees in the Hotel Chateau Study reported that the superiority of these luxury goods means that they must often be segregated from other objects, by being placed in display cabinets, etc. Where the size of the home and the nature of the furniture do not permit such display, or where the furnishings are so inferior that the luxury goods will be "out of place," their very superiority may result in them being consigned to the limbo of storage. In such cases it is not uncommon for young people to express the belief (or hope) that, "we will appreciate them much more in the future than we do now." What they really mean by this, of course, is that luxury goods are so irrelevant to their situation that they are not available for use in the present.

Practical gifts are not so obviously redundant. Indeed they may be thought to approach the limits of the gift economy, and perhaps of moral economy too. Here the rational calculation of the benefits to be derived from gifts is quite clear, whether the ends consist of helping another in need, exchanges of mutual aid, or a unilateral gain in social status. The utility of practical gifts for meeting the needs of others is openly stressed, and there is often a strong sense of obligation to attend bridal showers and to pay the equivalent of the cost of the plate at a presentation wedding.

Practical gifts often appear to take the form of simple transfers of resources to those in need of support. But appearances can be deceptive. As Mauss demonstrated, in communal giving gifts have to be looked at not in isolation but as elements in what he referred to as "the system of total prestations." They are inspired, he argued, by a complex notion – "a notion neither of purely free and gratuitous prestations, nor of purely interested and utilitarian production and exchange" (Mauss 1954: 70). In the flow back and forth of money, goods, feasts, and entertainments in these complex systems there may be few who end up significantly better off, or worse off, than they would have done if they had remained entirely outside the system. It may not be winning or losing that is important so much as playing the game.

The giving of practical gifts in general, and of *presentation* in particular, involves the kind of quantitative calculation or accounting which Weber referred to as formal rationality. It is characterized by "goal-oriented rational calculation with the technically most adequate available methods," expressed in "numerical, calculable terms," such as money (Weber 1968: 85). Weber contrasted formal rationality with substantive rationality. He admitted that the latter concept is full of ambiguities, but the difference between them may be simply put as the distinction between efficiency and adequacy in achieving the ends of action. Action is judged to be substantively rational, Weber says, by comparison with the ultimate ends of action.

In these terms *presentation* weddings may be formally rational, but they are not necessarily substantively rational. There are two related reasons for holding that practical gifts are usually substantively redundant. Firstly, where there is a direct exchange of values there may be little or no net gain derived from any one practical gift. That is often the case at Christmas (Cheal 1986) and at *presentation* weddings, where avoiding a loss is sometimes the best that the bride and groom can hope for. Secondly, even when there is no formal exchange of values there may still be reciprocal giving, as there is when young women give gifts at each other's bridal showers, or when *gifts* are given by those who are invited to a wedding. If the cost of the hospitality at a wedding is balanced by the value of the *gifts* received, then the *gifts* are made necessary in a practical sense only because of the expense incurred in providing the hospitality. Without that hospitality the guests' *gifts* would be unnecessary. Wedding gifts are therefore substantively redundant with respect to the criterion of benefit to the couple, since they only transfer resources that the couple, or their parents, would otherwise have been able to supply for themselves.

Instrumental redundancy and substantive redundancy have been described here as the foundations upon which the gift economy rests. Within the gift economy expressive interaction is instrument-ally redundant, and instrumental interaction is substantively redun-dant. There is in addition the third general form of redundancy, namely expressive redundancy, which is derivative. We have already come across some evidence of expressive, or communi-cative, redundancy in an earlier chapter. There it was pointed out that gift transfers sometimes consist of combination gifts, that is multiple gifts, rather than a single gift. The superfluity of signals within communicative acts happens quite frequently between family members at Christmas, but it can happen at other times too. For example, Mrs Anderson's plans for her parents' sixtieth wedding anniversary included giving three very different things in their honor. In her own words:

> The sixtieth anniversary, it's a diamond [anniversary]. We would like to give our parents a diamond – and I say we because the whole family's involved in our discussion of gift giving here, because obviously it's a very family-oriented thing. We realize that our parents would be excited and thrilled by the significance of a diamond. But we also know that their priorities go further than that, and so rather than going to a big diamond we might get a symbolic piece of jewellery with a small diamond. Where their priorities really lie are in church-oriented things. So we are going to give our anniversary gift to them by giving some-thing to the church, in honor of them at this time. The whole family has agreed, and this is the way we want to do it. And the other gift we're giving them is simply a scrapbook of memories of each of us. We're each putting something into it. It is our feeling, looking for their priorities, and yet finding a significant thing to do as well in connection with the particular occasion. So we've got occasion, giver, and receiver all involved in the kind of gift we're choosing.

From a semiotic point of view, Mrs Anderson's unprompted description of a multiple gift is charming. The three objects to be transferred achieve a remarkable balance of meanings between the communal and the intimate worlds of social and personal relation-ships. On the communal side, there is a "symbolic" (i.e. nominal) piece of jewellery, which is expressive and oriented towards the public meaning of a sixtieth wedding anniversary as a "diamond anniversary."[10] On the other side, there is a humble scrapbook, which is also expressive but oriented towards the intimate world of family members who have grown together over time. In between there is the "priority" gift, an instrumental donation in recognition of the individuals' personal commitments to a public institution.

The cultural logic of Mrs Anderson's gift is unassailable, and seemingly unquestionable. But, we may ask, why does one transaction have to be so complicated? Why is it not enough to just give a diamond at a diamond anniversary? One relevant factor that was discussed above is the nature of this occasion as a collective celebration. A sixtieth wedding anniversary provides the members of an extended family with the opportunity to demonstrate their individual and collective wealth, and hence their economic success. But that is clearly not all that is involved here. One of the gifts has no financial value whatsoever. It was chosen for what it has to say about the individuals involved, both recipients and donors. A wedding anniversary may be a family occasion, as Mrs Anderson says, but her symbolic gifts are not the emblems of a corporate kinship group. What her gifts do symbolize is described in our next chapter.

8

The social future

In the last five chapters original data have been presented about variations in gift behavior, and a number of ideas have been advanced to account for them. Our investigations into the gift economy are not yet complete, but enough information has now been presented for us to begin to see how some of it fits together. It is therefore possible to pay more deliberate attention to integrating a number of the issues raised in the preceding pages, as we have in fact just done for the theory of gift redundancy.

At the beginning of this study Durkheim's science of social order was introduced as the historical base from which the modern anthropology of the gift has grown. I shall argue here that his work still has a useful place in the sociology of gift transactions, only it does not lie in the direction that Mauss took. We shall see that there is much to be learned from Durkheim's sociology of morality.

Durkheim claimed that modern society had created a form of moral individualism which he referred to as "the cult of the individual" (Durkheim 1953: 59).[1] He argued that as the influence of collective religions has declined, so "the individual becomes the object of a sort of religion" (Durkheim 1964a: 172). In his view this "cult in behalf of personal dignity" was a consequence of the growth of large urban populations, integrated at the societal level by the laws of the nation state. He was convinced that at the level of everyday life, increased population size and the falling barriers to association between groups had produced a dynamic environment of expanded social interaction, into which all individuals were increasingly drawn. In turn, this state of affairs had brought about both a greater integration of the individual into society, and an increase in the freedom of individuals from detailed social regulation of their activities (Durkheim 1964a: 262–301, 1964b: 113–15). Both circumstances, he thought, had raised the moral status of the individual member of society. On the one hand, the individual citizen participated in the societal culture and thereby benefited from the idealization of humanity in modern secular ideologies (Durkheim 1953: 53–9). And on the other hand, the indeterminate nature of moral codes under conditions of cultural pluralism had opened up a space for individuality, for which guarantees were obtained in the form of rights to individual autonomy (Durkheim 1964a: 299). He concluded that the effects of this sweeping social change were visible in face-to-face interaction, particularly within the family.

Durkheim did not write extensively on the family, but what he did have to say contradicts the all too common view of his work as dealing only in positive social facts which are objective and external to the individual. To simplify his argument for present purposes,[2] he stated that moral individualism created the conditions for an expanded personality development, and thus for the divergence of interests between individuals, each of whom "increasingly assumed his own character, his personal manner of thinking and feeling" (Durkheim 1978: 234). In these circumstances the identity of consciousness which had sustained the traditional family system was no longer possible and so the family's ties of economic cooperation were internally weakened. He referred to this as the disappearance of domestic communism.) The consequence of all this was a contraction in the size of the domestic family (that is, of the familial household), *and* a change in the constitution of family life. Durkheim put it thus: "The family has developed by becoming concentrated and personalized. The family continues to contract, and, at the same time, relations continue to assume an exclusively personal character" (Durkheim 1978: 239).

Translating Durkheim's discussion into the terms that have been employed here, interaction within the family has shifted from an emphasis upon social relationships to an emphasis upon personal relationships, and family life has become more sentimental. His comments on "the bonds of relatedness" in the family are worth quoting in full for their relevance to our analysis of moral economy:

> What is certain is that [domestic solidarity] is transformed. It depends on two factors: persons and things. We retain solidarity with our family because we feel solidarity with the persons who compose it; but we also retain solidarity with it because we cannot do without certain things and because, under a system of familial communism, it is the family which possesses them. The result of the breakdown of communism is that things cease, to an ever greater extent, to act as a cement for domestic society. Domestic solidarity becomes entirely a matter of persons. We are attached to our family only because we are attached to

the person of our father, our mother, our wife, or our children. It was
quite different formerly, when the links which derived from things took
precedence over those which derived from persons.

(Durkheim 1978: 234)

According to Durkheim, modern family life is not only structured by relations between persons and things, but is also, and
primarily, founded upon relations between persons. It is, in our
terms, a moral economy rather than a political economy. Furthermore, the modern family is not a corporate group because its
members do not act in common in most respects. The solidarity
of the family therefore depends upon personal attachments between
its individual members. It is these personal attachments that are
celebrated on ritual occasions such as wedding anniversaries.

The cult of the individual

Most people in Winnipeg recognize that the social definition of a
particular ritual occasion has some bearing upon their choice of
what to give. But that is not the most prominent factor in their
minds when they go shopping for a gift. Mrs Anderson's remark,
"I think first of all of the person who I'm giving it to," was echoed
by almost all of the interviewees. Anne Baker – a university student
whose sociable life style was described in an earlier chapter (see
pp. 55ff.) – said that the most important consideration for her was:

The person I'm giving it to. I wouldn't give my parents a bottle, you
know. I'd prefer to get them something for the house. Basically it's
decided by what the person would like, what they've liked in the past.

Gifts in Winnipeg, as in Middletown (Caplow 1982: 387), are
usually transfers from individuals or couples to individuals (see
Table 8.1). The nature of the personal relationships that individuals
have with one another, and the unique characteristics of individuals
and the personal relationships between them, determine both the
content and the frequency of their gift transactions. Much of the
expressive redundancy of gift giving is accounted for by the desire
of people like Bernice Genyk to show their love for particular
others at every opportunity. The consequence of this is repetitive
giving, when every occasion becomes much like every other
occasion. Bernice said that the most influential factor in her
decision about the kind of gift to be given is:

The person. If I was giving a gift to my godchild, she's like mine, and
whether it's a birthday or Christmas or whatever, she's my godchild

and I think a lot of her. I would give her anything if I could. So it doesn't really matter whether it's a birthday or Christmas or Valentine's, she's remembered on all these occasions.

The fact that gifts for all occasions are chosen according to what the individual recipient will like has had enormous consequences for the ritual cycle in modern society. Regardless of the type of occasion, a wide range of things will be given whose variety reflects the projected likes and dislikes of the intended recipients. This is the principal cause of the weak symbolic differentiation of ritual occasions that was noted in chapter 5 (see pp. 93ff.). There it was observed that seven (almost half) of our ritual occasion categories are not marked by distinctive gifts. The modern gift economy is a de-differentiated ritual system, in which the semiotic order of objects is defined mainly at the level of interpersonal relations, rather than at the level of societal values or of mass media corporations (see Cheal 1987a).

Table 8.1 *Number of actors in gift transactions*

Number of actors	Per cent gifts by givers and receivers	
	Givers %	Receivers %
1	38.9	89.2
2	41.3	9.8
3	6.3	0.9
4+	13.5	0.1
Totals	100.0	100.0

The first point to be made about the cult of the individual, then, is that it is responsible for the absence of a coherent culture of differentiated occasions such as anthropologists have described for non-western societies (see, for example, Wilson 1957). This is to be expected, for, as Durkheim stated, the cult of the individual turns attention away from society and therefore away from societal values (Durkheim 1964a: 172). The relevance of his analysis of the cult of the individual can be shown to go further than that, however. It can also help us to explain why it is that some ritual occasions are more important than others.

In chapter 4 we saw that the two great times for giving are Christmas and birthdays (see Table 4.1). Their importance so far outranks that of any other occasion that it is tempting to treat them as exceptional events with unique properties. Yet we have seen in subsequent chapters that in other respects, such as the degree of ritual specialization and the financial values of gifts, birthdays and Christmas occupy a definite place within a general system of meanings. We will therefore pursue that general analysis here in order to see if it might also explain the magnitude of gift giving at these times.

According to Durkheim the cult of the individual has two main sociological features. In the first place its object is of course the veneration of individuals. But he used the term cult here in order to describe the fact that it is not only individuals who are involved in this practice. It is a common (shared) practice "in so far as the community partakes of it" (Durkheim 1964a: 172). Just like any other common cult, "It is still from society that it takes all its force," he concluded. It is this dual aspect of the cult of the individual, its duality of structure we might almost say (Giddens 1982: 36–7), that accounts for its peculiar force in those societies in which individual agency is encouraged.[3] At the level of interpersonal relations the duality of community and individualism appears as the duality of community and intimacy.

At the end of chapter 6 the point was made that intimacy and community are contradictory structures that could be combined effectively only under special conditions (see p. 120). The nature of those conditions could not be theorized at the time, but we are now in a position to provide a solution to that problem. Intimate relations and communal relations are integrated within the cult of the individual on those occasions when communal relations have been entirely subordinated to the purposes of intimacy.

In the study of wedding gift rites reported in chapter 7 we saw that the personal relations of intimates, and the status systems of communities, are not easily reconciled within the same occasion. Having to choose between them can lead to open disagreements about procedures, and sooner or later a collective preference for one or the other is likely to emerge. At least, that will be the case if value-laden claims are made by different groups that either the symbolizing of intimacy, or the practical achievement of community membership, is the ultimate purpose of ritual organization. That has been the case with wedding gifts in Winnipeg in recent years because of the particular conjunction of ethnic traditions that was described above (see p. 123). But it has not been the case for other ceremonial occasions, where interests in community and intimacy have typically coexisted with little difficulty.

Our earlier analysis of intimacy and community (chapter 6) concluded that Christmas and birthdays are among a number of occasions within which intimate and communal forms of social organization are linked. The foci of these occasions are individuals and the relationships between individuals. At the same time they are occasions for visiting, and hence for collective rituals. They are also times when individuals who are living so far away that they cannot be present in person send gifts as signs of their continued attachment. These ceremonial occasions are therefore both communal (in the mobilization of members) and individual (in the structure of attention). They are, in other words, relatively pure forms of the cult of the individual.

If that conclusion is accepted, there remains only one obstacle to accounting for the extraordinary importance of Christmas and birthdays. According to our earlier analysis there are seven types of occasions in which intimate and communal principles of social organization are linked (see Figure 6.1). They are, in addition to birthdays and Christmas: visits, parties, Father's Day, Mother's Day, and births. Why are the first 2 of these 7 occasions so much more important than the last 5? By comparison with some of our earlier problems, the answer to that question is quite straightforward. Birthdays and Christmas are diffuse calendrical rites. That is to say, they occur in annual cycles and their relational contents are unlimited. They therefore provide regularly recurring opportunities for individuals to recognize any or all of their significant others. The transaction possibilities for visits, parties, Father's Day, Mother's Day, and births are much more limited.

At Christmas and on birthdays anybody who has an appropriately close relationship with an individual can give something to him or her, and expect to have it accepted. That is because they are diffuse occasions. Mother's Day and Father's Day, on the other hand, are much more specific occasions. In principle, their relational contents are restricted to the bonds between children and their parents. In practice, children may also give to their grandparents (because they are the parents of their parents) and spouses may give to one another (in so far as they have shared the parenting of each other's children). The possibilities for further expansion of these occasions would seem to be limited, however. Certainly they could never approach the generality of that most diffuse occasion, Christmas, when anybody may give to anybody else.

Christmas and birthdays are calendrical rites, and therefore come around for everybody every year, unlike visits, parties and births which happen irregularly. Visiting, partying and giving birth go on all the time, of course. But they do not happen so often that every individual could be acknowledged by every other individual in her or his personal network every single year. Few women in North America give birth every year, and these days nobody does it for the duration of the normal life span. Visiting and partying happen more frequently, but confidants can go for considerable periods of time without coming together on either type of occasion. That is because visits and parties are face-to-face encounters, and being together in the same place can be very difficult for those who live far apart.

As diffuse calendrical rites, Christmas and birthdays are uniquely opportune times for staging the cult of the individual. It is for this reason that they have become the dominant rites in the modern western societies. There is an important point that follows from this for our understanding of interpersonal relations in mass societies, which requires us to return to the theory of ritual.

Passages and progressions

Since van Gennep we have become used to thinking of the structural consequences of ritual almost entirely through his model of rites of passage (see, for example, Glaser and Strauss 1971). Those rites continue to be important. The majority of the categories of rites that have been analyzed in the Winnipeg Ritual Cycle Study are rites of passage. Gifts at times of visiting, parties, farewells, and reunions are rites of passage from one point in space to another, which van Gennep referred to as territorial passages. They are passages into and out of the home (visiting and parties), or out of and back into the local region of accessibility (farewells and reunions). Then there are the rites of social placement. Births, pre-wedding events, and weddings are life-course passages through which individuals gain entrance into small social worlds. Social distribution into the larger world of formal organizations is achieved through high-school and university graduations, which we have included in the "other" category of occasions. Finally, there are the rites associated with the individual's encapsulation in life worlds which are different from the everyday life world. These are the sympathy rites, which deal mainly with passages into and out of the sick role, or the role of bereaved person, sometimes accompanied by rites of territorial passage into and out of hospital.

Rites of passage may comprise a majority of the special occasions that have been described here, but they are not responsible for the majority of gift transactions. Using the most generous estimate, they account for only 18.7 per cent of all gifts recorded in the Winnipeg Ritual Cycle Study (see Table 4.1). The other occasions, and the overwhelming majority of gifts, belong to a different ritual system. These are the rites of progression (Cheal 1988a).

Anniversaries, birthdays, Christmas, Easter, Father's Day, Mother's Day, and Valentine's Day together account for 81.5 per cent of all gifts, and 72.8 per cent of all gift expenditures, as recorded in the Winnipeg Ritual Cycle Study. They therefore deserve to be placed at the forefront of any theory of ritual in modern society. These ritual occasions are, in the first place, calendrical rites. However, that is only a formal property. It tells us that they occur in annual cycles, rather than irregularly, but it tells us nothing about their social contents or social significance. The important question is: why are these calendrical rites so highly valued? Certain possibilities can be dismissed immediately. These are not the rites of an agrarian society, dependent upon the natural cycle of the seasons. Nor are they primarily religious rites (although two of them have their origins in religious rites). They are, in fact, rites that affirm the maintenance of social bonds. They confirm the continued physical being of individuals (birthdays, Christmas), or their continued involvement in a personal relationship (Easter, Valentine's Day), or their continued occupancy of a role in a social relationship (Mother's Day, Father's Day, anniversary). They are therefore the opposites of rites of passage.

Rites of passage socially define an individual's separation from one social position in order to enter into another social position. The thematic core of a rite of passage is therefore always the contrast between that which is in the process of being left behind and that which is to be taken up. Rites of progression are similar to rites of passage in so far as they are both concerned with changes that occur over time, but there is an important difference of emphasis. In a rite of progression what is emphasized is not change through opposition to what went before, but change through the potential for growth in what already existed. Rites of progression are therefore rites of extension rather than contrast. They are, in fact, pure rites of extended social reproduction.

Rites of progression are rites of seriality. They are dramatic social constructions of social time in which the past, the present, and the future are linked in a ritual series. At the level of interpersonal interaction they are ritual constructions of relationships in time as successive encounters. As such, rites of progression have a vital importance in modern society. One of the consequences of the expansion of social life in mass societies has been that, as more and more opportunities for interaction have been opened up to individual choice, so the continuity of relations between particular individuals has become less certain. This does not mean that individuals necessarily have fewer continuous relationships. But it does mean that relational continuity is not often guaranteed by the limitations of a narrow social existence, and so it must be deliberately constructed through invented traditions. Anniversaries, birthdays, Christmas, Easter, Father's Day, Mother's Day, and Valentine's Day are the principal occasions for the enactment of intimate traditions within small social worlds. The subjective reality of these traditions is grounded in the frameworks of mutual knowing between individuals whose lives have grown together as relationships in time.

Relationships in time

Some relationships are stronger and last longer than others. Put more formally, some relationships have higher levels of presence-availability, attachment, sentimentality, sociability, and economic cooperation for longer periods of time than do others. These elemental social bonds are nowhere more powerfully combined than they are among individuals who have chosen to live together in the same household, for it is here that presence-availability is at its peak.[4] Enduring relationships within the household are thus the most socially influential relationships in time.

Durkheim believed that the greatest force for change in the modern family had been the lessened dependence of adult children upon their parents. As a result, he noted, children leave their parents at a comparatively early age in order to set up independent households, and the only permanent members of the household are the husband and wife (Durkheim 1978: 230). It is thus the conjugal, or spousal, relationship that is the basis for modern family life, he concluded.

Durkheim does not seem to have attached much significance to conjugal love as a social force, since he thought that spouses "cannot be for one another an object sufficient to tear them from the search for fleeting sensations" (Durkheim 1978: 238). Anticipating themes that have become prominent in family sociology in recent years, he argued that marriage had become "almost completely indissoluble" owing to its coercive regulation by the state and to the tightened economic bonds of community property between spouses (Durkheim 1978: 237). In recent decades state policies towards marriage have changed in almost all of the western societies, and marriage is no longer indissoluble. To be sure, economic bonds between the spouses continue to exist (Pahl 1983; Dulude 1984), but their restraints have clearly not been so great as to entirely prevent couples from separating. Under contemporary circumstances the nature and limits of conjugal love deserve somewhat more of our attention than Durkheim was prepared to give to them, for they have important effects upon the gift economy. Marriage is both a social relationship and a personal relationship. Marriage as a social institution is socially valued, but each particular marriage relationship is expected to last because the spouses want it to last. Its continuation is therefore signified not only at wedding anniversaries, but also at other rites of progression, as we see in Carol Brown's Christmas.

Case study: Carol Brown

Carol Brown is 33 years old. Her husband, Barry, is a manager in a large financial services company. His salary and investment income are enough to give them a very comfortable way of life in one of the most desirable residential areas of the city. Mrs Brown has chosen not to work outside the home in recent years, so that she could have more time to spend with her two children (now ages 5 and 8). Carol has enjoyed the close relationship that they have had, and she likes to talk about the things they have done together.

Relationships that last, with people for whom she cares deeply, are very important in Carol's life. This includes relatives and old friends of hers, and of her husband, and their spouses now that they are all married. At Christmas her gifts include presents to Lorraine and her husband Bob. Lorraine has been her good friend since the days when they were at school together. Carol says in explanation: "Lorraine, I've known [her] for so long. We've always done it, ever since we were so high." She also gives to Lorraine's children, and to the children of Duncan, her husband's best friend.

Carol Brown gets a lot of pleasure out of buying, and making, little things for her children and the children of her friends. Christmas, she says, "is basically for kids." The dollars and cents of Carol's gift transactions confirm that claim, but they also tell a different story. Most of her Christmas gifts are inexpensive, and the majority of them are under $20. The value of Carol's gifts to her children is well in excess of that amount, falling in the $100 range. (Her daughter Kim received a pyjama bag, slippers, and a fully equipped doll's house, worth altogether approximately $112. Her son Jonathan was given a sports bag, slippers, and a motorized construction toy, worth $92 in total.) Mrs Brown's gift to her husband was at a distinctly different level again, and was by far the most expensive transfer of all. Her presents to Barry, of a wide-angle lens for his camera and a sweater, came to $190.

Carol treats Barry differently in other respects too. When asked what she would do if people forgot to give her things at appropriate times, she indicated that nothing would happen. Then she added: "I got ticked off once when I didn't get a card, but that was from Barry, so I can get as ticked off as I want."

Mrs Brown's pattern of gift giving is not unusual. Survey data for Winnipeg show that the most valuable Christmas gifts are given more frequently between spouses than in any other social relationship (Cheal 1986). Carol Brown's view of marriage is conventional in other respects too. It combines the highest possible valuation of the spouse as a uniquely important person with an openness and freedom of feeling and communication that would not be accepted in any other relationship. This romantic love complex has become the dominant cultural definition of the spousal relationship in the western societies (Sarsby 1983). It is an ideal of intimacy that is not realized in every marriage.

Love culture revisited: personal love and impersonal love

We have seen that Durkheim thought the conjugal, or spousal, relationship lay at the center of modern family life because the presence-availability of spouses is greater, and lasts longer, than that of children. However, he also realized that although the conjugal relationship might last longer, it does not last for ever (Durkheim 1978: 237–8). Sooner or later the spouse dies (or the spouses separate) and the spousal relationship is dissolved. The family therefore "has not sufficient continuity to acquire a personal aspect, a history of its own, to which its members may feel attachment" (Durkheim 1951: 377).

He came to believe that in the long run individuals would find that the most effective guarantees for their social future lay in commitments to occupational organizations, such as professional associations (Durkheim 1951: 378–9; 1978: 238). His prediction about occupational organizations has proved to be wrong,[5] but there is still something to be learned from the larger argument. In modern societies a variety of communal organizations exist that provide an alternative sense of continuity between past, present and future to that provided by family ties.

Alongside the primary gift economy of interpersonal relationships there is a secondary gift economy of community organizations. In Winnipeg, and in Canada as a whole, the most important of these organizations are the churches (Cheal 1987b: 215). According to Durkheim a church is a moral community (Durkheim 1947). (Indeed he thought this point was so important that he made it one of two equal criteria in his definition of religion).[6] By this he meant that a church is a group whose members think in the same way in regard to sacred things, and who translate these common ideas into collective practices. Although he felt that collective phenomena were always more important than individual phenomena, churches and other community organizations are in fact of only secondary importance in the gift economy since individuals give much less to them than they spend on gifts for each other (Cheal 1987b: 214–15). It is for that reason that we have dealt only with interpersonal relationships in this study. However, organized religion is not entirely irrelevant to our subject. Religious groups have sometimes attempted to control the economy of interpersonal giving as one consequence of a rationalized religious ethic. Sometimes the results of that ethic strike outsiders as rather strange, as we shall see in a moment.

In recent chapters it has become apparent that the gift economy is a dynamic ritual system whose interaction processes are best understood as outcomes of the dialectic of intimacy and community.[7] We have seen how that dialectic works in wedding rituals, and in the contrasts between occasions such as bridal showers and Easter. The dialectic of intimacy and community also has visible effects at a level we have not yet considered. That is the level of the interrelationships between the primary and secondary gift economies.

It was claimed above that in modern societies the primary gift economy of interpersonal relationships is dominated by the cult of the individual, whose defining characteristic is the subordination of community to intimacy. The dominant characteristic of the secondary gift economy of community organizations is the subordination of intimacy to community. It is because they have these contrasting features that the system of interpersonal rituals is normally more important than the system of communal rituals in the modern western societies. Long-term relationships are constructed within small social worlds whose continuity depends upon personal attachments rather than category memberships. Fellow church members are sometimes incorporated into these small worlds, as individuals. But religious organizations as such are rarely small enough to be viable alternatives to kinship-friendship networks. The main exceptions to this are the sects. Their worlds are not only small, they are also different. As Max Weber observed, religious virtuosity "always leads to the control of relationships within communal life." That is because the domain of personal relationships is seen as a realm of temptations, and because it is believed to foster in the religiously average person a "complacent self-sufficiency and self-righteousness in the fulfillment of common obligations, at the expense of the uniquely necessary concentration on active achievements leading to salvation" (Weber 1965: 164–5). From within the sectarian world view that complacency must be avoided, and interpersonal relations must be subordinated to the cult of the moral community. Consider the case of Mrs E.

Case Study: Mrs E.

Mrs E. is a Jehovah's Witness. She is an old acquaintance of Mrs Caruk, who was interviewed in conjunction with the Winnipeg Ritual Cycle Study. Mrs Caruk is a tall woman who often cannot find clothes that she likes in her size. From time to time she has therefore hired Mrs E. to make clothes for her. Over the years that the two women have known each other Mrs Caruk has given Mrs E. a number of spontaneous gifts, mostly baking and other home produce. Mrs Caruk's transfers to Mrs E. have thus exceeded her contractual obligations, and so Mrs E. has felt that she wanted to reciprocate in some way. One day Mrs E. appeared with an afghan that she had voluntarily made for Mrs Caruk. With a stern look on her face Mrs E. thrust it at her, adding the gruffly spoken words: "It's not a gift." When Mrs Caruk told this tale in her interview she laughed, shook her head, and said, "But it was a gift. And a beautiful one too."

The behavior of Mrs E. makes sense once it is known that the Jehovah's Witnesses are strongly opposed to gift exchange, and to other "pagan" customs such as Christmas festivities, because they distract the faithful from Jehovah and his work (Stroup 1945: 141; Rogerson 1969: 110; Botting and Botting 1984: 29, 120). It makes even more sense when we consider that from within the dialectic of intimacy and community a strong move towards one pole or the other inevitably creates its own opposition. Durkheim observed that the growth of the cult of the individual "is possible only by the ruin of all others" (Durkheim 1964a: 172). We should not be surprised to find that the threat posed by moral individualism has been recognized, and that it has been resisted in socialism and in Christianity.

Jehovah's Witnesses are not the only Christians in Canada who are critical of secular gift rituals. The secularization of Christmas is deplored by many people, although opposition to it within the mainstream churches is usually phrased in terms of objections to "commercialism." From the religious viewpoint the commercializing of Christ's birth is seen to have created two major problems. Firstly, there is the fact that religious messages have been used to sell consumer goods, with the result that their contents have been trivialized. One interviewee apparently refused to enter department stores in November and December because she was disgusted by their constant playing of Christmas carols and hymns over the heads of busy shoppers. The other objection that devout Christians often have to secular Christmas is that the expansion of gift giving, and related interpersonal rituals, has resulted in an enormous collective expenditure that serves no religious purpose. Liberal Christians, such as members of the United Church of Canada, sometimes neutralize the implications of this for their own consciences by adding to their "Christmas lists" gifts to churches and to other good causes such as foreign aid agencies. The radical solution has been to undercut the primary gift economy at its base. In the Winnipeg Ritual Cycle Study that economic ethic was most evident in the interviews with members of Protestant sects.

No sociologist has contributed more to our knowledge of the economic ethics of religion than Weber. By the term "economic ethic" he meant "the practical impulses for action which are founded in the psychological and pragmatic contexts of religions" (Weber 1948: 267). The psychological context of religion usually includes beliefs about the connections between present actions and a social future for the individual after death. That belief is in fact a uniquely important property of religion as seen from the constructivist approach which we have followed here.

The possibility of access to an everlasting social future – in Christianity, the problem of "salvation" – has been of great historical importance. Its effect has been greatest where those who claim to have a privileged access to the future – the religious "virtuosos" as Weber called them – have combined into an ascetic sect whose task is to create the preconditions for that future (Weber 1948: 290–1). Under such conditions the religious virtuosos must prove themselves to themselves, and to each other, in their everyday work in "the world." For them the world of the here and now is religiously devalued by comparison with the future kingdom of God, and worldly values of pride in social status, enjoyment of beauty, and acquisition of goods are rejected. Instead, everyday work, including economic conduct, is methodically rationalized in the service of the Lord.

Weber pointed out that in this ascetic systematization of the life world, religious rationalism does not remove all irrationality from social life. On the contrary, he argued that in fact the irrational elements in religion become *more* influential, because they are made more explicit (Weber 1948: 281–2). A domain of irrational beliefs and values provides the irreducible core from which a consistent way of life is derived. It also provides a set of sacred values against which the demystified contents of the modern world can be measured and weighed.

According to Weber the most methodical rationalization of conduct in the world occurs when a religious ethic takes the subjective direction of constructing "a religious total personality pattern." Inwardly, discrete actions are treated as "symptoms and expressions of an underlying ethical total personality. The religious significance of any act therefore depends upon its being one outcome of a total character of goodness. Where that character of goodness is seen as something that has to be acquired through training, good works come to be valued as instruments of self-perfection" (Weber 1965: 155–6). As a result, the effects of an individual's actions upon others may come to be seen as less important than their relation to the self and its ascribed motives. Religious absolutism therefore replaces ritualism (Weber 1948: 328).

Weber argued that communities of virtuosos have invariably

developed a distinctive vocabulary of motives based on an ethic of brotherliness. That ethic was formed initially in the opposition between the sect and the world. Out of that experience the idea arose that the individual member's relationship with his brothers in the faith should be stronger than any other relationship, including family ties to a spouse, parents, or siblings. Weber maintained that this notion of in-group brotherliness transformed the elemental principle of reciprocity between neighbors into an obligation to render services to members of the religious community who were in distress.

> What had previously been the obligations of the noble and the wealthy became the fundamental imperatives of all ethically rationalized religions of the world: to aid widows and orphans in distress, to care for the sick and impoverished brother of the faith, and to give alms. . . . The principle that constituted the communal relations among the salvation prophecies was the suffering common to all believers. And this was the case whether the suffering actually existed or was a constant threat, whether it was external or internal. The more imperatives that issued from the ethic of reciprocity among neighbors were raised, the more rational the conception of salvation became, and the more it was sublimated into an ethic of absolute ends. Externally, such commands rose to a communism of loving brethren; internally they rose to the attitude of *caritas*, love for the sufferer *per se*, for one's neighbor, for man, and finally for the enemy.
>
> (Weber 1948: 329–30)

Once freed from the bonds of intimacy, this economic ethic of love and service has been capable of development in many different directions. The overall tendency, Weber thought, was for brotherliness to be generalized into an impersonal ideology of love. Weber thought that in the western societies a rational ethic of depersonalized and objectified love achieved its purest form in Protestantism, and particularly Puritanism (Weber 1958). Yet there is an inconsistency in Weber's work here. He himself pointed out that Calvinism replaced the universalism of love with a "vocational asceticism." Puritanism therefore produced a "standpoint of unbrotherliness" that "was no longer a genuine 'religion of salvation' " (Weber 1948: 333). Today a genuine religion of salvation can still be found among the Jehovah's Witnesses, which is why their numbers have continued to grow in troubled times. One of their members in Winnipeg is Verna Romaniuk.

Case study: Verna Romaniuk

Verna Romaniuk is 51 years old. One of ten children born to immigrant parents, she has led a narrow life constrained by the poverty and low education of her childhood, and by the control exercised by her parents and husband. Her parents came to Canada from Poland after the end of the First World War, and homesteaded in Manitoba. Years of hard work and struggle with the land went by before they had a viable farm. It was during this period that her father left the Roman Catholic Church and joined the Jehovah's Witnesses. According to Verna:

> My father left the Church because he had seen a lot of unjust things being done by the parish priest. It was shortly after my parents came from the Old Country. You know, when you start up farming you have to cut the bush down, you've got to cultivate the land. You know, you really start from scratch, eh. So if you're fortunate enough to have a cow and a few chickens, you have something to eat. But these things are being taken to the parish priest. So if you take him cream or cheese or milk or eggs, your family goes without. But you take [them to him] because this is part of their belief that you support the priest. Well, the priest had up to here [gestures] . . . and the farmers had very little. So when my father seen that he says, "No." He says we should all have the same. Regardless, you know. "The priest has so much. Why should we give him more?" So this was just the start of him really examining things, and then he found out that their beliefs weren't according to the Bible's principles.

In her teens Verna Romaniuk broke away from the Jehovah's Witnesses in order to try out the things of "the world." Later she "returned to the Bible," and at age 35 she joined the Jehovah's Witnesses. By then she was married with two young children. Mrs Romaniuk had started reading the Bible again at the time of the Bay of Pigs Invasion crisis, when many people were afraid that a nuclear war was about to break out between Russia and the United States. Mrs Romaniuk remembers:

> My girls were in school, and I was washing the kitchen floor and I was crying. I was really afraid. My husband was at work. I was just hoping that if that bomb was going to be dropped, my husband [would be] home from work and that my children would be home from school.

Whether or not the world as we know it will someday be blown away in a nuclear Armageddon, Mrs Romaniuk knows exactly what her social future will be. Jehovah's Witnesses believe that after the Battle of Armageddon they will live in an everlasting paradise on earth with those whom they have known in life, and for whose resurrection they will prepare. Verna Romaniuk is personally convinced that the "perfect peace and harmony under God's rule" which prevailed in the Garden of Eden will return: "It'll come back. The Bible promises it will come back."

Mrs Romaniuk says that her beliefs are related to her gift giving, because: "We all strive to live according to Bible principles." According to the requirements of her faith, Mrs Romaniuk does not give gifts at Christmas or at the other calendrical rites that are celebrated by most other Christians in Winnipeg. In fact the most distinctive feature of her gift behavior sociologically speaking is that she never gives gifts at rites of progression. All of her gifts on special occasions were given at rites of passage – sympathy at an illness (2), farewell (2), pre-wedding (bridal shower), wedding, and birth (baby shower). That is not the end of her gift giving, however, since she says of herself and her fellow congregation members that:

> The important thing about gift giving is that we don't wait until a particular time of the year. We give gifts whenever the need arises or whenever the occasion arises. Like, for instance, if somebody should get ill, or [go] in a hospital or in a home, or if we go away on trips. Or if we happen to be shopping and we see something that a friend or family member would like, we buy it. So it's no special time or occasion. We give because we love the person.

Whenever Verna Romaniuk talks about love of the person in this connection, conjugal intimacy and sentimentality are not what she has in mind. She and her husband do not have an affectionate relationship. Under the circumstances she feels that to celebrate their wedding anniversary would be hypocrisy, and so she has asked her grown-up children to stop sending cards or buying gifts for them at that time. She says: "My husband and I don't celebrate [wedding] anniversaries because celebrating an anniversary is [a sign of] a happy marriage, and this we don't have." When Verna Romaniuk talks about love in her life, then, she is referring to the love of Christ brought down to human level, and turned into a rational, universal principle for the regulation of social behavior.

> Jesus, when he was here on earth, everything he did was motivated by love. [What is important is] love for friend or family, for neighbors. And by neighbors, that doesn't necessarily mean your neighbor living right next door. It could be your neighbor in any part of the city you're living in, even any part of the earth, because the whole earth is man's home. So anyone is your neighbor. It's love towards neighbors;

showing consideration. And of course you must be aware of the Golden Rule: "Do unto others as you would like them to do unto you."

That is not always easy to do, and sometimes Mrs Romaniuk has to fight against feelings of despair about women's lot in this world. She described her husband frankly as stingy, demanding, and unreasonable. As a result she has sometimes found it hard to participate in celebrations held for young brides.

> [I did not want to go to the bridal shower because] I just thought that weddings were coming around too often. The ones that were getting married were too young, you know, and I thought they shouldn't get married. And of course [I was] thinking this way because I don't have a happy marriage myself, so I thought it was foolish for them to get married at such an early age. They should go out and go to work and learn what it's like to earn your own money, and to have to save some and to spend some on necessities and maybe some on luxuries. Rather than getting married and maybe getting children right away, and [then] your life is full of responsibilities. . . . But then as I thought about it, I said to myself, "Well, you know, that's not nice thinking that way. I bought gifts before and I didn't object, so why am I objecting now?" It's mostly because I'm just not in a good mood at that time. Maybe something had happened to put me in a bad frame of mind. I think there for a little while I wasn't feeling well, I was going through my menopause and I guess this kind of contributed to my thoughts. Or, you know, maybe my husband was unfair in talking to me or accusing me of something. Anything like that puts you off, you know. And then right in the middle of all this you get this invitation, and you think to yourself, "I don't need this. I've got enough [problems] of my own." But then when you sit down and you think things over you get your thoughts, your thinking, straightened out, and you put your priorities straight.

For Mrs Romaniuk, putting her priorities straight about bridal showers is part of a larger process of self-perfection, and self-control. That process includes the management of her emotions, to which she pays continuous, explicit attention. Unlike the young women whom Mrs Romaniuk sees rushing into early marriage, she knows that living a life of love is hard work.

> Like I said, during that time when I wasn't feeling well and I was going through my menopause I was kind of rebelling against a lot of things. Because not having a really happy childhood and not having a happy marriage, eventually it gets to you sometimes, you know. . . . [So] you always try to have the right kind of motives. . . . If you give grudgingly or unwillingly it doesn't count, so you might as well not bother giving. But when you [do] give a gift you give it because you want to, and it's because you care for the person, or persons. These are my beliefs

because, studying the Bible, you're striving to make your personality over. Because there's many weaknesses and there's many terrible things to a person's character, eh. . . . You know, there are a lot of people who tend to be very dishonest. Others tend to be just a little dishonest. Now, by studying the Bible you strive to be honest in all things. That includes your motives for doing things. . . . My style of behavior is not to be selfish. If I get selfish moments I sit down and I think, and I set my thinking straight. So I get over this feeling, and I just keep on doing the kind of things like the way I'm supposed to behave.

Having the right kind of motives includes giving practical gifts that are needed and that will be used. Mrs Romaniuk says that she gives a lot of thought to choosing her gifts. For a wedding she will buy something like a can opener, because when "a couple is starting off . . . a can opener is not a glamorous thing to buy, but it's one of the first things that you need, eh." She would buy a manual can opener rather than an electric one "because listen, if your electricity goes off you don't eat if your can opener won't work." At weddings, and at other times too, she says that: "My gifts are not so much personal as more functional, like for the house."

This instrumental view of gift giving, which Mrs Romaniuk has always had, has been accentuated in recent years because of "the times we live in."

We're living at the time where our money's not worth very much, and there's so many people that don't have jobs any more. I have the tendency to make do with what I have, and when I buy gifts for somebody I tend to buy gifts that will last and that'll be useful – something really practical.

It is above all the practical, domestic side of family life that Mrs Romaniuk thinks of as doing what she is supposed to do. For most of her married life she has not worked outside the home. Although she does not give her husband gifts, she says that she makes it up to him in other ways. "I make up his favorite dishes. Right now he's hooked on all sorts of sweet desserts. I'm always baking for him."

There is, surely, a paradox in Mrs Romaniuk's life. By her own account her relationship with her husband has not been a happy one, yet she continues to provide domestic services for him. More than that, she finds ways of serving him that will bring him pleasure. Mrs Romaniuk's life history has been presented in greater detail than usual here, not just because of its intrinsic interest, but because the nature of that paradox is theoretically important. It is the final piece in our theory of intimacy and community in the gift economy.

Conclusion

In chapter 6 the question was raised of whether or not the gift economy might contribute to the reproduction of patriarchy through asymmetrical transactions within marriage. It was pointed out that a woman's dependence upon her husband could not have a total effect upon her social life if she was integrated into a wider network of transactions with female kin and friends (see also Bott 1957). At that time it was argued that focusing on either structures of intimacy or structures of community alone would inevitably give an inadequate picture of the social organization of the gift economy. We can now return to that issue with the benefit of additional data, and with the benefit of the broader perspective that we have developed in this chapter. Intimacy and community are not simply the alternative poles of a universal axis of the differentiation of social systems. They are units of social construction that are used, and sometimes combined, in complex ways within a dynamic interactive process. Sometimes community is subordinated to intimacy, as it is in the cult of the individual. And sometimes intimacy is subordinated to community, as it is in millenial sects. Sometimes, too, both structures are linked in a continuous chain, or cycle, of social reproduction (see Figure 8.1).

Figure 8.1 The cycle of social reproduction in the gift economy

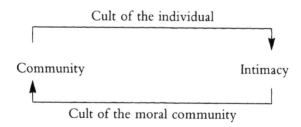

Cult of the individual

Community   Intimacy

Cult of the moral community

In the Winnipeg gift economy, the most dramatic community-intimacy cycle which reproduces patriarchal relations in marriage is to be found at bridal showers (Cheal 1988b). We saw in chapter 5 that bridal showers, in particular hall showers, are times when female communities assemble to help women set up homes in which they will serve their husbands. They are, in other words, times when the collective resources of female communities are pooled, in order to facilitate the intimate services of women to their spouses. At the same time hall showers are occasions when the power of the female community, and especially a married woman's reliance upon it for personal security, are dramatized in initiation rites that subordinate the privileged status of the bride to the collective whims of her female peers (Cheal 1988a).[8] In short, bridal showers circulate women into the domestic intimacy of marriage by passing them through the collectivity of the female community, while women collectively subordinate their communal organization to marriage and its obligations of intimate services provided by individual women.

Other community-intimacy cycles are less visible, but are nonetheless real. Mrs Romaniuk's commitment to her husband is due to one such cycle. Part of the explanation for Mrs Romaniuk's continuing service to her husband is undoubtedly that she is dependent upon his wage to maintain herself and her youngest daughter, who still lives at home. Verna Romaniuk's education ended at grade eight, and she explains that at her age, and with her lack of work experience other than domestic labor, her opportunities for employment are very limited. But simple economic dependence is implausible as the sole basis for marriage, if the husband is seen as having provided inadequate support for the wife, and when in any event it is not consumer goods that make people really happy.

Mrs Romaniuk says that her husband has kept her short of money for most of their life together, because he has an attitude of "what's mine is mine and I'm not going to share it." He is "reluctant to spend money on someone other than himself," so when she does have money of her own she says: "I buy things that a husband should buy a wife. Since my husband doesn't buy it for me, I'll buy it for myself." Her rebellion against her circumstances a few years ago included working as a domestic cleaner so that she could buy some luxuries for herself. One of those luxuries was a mink fur coat, which no longer gives her any pleasure.

> I went to work. I slugged it out, I worked hard. So I got myself a beautiful mink coat. But every time I look at that mink coat I don't enjoy it. I think that was a very – not a very wise decision, because I keep thinking how many dirty toilets I had to clean for somebody else to pay for that mink coat. This is one luxurious item that I bought for myself that I'm not enjoying.

Perhaps Mrs Romaniuk's dissatisfaction with her unwise

purchase has been deepened by the knowledge that the one thing
she did not get from her economic independence was freedom. We
are therefore thrown back upon the paradox that Mrs Romaniuk
continues to act in the way that she is "supposed to behave,"
despite the fact that she is unhappy with her life. That paradox
is only the reflection of a deeper contradictory consciousness of
community and intimacy.

Mrs Romaniuk subscribes to a universalistic ideology of helping
her "neighbor," whoever that neighbor might be. Her transaction
practices are rather different, however. In practice, most of her
help is given to very particular persons, and mainly to her husband
and her daughter still living with her. As Mrs Romaniuk put it:

> We're all different people with all different personalities and nature, and
> so we can't love or like everybody to the same degree. The more you
> know a person, and if you like him just a little bit more than you like
> somebody else, that has a deciding factor [on giving to him].

We see in Verna Romaniuk's case that received ideas of an
impersonal communal morality are held at the same time as practical ideas which emphasize intimate, personal relationships. There
is nothing unusual about this contradictory combination of ideas,
for it is typical of all salvation religions that have believed in a
social future on earth. The realization of that future depends upon
the extended social reproduction of the sect in time, and space,
and in population size. Population expansion is achieved through
the conversion of outsiders, and through the biological reproduction of members. In sects such as the Jehovah's Witnesses the
universalism of an ethic of brotherliness has provided the motive
for efforts to convert strangers, and the particularism of an ethic
of family has provided the motive for bearing and raising children
in the faith. The extended influence of the community of virtuosos
through population growth has thus required the intimacy of the
family, including the wife's dependence upon the family wage.

At the same time the intimacy of family life cannot be religiously
justified by such personal attachments as may form between
particular individuals. That is partly because such bonds draw
people away from the community and into closed circles of interpersonal intimacy. But, as we have seen in the case of Mrs
Romaniuk, it is also because only an impersonal ideology can
legitimate a personal relationship that has failed. When interpersonal feelings are weak, or negative, service to the other may still
be defined as the kind of unselfishness that anybody who has the

proper feeling of love towards humanity can be expected to hold. The feelings that arise in intimate relationships are thus subordinated to the communal goal of family maintenance. In particular, the resentments of women towards their disadvantageous position within the family are controlled by an ethic of self-perfection. That ethic requires that all actions conform to a motive of impersonal love for those whose needs are to be served, in whatever social position the individual happens to occupy. Where that position is one of intimate service to a spouse, it may be only impersonal love that keeps the family going.

No gifts are more redundant than those that are given out of impersonal love. These gift transactions may have the appearance of formal rationality, in the sense that objects are chosen for their practical contributions towards socially valued activities, such as setting up a new home. Mrs Romaniuk's gifts to brides are of this nature. They are also substantively redundant transactions with respect to her own sense of the recipients' needs, since she believes that the women she is "helping" will only suffer as a result of her actions!

It was for this reason that Mrs Romaniuk rebelled against giving bridal shower gifts and wedding gifts during the time when she was "not feeling very well." She seems to have believed then that her gifts were merely being used to facilitate the early marriages of young women who would soon be paying for their haste with their own loss of freedom. Subsequently, Mrs Romaniuk set her thinking straight about wedding gifts, but she does not seem to have changed her opinion about marriage and its consequences for women. Her carefully chosen gifts are therefore ultimately redundant because they are given out of an impersonal ethic of helping one's neighbor, regardless of the long-run consequences of what she is doing to herself. In these transactions it is not the recipient's well-being that is the criterion for giving. It is the donor's compulsion to have, and to display, the right motive.

The right motive in this context is an impersonal ethic, not only of helping one's neighbor, but more specifically of keeping the family going. I have tried to show in this chapter that there is in modern society an ethic of keeping the family going which belongs to a community-intimacy structure of extended social reproduction. That structure has its historical roots in salvation religions. It is therefore most evident today in the behavior of members of sects such as the Jehovah's Witnesses. However, it is unlikely to be confined to them, or to other Christians. As Max Weber showed, salvation religions have had profound historical effects upon the western societies. Their influence has continued in a socially valued love culture, which is now carried by many groups in addition to those in which it was formed. The modern love culture has therefore been shaped by many influences, some of which have been described in this book.

9

Conclusion

In this study gift transactions have been described as belonging to a moral economy within modern society. How that moral economy works, and the social processes that separate it from the political economy of capitalism, have been shown to add to our understanding of interpersonal relationships in general and of family relationships in particular. In chapter 1 the moral economy of modern society was described as consisting of that complex of motives, rituals, distribution rules, institutionalized ties, and modes of discourse by which small social worlds are produced within mass societies. The means by which resources are acquired, and the rules according to which they are distributed, have not received much attention here, although relevant investigations have been reported elsewhere (Cheal 1986, 1987c). The social dimensions of distribution processes in domestic units are to be taken up in a second study of moral economy, which is in progress. In the present study certain aspects of distribution rules were described in chapter 3, but the greater emphasis has been upon emotions, rituals, ties, and discourse, and upon the interconnections between them. The reasons for that choice of emphasis should be clear by now. These dimensions of interaction are central to the post-modern alternative to sociological elementarism, and they have been neglected by most schools of political economy. There is one important exception to the latter statement, and that is Collins' conflict theory.

Collins has consistently maintained that both Goffman's analysis of interaction rituals and its basis in Durkheim's theory of religion deserve to be recognized as major contributions to sociological theory (Collins 1975, 1980, 1981a, 1985). He considers Durkheim to be important because the latter "demonstrated that interaction is not simply a matter of cold-blooded bargaining, but that strong social ties are based on emotional bonds to which we attach moral ideals" (Collins 1975: 42). Similarly, he has argued that Goffman's work is valuable for its emphasis upon the ways in which social reality is constructed in interaction, an idea that he has developed in his own concept of interaction ritual chains (Collins 1981a, 1981b).

His ideas about interaction ritual chains have certain similarities to themes developed in this study. Nevertheless the present work breaks with his, as it does with any other school of political economy, in its insistence that the social order of mass society consists of a plurality of interrelated, *and irreducible*, systems of social organization within an ecology of games. In particular I have claimed for the gift economy a relative autonomy from social determination, which means that the sociology of gift transactions cannot be reduced to conflict sociology in general, or to class analysis and the theory of patriarchy in particular.

Collins has borrowed selectively from the insights of Durkheim and Goffman in order to round out a theory of social stratification (Collins 1975: 42–3). He has recently restated that position in his claim that the micro-analysis of interaction can be built into a macro-analysis of the state, of organizations, and of classes. In this way, he argues, "the Durkheimian tradition fills in the essential underpinnings of the conflict tradition." Solidary rituals are thought to define the cultures of social classes, and deference rituals between the members of different classes define their positions within a status hierarchy. In his view what ties micro-analysis and macro-analysis together "is a theory of stratification: the paramount reality on both levels." He has explicitly stated the implications of this position for the sociology of gift transactions in the following terms:

> Thus, the mechanism of microrituals adds up to a larger pattern, the entire society on the macrolevel. Mauss filled in this model in a crucial way by showing how gift-type exchanges create status claims and obligations to replay the exchange ritual. He also showed how the ritual charges physical objects with social significance – variously defined as magic, money, or perhaps other things – that can circulate as surrogates for a social presence. These symbolic objects tie together people and situations that are far apart and that may never actually see each other face to face. Out of this charging of objects with social energy comes the phenomenon of property. The Maussian perspective becomes a fundamental underpinning for Marx.
>
> (Collins 1985: 170–1).

Whether or not Mauss leads directly to Marx, his views about the gift clearly have encouraged energy flow models of social life. In turn, such models are easily reconciled with Marxian accounts of capitalist society as a totality structured by laws of the motion of capital. We have in fact encountered this sort of development once before, in Gregory; a claim that it is the spirit of the gift (that is, its emotional charge) that links individuals into systems of relations in non-market economies. Detailed criticisms of Gregory's point of view were presented earlier and will not be repeated here, but the conclusion drawn from them is worth re-emphasizing. What is lacking in these energy flow models of social order is a theory of the institutionalization of ties as social bonds.[1] We have seen that the paramount reality in the institutionalization of the moral economy of everyday life is not social stratification but social reproduction. That does not mean that gift rituals are unrelated to social inequality. But it does mean that any theory of the social construction of inequalities within a moral economy has to begin with an understanding of how social reproduction is organized.

Parallel systems of social organization

Moral economy and political economy are twin principles of social organization. That is true for any society but their interdependence is most obvious, because it is most visible, in those societies where they have been institutionally separated to a high degree. In a modern society the moral economy of family life and the political economy of the market are interdependent systems, because the latter generates the resources for use in the former, and because the former generates the motives for acquisitive effort in the latter (Holton 1986: 56–62). In his study of suicide Durkheim observed that by themselves economic gains could not provide lasting satisfaction for most people, because there are no ultimate values by which success or failure can be determined in market exchange (Durkheim 1951). For that reason, he claimed, economic achievement could be an effective principle in social life only insofar as it contributed to some goal of the individual whose object lay outside of the market economy. Keeping the family going is one such purpose.

He maintained that in the long run the most lasting sense of purpose is that provided by the indefinite extension of personal attachments into the future, in the form of service to members of the next and succeeding generations. He further noted that one of the principal conventional forms that this interest has taken is the hereditary transmission of property (Durkheim 1978: 236). The inheritance of property perpetuates existing inequalities and thereby contributes to the maintenance of a stratified social order, as Durkheim pointed out. That situation is not the result of a hierarchy of status rankings or the unseen hand of the market for emotional and cultural resources. It is, rather, a consequence of the personal interests of individuals in the well-being and enrichment of their children. As he saw it, the basis for family life in modern society is the social organization of social time. One of the consequences of that fact everywhere is the social construction of intergenerational inequality.

The intergenerational transmission of property is only one form of social reproduction. In a modern industrial society it is certainly not the most important determinant of the life styles and life chances of the mass of the population. What is far more important in the lives of most people is the transmission of memberships in, and the means for gaining access to, systems of social organization. There are many such systems, including formal organizations and markets. In small social worlds the principal systems of social organization are based in structures of intimacy and structures of community. What those systems organize, and how they do it, must now be formally described.

During the course of our investigations we have seen that the gift economy is constituted by a series of contrasting features of social life, such as intimacy and community. Some of the links between these contrast sets have been explored, but they have not yet been drawn together in a formal way. It is now possible to show that the gift economy consists of two parallel systems of social organization. Each system contains within itself a complete set of components for the social organization of social reproduction, consisting of the elements of a way of life and the elements of a ritual process (see Figure 9.1).

Figure 9.1 Organization of social closure

Components of social organization	General closure	Privileged closure
Way of life		
Social form	Community	Intimacy
Social motive	Impersonal love	Personal love
Social object	Cult of the moral community	Cult of the individual
Ritual process		
Ritual form	Rite of passage	Rite of progression
Ritual motive	Instrumental	Expressive
Ritual object	Practical gift	Symbolic gift

The system of social organization with which we have been most concerned in this study is based in structures of intimacy. These are the smallest of all small worlds, sometimes consisting only of dyads, such as the spousal relationship which Durkheim perceived to be the core of the conjugal family. Ways of life in intimate structures have the following characteristics. They consist of: 1) a small number of individuals who have; 2) a common social future, on the basis of which they maintain in the present; 3) personal relationships of high presence-availability and/or attachment and/or sentimentality, which are defined as; 4) belonging to an intimate social form, such as "the family" or "best friends," and as; 5) involving relatively unrestricted access of the parties to each other, by comparison with their accessibility to non-members, and who therefore; 6) have special rights, or privileges, in the use of all or most of each other's resources (physical, emotional, cognitive, and economic resources). Within the intimate forms of family and friendship, personal attachments are more important than group norms. It is therefore the individual person (rather than the family, etc.) which is treated as the object of ultimate value within a common cult of the individual.

The exceptionally high valuation of the person within the cult of the individual is articulated in an intersubjective vocabulary of motives, consisting mainly of an ethic of personal love. Gift giving is seen as the spontaneous outcome of such socially approved motives as "maternal love" and "falling in love." Gift rituals take the characteristic form of rites of progression, in which the duration of long-term relationships between persons is measured. The value that significant others attach to the durability of relationships is expressed in symbolic gifts that are instrumentally redundant.

The second system of social organization that has been described in this study is based in structures of community. Ways of life in community structures consist of: 1) a substantial number of individuals (most of whom also belong to intimate social worlds, so that a communal structure contains a number of intimate social units) which have; 2) a common social future, on the basis of which they maintain in the present; 3) social relationships of great sociability and/or economic cooperation, between individuals and between intimate social units, which are defined as; 4) belonging to a communal social form, such as "the neighbors," "the church," or "the community," and as; 5) involving preferential access of the parties to each other, by comparison with their accessibility to non-members, and who therefore; 6) have general rights, or entitlements, to limited use of the parties' resources (particularly cognitive and economic resources). Within the communal forms of churches and ethnic groups, positions within social relationships defined by group norms are more important than personal attachments. Social action is therefore principally the performance of role obligations (such as the obligation to get married, which is followed by the obligation to keep the family together, etc.), and interpersonal relationships are thus consequences of the power of collective opinion. A reified, and idealized, image of that collective opinion (that is, of the collective conscience) is held within a cult of the moral community.

In moral communities (which in modern societies may take religious or secular forms) the superior valuation of the collectivity over the individual is articulated in a vocabulary of motives that is depersonalized. Religiously, impersonal love for one's fellow virtuosos (fellow church members) is required, together with a weaker recommendation to love all God's children. Membership in moral communities is achieved through rites of passage, in which the individual's voluntary submission to group norms is celebrated. Communal rites of passage are expensive, due to the large numbers of individuals involved in their festivities. The costs of these rites are underwritten, in part at least, by the reciprocal provision of practical gifts. Ritual transfers within community structures are therefore usually conducted for instrumental reasons, but are substantively redundant.

Stated in such bald terms the twin systems of social organization just described are clearly ideal types, as are the concepts of political economy and moral economy with which this study began. Like all ideal types they have been condensed and simplified for expository purposes. Whether or not they have any value for social research outside the context in which they have been produced remains to be seen. One thing is very clear, however. That is that it is no longer possible to talk about "the gift" in the way in which Mauss did, since we have found that in Winnipeg gift giving is structured by two very different models of action. In truth there is no such thing as "the gift," just as there is no such thing as "the family." In both respects the progress of social scientific inquiry has been hindered by the essentialist logic of elementarism – that is, by the idea that all social life consists of a system of universal elements, whose real essences can be discerned from studying the elementary social forms of primitive societies. In this study I have talked about "the gift economy" rather than "the gift" in order to avoid any confusion with that idea.

The major advantage of abandoning Mauss's elementarist sociology is that it has been possible to distance the theoretical approach developed here from his model of a system of total prestations, while at the same time incorporating what is valuable in that model into a broader view of the gift economy. In particular, we have taken very seriously the fact that the numbers of givers and receivers participating in gift exchanges in North America is different from the situation that he described for primitive societies. He claimed that "In the systems of the past . . . it is groups, and not individuals, which carry on exchange" (Mauss 1954: 3). We have seen that in North America it is mainly individuals and couples, and not groups, that conduct gift transactions. Mauss's assumption about the actors in gift transactions imposed a fundamental limitation upon the kind of theory that he could produce, as a result of which his claims are today of very little value for sociology. Once it has been assumed, as Mauss did, that *all* transactions are intergroup exchanges, then any distinction between social and personal relationships is unavailable, and the entire argument developed in the present study is made impossible. His followers have paid insufficient attention to this limitation in his work. Its effects have been most serious for the sociology of gift transactions in the western societies, which is to say those societies whose cultures have been heavily influenced by moral individualism, and by the associated ideology of personal love.

The labor of love

The individualist and collectivist types of the social organization of social reproduction that have been observed in Winnipeg do not exist in isolation. They have been described here as interrelated in the dialectic of everyday life, and in the process of ecological succession between ethnic subcultures. More than that, it has been suggested that they are linked by their location within an underlying structure of redundancy by which the gift economy is constituted. They may also be linked in other ways which we have not yet considered.

Gifts are not given to just anybody. They are given to individuals with whom the donor has personal ties, or who occupy social positions within a community to which the donor also belongs. The comembership of giver and receiver within some personal relationship or social relationship is thus a precondition for gift giving. It is ultimately this fact which accounts for the redundancy of the gift economy, since gift transactions create nothing but only add to and extend what already exists. An important consequence of this social arrangement is that gifts circulate within closed social worlds consisting almost entirely of people who have pre-existing relationships. As the interviewees in the Winnipeg Ritual Cycle Study put it, gifts are given to people we know, and who know us, and who we know that we like better than others.

The fact that gift giving occurs within frameworks of mutual knowing is so much taken for granted that we are likely to be surprised when we find that it does not always happen that way. In the Winnipeg Ritual Cycle Study it was found that 1.6 per cent of all personal network members involved in gift transactions with the interviewees had never met them. The curiosity provoked by this finding confirms the exceptional nature of such transactions in the gift economy. Gift transactions almost always occur between individuals who possess the kind of reciprocal interpersonal knowledge that can only be acquired in face-to-face interaction. From a sociological point of view one of the most striking single findings about gift transactions is their massive social closure. The Winnipeg Ritual Cycle Study interviewees had seen 3 out of 5 (61.2 per cent) of the personal network members with whom they were involved in gift transactions at least once a month during the preceding year.

Closed relationships permit a local monopolization of resources, which may be economic, religious, emotional, sexual, etc. (Weber 1968). General closure within communities has been common throughout history, as members have preferred to transact with other members, and have discriminated against outsiders. In addition, circles of privileged closure have usually existed within communities, the most common being family or kinship networks. The systems of social organization that are reproduced in the Winnipeg gift economy are systems of general (i.e. communal) and privileged (i.e. intimate) closure. Gifts are not used to mark the boundaries of these systems, but they are used to help maintain the bonds between members, without which they would soon cease to exist.

The bonds that most people are most concerned with are those that define their intimate ties with close friends, or especially, family members. The closed world of the private family has been much debated in recent years (see, for example, Barrett and

McIntosh 1982), and here we must return to one of the principal issues with which this book began. The majority of gift giving is carried out by women, alone or in conjunction with male partners (usually spouses) who play a less active role in what is done. It has been suggested that this gender bias in the gift economy is a result of the historical segregation of women in industrial capitalist societies (Cheal 1987a). Their location in the domestic sphere of family life has meant that women have had the primary responsibility for maintaining family and kinship ties. We are now in a better position to evaluate that argument, together with the general model of private and public spheres from which it was drawn. What relevance does the discovery of general and privileged systems of closure in this study have for the theory of public and private domains? And what implications do our findings have for a better understanding of the relationship between gender and caring?

In Marxist political economy the theory of public and private life worlds has been joined with a theory of the capitalist mode of production, in which women are situated as domestic workers in the household economy (see, for example, Fox 1980). Women have been described as being limited to the performance of domestic labor in the household in order to release men for wage labor in industry, and in order to reproduce the next generation of industrial workers. Women's work within the household includes caring for their husbands and children. Referring to the special consequences of this situation for women, Luxton has stated that, "Because their work is rooted in the intense and important relationships of the family, it seems to be a 'labour of love' " (Luxton 1980: 11).[2]

Luxton has explored the manner in which women's love relations are structured by the requirements of industrial capitalism in her study of Flin Flon, which is in the same province as Winnipeg. It would be hard to find a more favorable context in which to confirm Marxist feminist political economy than a study of working class nuclear family households in a place like Flin Flon, Manitoba. Flin Flon is a one-industry mining town in which, until very recently, women have had few opportunities for wage employment. The lives of married working-class women there are inevitably highly dependent upon a male world of industrial production. Life in Winnipeg is different. It is also more typical of contemporary Canada's highly urbanized population.

Winnipeg is a city of 600,000 people, comprising more than half

of the population of Manitoba. It has a very diversified economy
that includes a wide range of jobs in manufacturing, construction,
transportation, and service industries, in which both men and
women are employed. In this study we have seen something of
the diversity of life styles of women in Winnipeg today, and it is
worth reminding ourselves of just how great that diversity is. We
have encountered women who are dependent housewives (Verna
Romaniuk, Carol Brown), as well as women who support themselves (Orysia Caruk, Hazel Anderson) and their dependents
(Bernice Genyk, Mary Atamanchuk) by their own wage labor.
Some of them are working-class (Mary Atamanchuk, Verna
Romaniuk, Pat Chubey) and some of them are middle-class
(Orysia Caruk, Carol Brown, Hazel Anderson).

There are other important differences among women in
Winnipeg, beginning with ethnicity, which has been the subject
of explicit attention in this study. Also, some of the women interviewed in the Winnipeg Ritual Cycle Study are very religious
(Verna Romaniuk, Margaret Rose) whereas others are irreligious
(Anne Baker, Colleen Williams). However, the most important
differences occur in two dimensions of social life which take on
very particular forms in the conventional co-resident nuclear
family. Those dimensions are sexual affiliation and household
composition. The sexual affiliations of women interviewed in the
Winnipeg Ritual Cycle Study range from single and uninhibited
(Anne Baker) to single and going steady (Colleen Williams) to
unmarried but living in a common law relationship (Bernice
Genyk) to legally married (Hazel Anderson, Carol Brown) to
widowed (Mary Atamanchuk) and divorced (Orysia Caruk,
Margaret Rose). Their household arrangements are similarly
diverse. They range from living with a room-mate of the same
sex (Anne Baker) to living alone (Margaret Rose) to living with a
spouse only (Hazel Anderson) to living with a spouse and children
(Carol Brown) to living with an aged parent only (Mary
Atamanchuk).

With so many different experiences and values, it is only to be
expected that women in Winnipeg would not think about gift
giving in a uniform manner. Women with low incomes tend to
give fewer gifts, and working-class women from a Ukrainian background are particularly likely to think about gifts in an unsenti-
mental way, emphasizing practical utility, value for money, and
reciprocity. Middle-class women on the other hand tend to give
more freely, particularly if they have reached a financially stable

middle-age and no longer have children living at home, or if they are enjoying a financially comfortable retirement. The greater freedom of their giving is reflected in a greater number of gifts (although not necessarily in more costly gifts), and in the wider range of feelings and shades of emotional intensity which this allows them to express.

Most of the women interviewed in the Winnipeg Ritual Cycle Study stated that gift giving is an important activity in their lives because it facilitates the expression of intimate feelings. For these women relations of love are not merely coincidental outcomes of high intensity interactions with men upon whose wages they depend. Nor are gifts of love simply things that are hidden in the household, although the most valuable gifts often are given between spouses. Only 7 per cent of personal network members involved in gift transactions with the interviewees in fact lived with them in the same household. Social closure is important in Winnipeg, as it is in most cities, because it produces small social worlds whose members can be trusted (Fischer 1981). But the principal locus of closure is not the nuclear family household. It follows that the principal determinant of closure cannot be the family wage, and that the capitalist mode of production has not reduced love to mere domestic labor.

Love, personal or impersonal, is not confined to relations of nurturant dependence within the private domain of the household, although it may be at its strongest there. Personal love relations also occur between individuals living in separate households. That includes and is perhaps especially likely to include, those attachments that form between members of the same sex. Smith-Rosenberg has studied the intimate, loving relationships that often formed between American women in the eighteenth and nineteenth centuries, and has pointed out that these women inhabited two social worlds – one heterosocial and the other homosocial (Smith-Rosenberg 1975). As a result of the rigid sex role differentiation within the family, and within society at large, women's and men's lives were socially, and emotionally, segregated. Smith-Rosenberg claims that this did not mean that nineteenth-century American women simply formed an isolated and oppressed subcategory within an essentially male society. Rather, women had their own sphere whose integrity and dignity grew out of women's shared experiences and mutual affections.

The female world in the nineteenth century was based in extended female networks consisting of long-lived intimate relationships. It was a world of emotional richness and complexity, which was institutionalized in the rites of passage that accompanied virtually every important event in a woman's life. The ties between women took many forms, but were heavily influenced by the fact that girls were born into a female world. The mother's network of female friends and relatives was among the first realities in the life of the developing child, and many relationships that were to be important in later life were drawn from it.

> Central to this female world was an inner core of kin. The ties between sisters, first cousins, aunts, and nieces provided the underlying structure upon which groups of friends and their network of female relatives clustered. Although most of the women [studied] would appear to be living within isolated nuclear families, the emotional ties between nonresidential kin were deep and binding and provided one of the fundamental existential realities of women's lives.
>
> (Smith-Rosenberg 1975: 11)

The social condition of women in Canada today is of course not the same as it was in America in the last century. Nevertheless, there are important continuities between nineteenth-century America and late twentieth-century Winnipeg. In Winnipeg today it is still the case that many women, from all social classes, continue to value long-term relationships with other women living outside the household. In the case studies reported above we have noted Mrs Chubey's close relations with her aunts, and Mrs Brown's tie to her old school friend. These are not unusual examples, and other illustrations could have been given. In the Winnipeg gift economy women do the largest part of the gift work, not only for their husbands (if they are married) but also on their own account. Women are not only the largest givers of gifts, they are also the largest receivers (see Table 9.1). More than half of all gifts recorded in the Winnipeg Ritual Cycle Study went to women (see also Caplow 1982: 387), and it is likely that many of the gifts with joint male and female receivers were in fact also given to women. Georgina Baran (see pp. 179ff.) says, "You know everyone always buys for the woman when they buy in couples."

Outside marriage women who have the necessary financial resources and interaction skills construct personal networks of friends in which long-term relationships with other women are both socially and emotionally important (for example, Mrs Rose's "golfing group"). Within marriage men's incomes and family ties are transformed by women into the means for constructing

Table 9.1 *Distribution of all gifts reported, by sex of givers and receivers*

Gender of Givers	Gender of receivers			
	Male	Female	Male and female jointly	Totals
	%	%	%	%
Male	1.6	3.4	0.4	5.4
Female	11.8	22.1	2.6	36.5
Male and female jointly	20.5	30.4	7.2	58.1
Totals	33.9	55.9	10.2	100.0

extended female networks of love. We have seen in the case studies of Pat Chubey, and especially of Melvin Fisher, that in the social reproduction of structures of intimacy and community men are often merely auxiliaries in the life-course plans of women. Our final case study illustrates how strong female solidarity can be under such circumstances.

Case study: Georgina Baran

Georgina Baran is 22 years old. She has been unemployed since her position as a waitress in a hotel bar was terminated about six months ago. Her husband Gordon (known as Gord) is age 32. Gift giving is important to Georgina, at any time of year, because it enables her to express strong feelings that she cannot easily reveal in more direct ways. Her mother (who is Norwegian) has never encouraged her to be open about her feelings. Georgina loves her mother and says:

> When you love somebody and you care a lot about them, getting a gift is a special way – because we were never ones for saying "I love you" and giving your mom a big hug. Oh, when I'd had a few drinks I'd go and say, "Hi Ma! I love you!" – "Drunk again, eh?" – "Yeah, a little bit." It's just, I love to see the people I love happy. Buying gifts is another way of saying you love them. Like, for my mom I went and bought her a corsage the other day, and she said: "Well, what's this for?" So I said, "What the hell, it'll look good on your coat." It's just, we don't have to sit there and say "I love you," because we were never kissy-face in our family. When Gord comes up to give me a hug and a kiss I tell him to get away from me. "Go bug someone else for a while" [laughs].

Gord is a laborer in the pipeline construction business. Because of the nature of his work he sometimes spends a lot of time at home, but at other times he is out of the city for weeks at a stretch. When she was first interviewed, shortly before Christmas, Georgina was not looking forward to the festive season because she knew Gord would be out of town.

> Christmas this year is really going to be hard because I'll be by myself. Gord can't make it home for Christmas, so when I was putting the tree up – you get a sentimental feeling. When you get older you lose that excitement, but it's still there. But you're supposed to be adult enough, so they say. When my husband is home here for Christmas he's worse than a kid – "Oh, look how many I got, look at how many I got; I think you got one here too," you know.

Even though Gord is not always home for Christmas, he has more family life than Georgina's father has enjoyed. Georgina's father works at a military establishment in the far north, and he comes home for six weeks once a year. For the rest of the year he works and lives in a world of men, separated by distance and social organization from his wife and daughters. Georgina has therefore grown up in a female world, which she assumes will continue to make a place for her. Georgina's marriage to Gord was accompanied by her inclusion in a new women's world, namely that of her husband's female relatives. She says:

> When you're married you've got his family to hope to God you're going to like. And they love me. It's funny really, because Gord's family (I hate to say this, but he knows it) they love me a lot more than they love him. Because he is family, [but] I've really won them over. We're very, very close. I see [Gord's sister] all the time. And she complains about him – "That brother of mine" – so I told him, you know. And his mom. I got a note from her – "You come and see me and you leave Gord at home. We need some time together, just me and you. We'll spend a week together." I'm closer to his family than Gord is. Gord doesn't sit and talk with his parents or pop in for coffee to see his sister. I'm always over there complaining. That's what family's good for is to complain, you know. And having his nieces and in-laws liking me as much as they do it's even better. Before I only had my own family. But with Gord's family I've got twice as much as what I had before. They love me and I love them. It's better to have more people love you. Having his family also is twice as better.

In Georgina's life world social interaction is not so much structured by household boundaries or kinship groups or generation gaps, as it is by the differences in feelings between men and women. Georgina feels a lot closer to her mother and mother-in-law than she does to her father and father-in-law, and the solidarity she feels with her two sisters in their relations with men overrides their differences of opinion on other matters.

> I always get nice little letters from my mother-in-law. She signs them. "Love Joe" – but it's not Joe talking, it's her. And my mother, we're very, very close. My dad and I are close in one way where we're friends more than daughter and father, 'cause he was never really home for us to say "Dad" [to]. For me to say "Dad" is really funny. My mom, we're sort of pals, but I respect her because she's my mother and I'd never argue with her. As much as I'd love to. [Me and my sisters] we stick together no matter what. In other words, if the husband does something (to her older sister, who is also married) we'd kill him. We love him, but before they got married we told him – "you never hurt my sister. If you ever do any damage to my sister you'll be sorry." And the same thing with [her younger sister, whose fiancé lives in Alberta]. She's engaged now to be married, and I told him over the phone – "If you ever hurt her, don't you ever come to Winnipeg." And it's the same thing with me, they said the same thing to Gord. . . . When we were kids we were always together, and then when you're older you're not together as much as you used to be. You're starting to go out with boys, and you miss out on a lot of family dinners because your boyfriend asked you to go out. It's a choice, a toss-up between family and boyfriend. Well, you got to go with the boyfriend. And then when you get married it's, "Should we go to his family's house for dinner at Christmas, or should we go to mine?" You miss being that family you used to be. You're not together as much as you once were. We were together every day. You get up in the morning, and there were three of us all fighting for the washroom. When you get older you don't have to fight for the washroom and, like, who's using whose stuff. Here I've got Gord. Gord doesn't wear any make-up [so] I can't argue with him about that, or about who's wearing my clothes again. God, you lose so much when you get married, when you actually think about it.

Conclusion: the discourse of relationships

The principal locus of social closure in everyday life in Winnipeg is the division between women's worlds and men's worlds. Whatever the situation may be in other areas of social life, within the gift economy the small social worlds of women are more likely to be closed than are those of men. Women are not only more likely to give and receive gifts than are men, they are also much more likely to give to individuals of the same sex (see Table 9.1). Most of the things that men give are given to women, but most women's gifts are also given to women. Giving at bridal showers is of course the classic example of sexually segregated giving. Here women give only to other women within a self-consciously closed female world.

Women's greater involvement in gift transactions than men is not a result of privatized experiences such as domestic dependence or child care, since they are no longer events that all women experience. Nevertheless, women's giving has been affected by the fact that those experiences have historically been more common among women than they have been among men. If there is an apparent paradox here, it is largely because the boundary between women's lives and men's lives has been changing.

Gerson and Peiss have recently stated that changing gender relations, especially the fact that more women are now wage earners, raises important questions with which sociology has not been well-equipped to deal (Gerson and Peiss 1985). How, they ask, have gender boundaries been reconstituted under new conditions? And what boundaries remain, or have become significant, in defining gender differences as traditional divisions become less sharp? The notion of separate spheres of public and private activities is increasingly problematic, even though significant gender differences remain, because it does not capture the complexity of social and cultural divisions in contemporary urban life.[3] The reality of division within complexity is today best captured by the contrast between political economy and moral economy, as it has been analyzed in this study.[4] It is a division which cuts across groups and role structures, in industrial organizations and in families. The reason it is so powerful, and the reason why it is so little understood, is because political economy and moral economy are parallel systems of social organization that can be found wherever there is social interaction.

Although systems of political economy and moral economy are found in all social groups, not everybody is influenced equally by both of them. In fact it is normally the case that exposure to these systems is selective, so that appropriate motives and knowledge are socially distributed. Women and men are usually unequally exposed to systems of political economy and moral economy, due to the social separation of women's worlds and men's worlds. That separation begins in childhood, in the homosocial peer groups that children form at school, and in the social networks of their parents. Segregated worlds are encountered, and created, within which distinctively different kinds of meanings are constructed (Cheal 1988b).

Women's lives in industrial society have, until very recently, been centered around home and service to children, whereas men's lives have traditionally been centered around employment and service to the state. As a result, male conversation has typically consisted of the discourse of political economy, while female conversation has typically consisted of the discourse of moral economy. Women's greater involvement in gift giving today is not simply an effect of their immediate experiences in the household. Rather, it is the consequence of their participation in a discourse of relationships. Through that discourse the present generation of women, and their predecessors, have shared common experiences of moral economy, and have created their own relational cultures.[5] It has been within these female relational cultures that the modern meanings of gifts have evolved. The dominant social definitions in the gift economy today are derived from a feminized ideology of love.

Notes

1 Moral economy

1 Such gifts may be willingly accepted and politely, even enthusiastically, acknowledged. But they are not likely to arouse deep feelings of gratitude. For this reason the gift economy cannot be understood simply as an "economy of gratitude," as Hochschild (in press) has proposed. Gift giving is usually institutionalized (Befu 1968; Lebra 1976), and it is therefore governed by rules which define what individuals can expect to receive from others, and when they can expect to receive it, and how much it will be worth. In an institutionalized gift economy it is only "surprise gifts" or "generous gifts" which achieve the ideal of normative redundancy, and which are therefore framed as extraordinary transactions within an economy of gratitude.

2 The position taken here should be clarified in relation to the problem of the autonomy of agency, or put more simply the problem of agency, as it has been discussed in recent years (see, for example, Giddens 1976, 1979). Autonomy is not a property of subjects considered as social actors. Rather, it is a property of action within a certain context, or frame, as Goffman demonstrated in his comparison of front regions and back regions (Goffman 1959). It is, therefore, gift transactions and not gift givers that may be described as possessing (relative) autonomy.

3 At this point certain claims for the universality of political economy can be anticipated, according to which the laws of political economy are seen as the necessary foundations for an integral social science (see, for example, Fraser 1985). The position taken here is quite different, since it is not assumed that one theoretical framework can answer all of the questions that are worth asking.

The work presented in this study follows Weber's method of investigation by means of ideal types (see Hekman 1983). Weber maintained that sociological explanation involves constructing concepts whose various elements are abstracted from reality and recombined in a logically integrated fashion. Because of this logical integration by the observer an ideal type may never be found in real life. It is a theorist's concept, to which actual events will correspond with different degrees of approximation. The classical concepts of economic theory are, therefore, all instances of ideal types (Weber 1947: 96, 111).

The advantages of such concepts, Weber pointed out, are their precision and clarity, and thus their aid to reasoning. They facilitate the working out of general explanatory principles and provide guidelines for the development of hypotheses (1947: 109–11, 1949: 90). The heuristic nature of ideal types is evident in his insistence that no single type could describe the whole of social life. It is therefore necessary to develop a number of ideal types in order to describe the different aspects of the cultural significance of social phenomena (Weber 1947: 110; 1949: 91, 97, 1968: 262–4). From Weber's point of view, the concept of economic exchange is merely one such type (1949: 100).

Weber's methodology was criticized by Parsons for leading to the proliferation of unrelated constructs, and thus to an unsystematic "mosaic theory" of society (Parsons 1949: 607, 610). Parsons clearly believed that ideal type theorizing was a primitive method that would be superseded by the method of analytic reduction (1949: 616–24). Nevertheless, he allowed that ideal types might be used as a matter "of scientific convenience, of fact" (1949: 617), whenever the phenomena studied were "organic" (1949: 615, 625). As we can see in Parsons' subsequent work, a mosaic theory of society is in fact necessary where social life consists of different domains of meaning whose distinctiveness is maintained by social boundaries.

The general solution to this problem that he developed (Parsons 1951) was a model of society consisting of at least two levels, in which the superordinate level contains mechanisms for the differentiation and interconnection of subsystems (Cheal 1978a; Luhmann 1982). In this way it is possible to show at the macrolevel how contradictory social practices are related within a more general framework of social organization. At the level of the individual, this arrangement takes the form of the "pluralization of the life world" described by phenomenological sociology (P. Berger, B. Berger, and Kellner 1973: 63–69 especially).

An important consequence of the separation of life-world spheres is that the subjective contents of everyday life cannot be described by universal laws of the objective functioning of economic systems. The distinction between political economy and moral economy that is introduced in this chapter is therefore more than just a device for classifying social science paradigms. It is also a systematic sociology of social forms which can be used to analyze the division of everyday life into contrasting frames of action (see Goffman 1974). The relations between those frames, including their interpenetrations within concrete systems of relations, comprise the subject matter for socio-economics.

4 If the methodology for this study is neo-Weberian, then the approach to the study of gift transactions that is taken here is neo-Durkheimian. It is Durkheim's conceptualization of social order which provides the issues to be investigated. In the first place, the distinction between moral economy and political economy that is drawn here is modelled upon recent discussions of Durkheim's ideal types of mechanical and organic solidarity as coexisting forms of social action (Lukes 1973: 148; Cohen 1985: 24–5, 116–17).

Organic solidarity is characteristic of market economies and consists of the interdependence between individuals that arises from economic exchange under conditions of the division of labor. According to Durkheim, the problematic nature of exchange is resolved by a process of social regulation within a framework of social rules, such as contract law. Mechanical solidarity, on the other hand, occurs as a result of the affinity between individuals who hold the same beliefs and value the same things. It is, as he put it, a solidarity "born of resemblances." The precondition for a high level of identification between individuals is that they are organized into small groups, or segments, within society, such as kinship groups and domestic groups (Durkheim 1964a: 106, 175). The present work describes some of the features of mechanical solidarity within these groups.

Secondly, he claimed that the material advantage gained from the division of labor (and thus from exchange) is small by comparison with its "moral effect" in inducing feelings of solidarity. In this way, he argued, the social significance of the division of labor goes far beyond its relevance for economic interests (Durkheim 1964a: 56, 60–1). I have shown elsewhere that the substantive functions of gift giving have typically been overstated in conventional accounts of social support networks (Cheal 1986). It will be argued here that the most important dimensions of the gift economy are to be found in the construction of social solidarity via interaction rituals.

Durkheim's emphasis upon the moral effects of transactions is echoed in the work of Goffman, as Collins has pointed out (Collins 1980) Goffman's account of deference rituals rested upon Durkheimian principles that had been reworked within the conceptual framework of mass society theory. Expressions of deference in interaction rituals are, in his view, one of the ways "in which the person in our urban secular world is allotted a kind of sacredness that is displayed and confirmed by symbolic acts" (Goffman 1967: 47). Goffman made explicit reference to Durkheim's theory of religion in this connection, and claimed that Durkheimian notions about religion can help us to understand certain aspects of urban life (1967: 95). Like Durkheim, he thought that the decline of rituals involving belief in supernatural beings did not necessarily mean that religious phenomena are absent from modern social life. Rather, he recommended us to examine those interpersonal rituals which attest to the recipient's possession of a patrimony of sacredness (1971: 63). "Many gods have been done away with, but the individual himself stubbornly remains as a deity of considerable importance. He walks with some dignity and is the recipient of many little offerings" (Goffman 1967: 95). It is these "little offerings" to the minor gods of small social worlds that are the subject matter for our study.

5 For useful discussions see Bennett (1968), Lowenthal (1975), Hansen (1981), Meillassoux (1981), and Smith, Wallerstein, and Evers (1984).

6 The third theoretical approach that has provided the guiding principles for this study is the symbolic interactionist view of mass societies, as outlined by Tamotsu Shibutani. According to Shibutani, the principal characteristic of mass society is its cultural pluralism (1955: 566). Such

societies are made up of a multitude of social worlds whose meanings are often contradictory. The system of meanings which constitutes a social world is reproduced through communication, and the existence of a social world therefore depends upon the structured participation in communication channels that arises from differential contact and association (Shibutani 1955: 565–6; Cheal 1981). The diversity of channels of communication in mass societies is what makes a high level of cultural pluralism possible.

Unlike most historical societies, in which social life was organized within territorial communities, interaction in mass societies depends upon a variety of space-transcending transportation and communication technologies. Modern social worlds are therefore often geographically dispersed. Their cultural frames of reference are, for the most part, no longer coterminous with localized groups, but are diffused through ramified communication networks that cross a variety of social and physical boundaries (Shibutani 1955: 566–7; Unruh 1983). According to Shibutani, "Each social world, then, is a culture area, the boundaries of which are set neither by territory nor by formal group membership but by the limits of effective communication."

Extensive participation in the dynamic social milieus of mass societies means that individuals are exposed to, and committed to, a variety of frames of reference. The management of inconsistent meanings is thus a practical necessity for everyday life. This may be achieved through the segmentation of social worlds (Shibutani 1955: 567), although that is rarely a completely successful solution to the problem. Conflicts between discrepant meanings inevitably take the form of personal problems (Shibutani 1955: 565, 568; Cheal 1987a). Common adaptations to these problems bring about changes in social practices.

Changes in practices in one field of action often have consequences for activities in other areas, with the result that social life in mass societies is characterized by constant change. Transformations in social institutions, and adjustments in social relationships, are therefore continuous preoccupations for many people (Shibutani 1955: 569). Changing frames of reference and shifts from one situated frame to another, together with the awareness of a multiplicity of perspectives, mean that the selection of lines of action acquires an importance in mass societies which it could not have had in earlier societies (Shibutani 1955: 567–8).

Studies of collective action in mass societies have found that commitments to lines of action are not determined by the nature of the functions performed by social structures, or by a societal system of structural constraints (Cheal 1975, 1978b). Rather, they depend upon how actors define social objects, and hence in part upon the shared ideas that become available through communication channels (Shibutani 1955: 569, Cheal 1979, 1988a). Important communication channels include the mass media and face-to-face interactions with significant others.

It is, Shibutani claims, through communication, and especially through personal relationships, that social worlds are constructed (1955: 568). In their transactions social actors display and receive confirmation of the expectations that each holds of the other (1955: 564, 569). In this way they define the existence of a shared universe of meanings. These intersubjective meanings make action, and therefore social life, predictable and manageable.

> Each of these worlds is a unity of order, a universe of regularized mutual response. Each is an area in which there is some structure which permits reasonable anticipation of the behavior of others, hence, an area in which one may act with a sense of security and confidence. . . . A social world, then, is an order conceived (sic) which serves as the stage on which each participant seeks to carve out his career and to maintain and enhance his status.
>
> (Shibutani 1955: 566–7)

7 The deliberate neglect of attributes and attribution processes by many social networks sociologists (for example, Richardson and Wellman 1985: 776) is one of the most serious problems in structural analysis today. The unproblematic view of interaction that is characteristic of most structural sociology has been exacerbated in the structural analysis of networks by the excessively abstract, mathematical nature of much recent work. The bonds which hold people together have come to be described through unexplicated concepts of "connectedness" and "strength of ties." What is missing in this effortless, algebraic view of social interaction is the fact that social life, like any other condition of existence, has to be produced. The process of producing social ties is often hard work, and may require considerable resources of time, money, and emotional resilience. Success is never guaranteed, and is always limited by the conditions for action within a given social environment.

Sociologists working in the symbolic interactionist tradition have pointed out that networks of relationships are always based on a social-psychological infrastructure. Blumer's remarks on this point are worth quoting at some length. He has urged us to recognize that

> the diverse array of participants occupying different points in the network engage in their actions at those points on the basis of using given sets of meanings. A network . . . does not function automatically because of some inner dynamics . . . (but) because people at different points do something, and what they do is a result of how they define the situation in which they are called on to act. . . . It is necessary to recognize that the sets of meanings that lead participants to act as they do at their stationed points in the network have their own setting in a localized process of social interaction – and that these meanings are formed, sustained, weakened, strengthened, or transformed, as the case may be, through a socially defining process.
>
> (Blumer 1969: 19–20)

This socially defining process consists of the mutual signifying of meanings and the taking account of the meanings thus signified. Meanings may be transmitted in a variety of ways, both verbal and non-verbal, through various communication channels. Gift giving is one such channel of communication, whose importance in the social construction of social support networks has been described elsewhere (Cheal 1988a). It is for these reasons that the key concept in this study is that of moral economy, and not social network.

2 Tie-signs

1 Goffman himself disavowed any interest in the structural dimensions of anchored relations (Goffman 1971: 193). In contrast, the concept of moral economy advanced here presupposes that gift transactions are partly structured by rules which define the existence of a differentiated system of classes of actors (Cheal 1980: 39–40). Structural arrangements based on socially defined kinship and gender statuses are therefore likely to be of some importance for tie-signs such as gifts (Caplow 1982, 1984; Cheal 1986).

In a typically understated shift in approach, Goffman did in fact take up studies of the ritual order of gender statuses in the latter part of his career (Goffman 1977, 1979), although they have generally been overlooked (for example, by Collins 1980). There is still much to be learned from his work about microstructural models of interaction processes (Cheal 1988b).

2 Collins has extended this idea of Goffman's by arguing that social structure consists of repetitive actions which are organized as interaction ritual chains (Collins 1981a, 1981b). His development of this idea has been controversial, partly because it is conceptually loose and imprecise (J. H. Turner 1986), and partly because he has argued that all macrophenomena should be translated into combinations of micro-events (Giddens 1985: 290–2; Ritzer 1985). Among the objections to be made to this oversimplified conception of sociology is the necessity to explain the different forms that interaction rituals take. As Berger and Luckmann have pointed out, in the microanalysis of everyday life interaction must be studied as a dialectical process in which intersubjective meanings constructed at one point in time are reified and therefore define the probabilities for actions at later points in time (P. Berger and Luckmann 1966). In practice this involves making reference to the limits to the extension of interaction ritual chains that arise from the differentiation of structures of action (see, for example, Cheal 1987a, 1987b). It is for this reason that the present monograph begins with a macroanalysis of the gift economy considered as a structure of action that has been differentiated from other structures.

3 Goffman defined ritualization as "the standardization of bodily and vocal behavior through socialization, affording such behavior – such gestures, if you will – a specialized communicative function in the stream of behavior" (Goffman 1983: 3). Ritualization is therefore an

aspect of the institutionalization of action, as described in the previous chapter.

4 This gap in the empirical record has had theoretical consequences in the revival of American neo-functionalism, since there has been a tendency to see modern gift rituals as analogues of the forms of communal solidarity that are sometimes described for traditional societies. The resulting focus upon gatherings organized in conjunction with the celebration of Christmas and marriage has tended to reinforce orthodox functionalist interpretations of gift practices, according to which they objectify and confirm a societal role system (Caplow *et al.* 1982; Caplow 1984). What these interpretations of gift ceremonial have ignored, however, is the parallel existence of segregated and highly privatized celebrations, such as bridal showers and birthdays. Standard societal integration models of the ritual process do not provide the most useful accounts of the latter kinds of occasions, as I have suggested elsewhere (Cheal 1988a).

5 The work reported here has been supported by Grant No. 410–82–0041 and Grant No. 410–85–0082 from the Social Sciences and Humanities Research Council of Canada.

6 For an earlier report from the Winnipeg Ritual Cycle Study see Cheal (1987a).

7 Regrettably, it is necessary to correct a serious error made by the publisher in one of these papers. In "The social dimensions of gift behaviour" the beta coefficient for AGE and RECCOST in Table 3 is not positive, but *is in fact negative* (Cheal 1986: 430).

8 Interviewing for the Ritual Cycle Study was conducted in six districts of Winnipeg that could be identified (from Weir 1978) as possessing the theoretically desirable social characteristics. They were, in the first place, areas that did not have a high proportion of foreign-born residents or a high level of recent in-migration from outside the city. Secondly, they were either areas which contained relatively large proportions of people of British descent *and* relatively large proportions of United Church members, or they were areas which contained relatively large proportions of people of Ukrainian descent *and* relatively large proportions of people belonging to the Ukrainian Catholic Church. In Winnipeg the United Church and the Anglican Church are both predominantly British, and the Ukrainian Catholic Church and the Greek Orthodox Church are both predominantly Ukrainian. The United Church is the largest British denomination and the Ukrainian Catholic Church is the largest Ukrainian denomination. Those two denominations were therefore selected for special emphasis in the sample design. (For the theoretical assumptions from which this design was derived see the discussion in Cheal 1981.)

Most (63) of the 80 individuals interviewed were selected because of the ethnic distinctiveness of their family names as they were listed in the city telephone directory. (Lists of Ukrainian names were drawn from Kaye 1975, and lists of British names were drawn from The American Council of Learned Societies 1969: 175). The remaining 17 interviewees were selected from the memberships of the United Church or the Ukrainian Catholic Church in 4 of the 6 districts.

The use of ethnically distinctive names in sampling has the disadvantage that where there is considerable intermarriage between ethnic groups the social identities of women may be obscured by the names of their husbands. In the Winnipeg Ritual Cycle Study there were only two instances of this that resulted in a married woman claiming a non-British or non-Ukrainian ethnic identity. One woman identified herself as being Polish Canadian, and the other woman identified herself as American. (The only other self-identification as non-Canadian was made by an elderly Englishman who had lived in Canada since he was a young man.)

9 For a discussion of this problem in the context of historical studies of European societies see Plakans (1984).

10 It has been customary among some social anthropologists for kinship diagrams to use solid ideograms to refer to the dead and open ideograms to refer to the living (for example, Epstein 1981: 226–7). That procedure has been reversed here, since graphic emphasis should be in accordance with research purposes. In diagrams that are intended to depict networks of effective social ties it is desirable for the living to be more prominent than the dead.

11 The alphabetic abbreviations used here are based on the two-letter acronymic system introduced by Murdock (1947). His system is no longer widely used among social anthropologists, having been displaced for most purposes by a system of genealogical descriptors employing single letters (Barnes 1967). The latter system permits highly condensed descriptions of extended relationships but it has several disadvantages, including the professional closure that is sustained by arcane communications. Single-letter abbreviations are confusing for those not trained in their use, since some of the symbols are not acronyms and are therefore impossible to interpret intuitively (for example, since S stands for son, sister has to be represented by the letter Z).

12 The list of relational terms used in the RANK graphs has been truncated and the available information on social ties condensed in order to avoid visual distraction and confusion. All alters other than kin, friends, and pets were coded as "acquaintances" for the purpose of preparing the RANK graphs.

3 Transactions and relations

1 I would argue that it is precisely this combination within the western family system that makes modern family life such a peculiar, and irremediable, locus of interpersonal conflict. This argument will be developed in the course of future research on family economics.

2 Bloch also pointed out that kinship is not the only moral relationship. In an approach very similar to our description of a moral economy as an inclusive structure of interaction, presented above, Bloch stated that:

If the effect of morality is the existence of long term commitments then there is no sharp break between kinship and other commitments but rather we should regard kinship as the end of a continuum consisting of commitments of different terms.

(Bloch 1973: 77)

3 The twin terms *reciprocity* and *exchange* are inexact and thus overlap to a considerable degree in social scientific discourse. A useful distinction can nevertheless be drawn between them. Reciprocity is best regarded as that pattern in the flow of valued objects within a system of transactions in which a social actor who is the source of one transfer is the recipient of another transfer. Reciprocal transactions may be described as being balanced (i.e. symmetrical) or unbalanced (i.e. asymmetrical) depending on whether or not the valued objects given and received are equivalent according to the criteria of value used within the culture in question (Lebra 1969). If reciprocity can be taken to refer to a pattern of transfers, then an exchange is best regarded as a social-psychological process in which one transfer is identified as being a return for another, that is, as having been given in recognition of the other's bestowal (Cheal 1984: 145).

4 For a discussion of alignment as a social process see Stokes and Hewitt (1976).

5 A quantitative demonstration of the combination of symmetrical and asymmetrical gift giving at Christmas can be found in Cheal (1986).

6 I have discussed elsewhere the practical impossibility of ever disproving exchange propositions and how this has hindered the development of transactional sociology (Cheal 1984, 1988c).

7 Blum and McHugh have pointed out that the organizational uses of the ascription of motive include "members' methods for tracking and formulating biographies from a universe of possibilities, and the various rules for deciding the relevance of particular biographies as particular types of persons" (Blum and McHugh 1971: 108). The rules for ascription of motives are therefore rules for deciding upon interaction as a course of history, and for defining that history as a relationship in time. For the importance of the latter concept in the study of social worlds see Cheal (1988a).

8 On the arts of impression management see Goffman (1959).

4 Love culture

1 The concept of "work" used here refers to the deliberate effort that is involved in constructing, or building up, a line of action together with the resources and social arrangements that are necessary for its production (see, for example, Wadel 1979). This constructionist approach stands in sharp contrast to the critical theory of Baudrillard who has attempted to separate political economy and semiotics by claiming that a "rupture" exists "between symbolic exchange and work" (Baudrillard 1975: 45). From a constructionist point of view,

symbolic exchange as well as economic exchange involves acts of production in which pre-existing conditions are transformed through human effort. That effort may properly be identified as "work." In the absence of a comprehensive concept of work, such as that outlined here, Baudrillard is unable to theorize a *pragmatic* semiotics (compare Baudrillard 1981: 66, 123 with Cheal 1987a). It is this lack which is ultimately responsible for the failure of his account of autonomous transactions, since if the gift economy cannot be seen as work it can only be seen as waste (compare Baudrillard 1981: 31–3, 75–8 with Cheal 1986: 429–32, 1987a, and with the critique of Veblen in this volume).

2 The problem of the universality of the family posed in functional theory is not only an empirical question about the relations between structures and their functions, it is above all a question of definition. A classic illustration of this point can be found in Weigert and Thomas's analysis of the universality question. After a careful, logical discussion they arrived at a concept to which, they say, "we will somewhat arbitrarily apply the label 'family' " (Weigert and Thomas 1971: 193). In that "arbitrary" decision lies a host of unstated assumptions about words and life, and the relations between the two (see especially Flandrin 1979: 4–9; Leonard and Speakman 1986). As this example illustrates, the key concepts used in sociology are always culture-bound to some degree. It is therefore necessary to pay explicit attention in theory construction to the fact that social theories are ultimately grounded in the linguistic usages and shared meanings of some society or subculture (Winch 1958; Coulter 1979; Cheal 1980).

3 Recent Marxist theorizing on family and gender has often employed a functionalist logic, as a number of commentators have noted (Bruegel 1978; Kuhn 1978; Barrett and McIntosh 1982; Harris 1983; Elliot 1986). It has therefore retraced the familiar set of difficulties arising from the indeterminacy of social needs, which had earlier been demonstrated with respect to structural functionalism (Cheal 1975). This reworking of old ground under new slogans is perhaps one of the most distressing signs of the contemporary crisis in sociological theory (see especially Pedraza-Bailey 1982; J. H. Turner 1986).

4 For recent discusssions of social constructionism and social constructivism see Delia, O'Keefe, and O'Keefe (1982), Mehan (1982), Thomason (1982), Gergen (1985), and Harré (1986). See also Cheal (1988c).

5 It is worth pointing out, by way of comparison with Foucauldian discourse theory, that neither Mrs Rose nor any of the other people interviewed in the Winnipeg Ritual Cycle Study sought to legitimate their family practices with reference to the professional ideologies emphasized, for example, by Donzelot (1979). Whatever influence medical and psychoanalytic ideologies may have had upon state policies in Canada, they have not been extensively incorporated into the routine accounts of everyday family life used by most people in Winnipeg, even by those of them who have been trained in social work (see the

case study of Colleen Williams below). The reasons for this interesting state of affairs have not been explored here, but they may have something to do with the fact that although professional ideologies can be designed for the rationalization of interpersonal relations, they are not well-suited to the legitimation of systems of long-term relationships. Put simply, professional ideologies are open to continuous revision on the basis of new forms of technical knowledge, and so they cannot present even the appearance of stability that is achieved in invented traditions (see pp. 80–1). It can be argued that it is especially important for professional ideologies to avoid the *appearance* of stability, even when at the same time occupational closure is enforced through rigid professional practices.

6 The commonsense ideology of familism described here has been the basis for much psychological theorizing about family relations, such as "attachment theory" (Cicirelli 1983a, 1983b). According to this theory attachment is understood as an emotional or affectional bond between two people that is formed early in life and which typically persists throughout life. The sociological approach taken here is different. It begins with the fact that the persistence of sentiments itself has to be explained. From a constructivist point of view, attachment is a positively valued state (in oneself and in others) within intimate relationships, which actors must work to maintain through the management of emotions. The interpersonal rituals performed on special occasions such as Christmas are examples of this attachment work.

7 Analogizing about modern societies is the temptation to which all elementarist theories eventually fall prey. It consists of drawing an analogy between complex events and selected phenomena in simpler societies which are better understood and for which more powerful models are available. This can be seen on a grand scale in Pamela Shurmer's claims that the preoccupations of individuals in potlatching, New Guinea pig exchanges, and the Kula trade in the Trobriand Islands are power, prestige, political alliance, indebtedness, speculation, and brinkmanship, and that "all this applies to [gift giving in] our own societies just as much as to New Guinea or to Indian potlatching" (Shurmer 1971: 1242).

The attraction of the analogical mode of theory construction is that it enables social scientists to draw broad conclusions with relative ease. If the models are well-chosen, this can lead to significant advances in the prediction of some aspects of the phenomena under investigation. However, a facile transposition of models from one social system to another cannot be justified. The analogical method ultimately suffers from the disadvantage that an analogue model can only handle those features of the subject under investigation which are indeed similar to the system from which the model was abstracted. Features of the subject which are peculiar to local socio-temporal conditions must be described in some other way, through grounded theory (Glaser and Strauss 1967).

8 The relevance of structural functional family models for understanding the moral economies of advanced industrial societies would seem to have declined during the past three decades. In particular, fewer people are now living in co-resident nuclear families, and that trend seems likely to continue (Kobrin 1976; Wargon 1979: 40–2; Harris 1983: 218–19; Glick 1984). Feminist critics (for example, Eichler 1981; Thorne 1982), and others (for example, Cheal 1987c) have questioned the dominance of concepts of family functioning in mainstream social theory. It is especially necessary at the present time to describe the intimate ties of women living non-traditional life styles. This includes single women living in non-family households, such as Anne Baker whose case was discussed in chapter 3, as well as women living alone, such as Margaret Rose and Colleen Williams whose cases have been examined in some detail in this chapter.

The epistemological position taken here is that for sociology (as opposed to other forms of social thought) these life styles, and any others, are not to be understood as "deviant" or as "liberated," although they are "alternative." The analysis presented here follows the structural method of theorizing transformations, whose utility has been demonstrated elsewhere (Cheal 1983). A variety of life styles are presented in this monograph as consequences of the same underlying system of rules and resources for constructing relationships as that which is employed in the "normal" family.

9 See, for example, Colin Turnbull's account of the Ik (Turnbull 1972).

10 It should be clear that the approach taken here follows the common distinction drawn between family and household (Yanagisako 1979; Elliot 1986: 4).

11 The concept of "plausibility structure" was introduced into sociology by Berger. It refers to the social base which reproduces a social world by ensuring its subjective plausibility as a fact of life. This state of affairs is brought about by the systematic provision of experiences in everyday life which confirm the reality of that social world. Since any event may be experienced in a number of different ways, plausibility structures depend crucially for their effects upon the continuous mutual definition of experiences in the closed interaction ritual chains of dense social networks. In a pluralistic mass society the most effective plausibility structures are therefore segregated subsocieties (groups or communities) whose closure is the result of a continuous, conscious attention to the boundaries between inner and outer worlds. The private nuclear family is one such plausibility structure. (See P. Berger 1967: 45, 48–9, 133–4).

5 Social reproduction

1 Sociological theory has had little to say about altruism. An attempt to rethink this problem in non-functionalist terms, and in response to developments in other disciplines, has been made in Cheal (1988c).

2 The redundant nature of gift giving (and thus its relatively high degree

of autonomy from functional determination) as theorized in this volume is confirmed empirically in American investigations of consumer behavior. Levels of gift expenditure have been reported to be surprisingly sensitive to changes in the level of total consumption among the elderly, and among the retired elderly in particular, by comparison with younger age groups (Chen and Chu 1982; McConnel and Deljavan 1983). It would appear that gift purchases are highest among those with relatively large financial resources, as we should expect (Cheal 1986), *and* with fewer domestic and occupational needs that limit the uses to which they must put their resources.

3 Certain implications of the distinction between personal and social relations *within* intimate relationships have been described elsewhere (Cheal 1986).

4 The shorthand descriptive terms used for these categories refer to the following things:

Food: All foodstuffs other than confectionery and purchased meals eaten away from home.

Drink: Alcoholic beverages.

Candy: Confectionery.

Food and drink equipment: Equipment for eating and drinking – includes china, glassware, dinnerware, serving ware, and cutlery.

Food preparation equipment: Includes kitchen utensils and appliances, other food equipment, dining and kitchen linens.

Household essentials: Includes furniture, soft furnishings, bathroom furnishings, bedroom furnishings, tools, clocks, calendars, etc.

Decorative household objects: Includes art work, crafts, ornaments, silverware, crystalware, candles, etc.

Decorative vegetation: Flowers, plants, and wreaths.

Day clothing: Daytime attire in regular use – includes outer clothing, footwear, hats, etc. for everyday activities.

Night clothing: Evening and nighttime attire for domestic relaxation and sleeping.

Other clothing: Includes underwear, fabrics for home-made clothing, sports clothes, etc.

Play equipment: Includes dolls, stuffed animals, toys, games equipment.

Reading equipment: Books, magazines, newspapers.

Relaxation equipment and services: smoking utensils, restaurant meals, theater tickets, audio-visual equipment, records, tapes, joke gifts, etc.

Activities equipment and services: Includes hobbies equipment, arts and crafts equipment, sports equipment, sports club memberships, travel equipment, yard and garden equipment, photographic equipment, musical equipment, etc.

Personal accessories: Personal equipment in regular use – includes watches, pens, calculators, stationery, bags, purses, wallets, etc.

Body adornments: Includes jewellery, corsages, etc.

Body preparation equipment: Body care and body decoration items – includes toiletries, babycare equipment, cosmetics, razors, perfumes, lotions, etc.

Money: Cash, cheques, vouchers.

Personal relations media: Media for keeping in touch with significant others – telephone calls, telegrams, trips, photographs.

Miscellaneous: Other goods and services.

5 The fact that almost two-thirds of wedding gifts in Winnipeg consist of money has been confirmed by a city-wide random sample survey with 573 respondents. In the 1984 Winnipeg Area Study 65 per cent of wedding gift donors reported money as their sole or principal gift at the most recent wedding for which they had given something to the bride and groom.

6 Caplow has claimed that the giving of candy such as chocolate eggs and rabbits at Easter is consistent with a description of that occasion as one in which the "particularizing" of relationships is unimportant (Caplow *et al.* 1982: 238–40). He has stated that:

> These [things] may be given by anyone to anyone. The giving recognizes that there is a relationship, but it does not specify the kind of relationship. All relationships become more or less equivalent, because complementary social roles, such as parent and child or teacher and pupil, are blurred or ignored. The theme of these activities is clearly opposed to the theme of Christmas.
>
> (Caplow *et al.* 1982: 239–40)

The plausibility of Caplow's argument (and the model of a cultural system of segregated meanings from which it is derived) is undermined by his own observation that candy is a typical gift on Valentine's Day (Caplow *et al.* 1982: 237). The evidence from the Winnipeg Ritual Cycle Study shows that candy is by far the most typical gift on Valentine's Day, which is an occasion when emotional significance is undeniably assigned to particular relationships.

7 The difference between the number of guests (approximately 115) and the number of recorded transactions (65) is due to the fact that a few women gave monetary contributions but no goods, while other women pooled their resources to purchase joint gifts.

8 The reasons for this narrow research focus are no doubt due in part to the connections between the study of informal social supports and social policy issues, and through them the funding programs of government agencies (see, for example, Wenger 1984; Cohen and Syme 1985; Sarason and Sarason 1985; Wellman and Hall 1986; Finch 1987).

9 The variations around this theme have been considerable, and the underlying unity of approach has not always been acknowledged. Prominent resource flow models of interpersonal relations have included the "resource theory" of family power relationships (Blood and Wolfe 1960), and discussions of "aid" in extended families (C. Bell 1968, 1971) and of "informal social support systems" or "support

networks" in communities (Craven and Wellman 1973; Wellman *et al.* 1973; Stephens *et al.* 1978; Cantor 1979; Lee 1985).
10 For important recent discussions of the distinction between expressive interaction and instrumental interaction, and the connections between them, see Cancian (1985, 1986). Cancian has made the valuable point that the sexual division of labor, and the consequent separation of public and private spheres, has resulted in the feminization of love as an expressive relational style.

6 Intimacy and community

1 My purpose here is not to question the reality of affections. Rather, our interest is in the ecology of interpersonal constructs. The approach taken here therefore follows that of Goffman, who pointed out that questions concerning the real sincerity or insincerity of actors are less important than questions about the nature of sincerity as a property of systems of action (Goffman 1959: 70–1).
2 An ideology of love is not the only possible solution to the problem of the synchronization of life plans. The major alternative, which would seem to be the dominant notion in Japanese civilization, is an ideology of indebtedness (Befu 1967, 1974; Lebra 1969, 1976; Johnson 1974, 1977). It will already be apparent from the case studies presented above that in Winnipeg transactions which might create indebtedness are either avoided or redefined in such a way that their social-psychological effects are minimized. The reasons for that state of affairs are not entirely clear, but are probably related to the culture of individualism in western civilization discussed below (pp. 142ff.). This point is worth emphasizing because it is always necessary in empirical investigations to take into account the historically conditioned forms of different societies. The more general point for sociology is that culturally distinctive features of selected societies should not be confused with a supposedly universal system of industrial capitalism (see also Blumer 1960; Cheal 1978b). That point has been made repeatedly in recent historical and theoretical work on western family life, as summarized by Barrett:

> [Although] it is difficult to establish that capitalism itself requires, and so constructed, a realm of privatized family and personal life, it certainly appears to be the case that the bourgeoisie as a class articulated this ideology very strongly. I would suggest that it is more useful to pose these arguments in terms of a struggle between the familial ideology of the emergent bourgeoisie and the practices of other classes, than in terms of a strictly necessary logic of capitalism.
> (Barrett 1980: 202)

3 The practical importance of life-course planning (and therefore life-course management) in modern social life has recently been restated (Elder 1984: 107–9 especially). See also Cheal (1987c).
4 Adorno's critique of Veblen is unexpected, because in other hands

critical theory has been receptive to the latter's rejection of consumerism (see the discussion in Kellner 1983). However, the goal of early
critical theory was to insist that the advanced capitalist societies must
be theorized on their own terms, as constituting a unique type of social
system in which social processes, like prisms, have more than one
face. It is for this reason that Adorno considered Veblen's approach to
be unsatisfactory, as we can see in the following selected quotations:

> [Veblen] confronts society with its own principle of utility and
> proves to it that according to this principle culture is both a waste
> and a swindle, so irrational that it raises doubts about the rationality
> of the whole system. . . . The concepts of the useful and the useless
> presupposed in such thinking are not subjected to analysis. Veblen
> demonstrates that society functions uneconomically in terms of its
> own criteria. This is both much and little; much, because he thus
> glaringly illuminates the unreason of reason, little, because he fails
> to grasp the interdependence of the useful and the useless. . . . As
> economist he is all too sovereign in his treatment of culture, cutting
> it from the budget as waste. . . . He fails to see that its legitimacy
> or illegitimacy can be decided only through insight into society as
> a totality. . . . The deceptive images of uniqueness in an era of
> mass production are only vestiges for him, not responses to highly
> industrialized mechanization which betray something of its essence.
> The world of these images, which Veblen unmasks as that of
> conspicuous consumption, is a synthetic, "imaginary" world. It
> represents the futile but compulsive attempt to avoid the loss of
> experience involved in modern modes of production and escape the
> domination of abstract equivalence through self-made concretion.
> Men prefer to deceive themselves with illusions of the concrete
> rather than abandon the hope which clings to it. . . . Luxury has a
> dual character. Veblen concentrates his spotlight on one side of it:
> that part of the social product which . . . is squandered in order to
> preserve an obsolete system. The other side of luxury is the use of
> parts of the social product which serve not the reproduction of
> expended labour, directly or indirectly, but of man in so far as he
> is not entirely under the sway of the utility principle.
>
> (Adorno 1981: 83–6)

It should be apparent by now that it is with the reproduction of
"man," and therefore with the actions of men and women when they
are not entirely under the sway of the utility principle, that we are
most concerned in this volume.

5 Critics of the approach taken in this volume may wonder if I have
merely reversed Veblen's emphasis, and subordinated the analysis of
substantive values to the analysis of ceremonial values in a theory that
equally fails to describe the dialectical relationship between culture and
action. That such is not the case can be seen in my account of the
dialectic of intimacy (Cheal 1987a) in which it is shown that the

probabilities of ceremonial acts of various kinds are heavily conditioned by the substantive values of an hegemonic market economy.

6 Using gifts to make claims about social status may be more common among men than among women, in which case the sex-biased sample in the Winnipeg Ritual Cycle Study would have an effect upon the results reported below. In my opinion that is unlikely to invalidate our test of Veblen's thesis, since women, too, engage in status rivalry through gift giving, particularly at events such as the hall shower described above. What is most apparent is that observations about rivalrous male giving are derived almost entirely from public forms of giving, such as philanthropic donations (see, for example, Schwartz 1967: 2). Rivalrous female giving, on the other hand, occurs mainly at segregated occasions which have been neglected by the social sciences and about which we know very little. Any final judgment about the effects of sex bias in this case must therefore wait upon a comparative knowledge of men's worlds and women's worlds within the gift economy.

7 There is a point to be made here about the structure of attention, and by implication about the sociology of knowledge. Valuable gifts can be used to attract attention to personal wealth, and thus to make claims for social status, only because they are rare. If they were not rare they would obviously be just like any other gift and they could not succeed as marks of distinction. For the same reason valuable gifts which stand out against the background of social life have become the basis for most social theories of the gift economy. It is because of their extraordinary visibility, and not because they are truly indicative, that extravagant gifts have received so much attention from social scientists. The effects of this bias are most pernicious where the data are apocryphal (see, for example, Douglas and Isherwood 1979: 59).

8 The interpersonal financial value transferred per gift transaction has been calculated by weighting the total financial value of each transaction by the number of givers and receivers involved in the transaction, according to the following formula: $\dfrac{1}{T(P+1)}$ where T = ego's transactors (that is, the person or persons to whom the gift was given) and P = ego's partners (that is, the person or persons, if any, with whom the gift was given).

9 It might be surmised that since the major part of giving is from 2 or more persons acting together, predatory giving could take the form of rivalry between corporate groups (especially kinship groups) as found in some tribal societies. That cannot be the case here since only 13 per cent of gifts are from 4 or more people acting in concert. The overwhelming majority of gifts (four-fifths) are given by 1 or 2 persons. They are, in other words, interpersonal gifts between individuals and couples and not group gifts (see Table 8.1).

10 The corollary of this point is that the power of advertising executives as "captains of consciousness" (Ewen 1976; Ewen and Ewen 1982)

would seem to have been considerably overrated in much contemporary critical theory. Among the occasions for gift giving in Winnipeg, Father's Day is the only one that can be unambiguously identified as a commercial creation largely unsupported by other social institutions. It is therefore worth pointing out that Father's Day is not a popular occasion with everyone. It is far less important than Mother's Day, both with respect to the volume of gifts (Table 4.1) and the costliness of gifts (Table 6.2). One conclusion to be drawn from these observations is that the sociology of reference groups (Shibutani 1955), is likely to be of greater value for the social history of the twentieth century than the Marxian media studies.

11 For a Durkheimian analysis of the social value of rituals performed for the ancestors see Swanson (1960).

7 Gift games

1 Money is one of the most important cultural constructs in capitalist society. The pursuit and possession of money, the benefits derived from it, and the deprivations suffered from the lack of it have all been intensively studied. The interactional uses of money, on the other hand, have received comparatively little attention, and sociological discussions of money have tended to be metaphysical in nature (see, for example, Simmel 1978; Smelt 1980). We have been too much concerned with the essence of money, and not concerned enough with situated variations in its usage. The study of variations is important if we are to understand the social organization of economic relations under different historical conditions. Cutler and his colleagues have suggested that sociologists should be less concerned with what money represents and more concerned with "the analysis of the concrete conditions under which money exists, the form it takes, and the role it performs under particular conditions" (Cutler *et al.* 1978: 14). What is most needed, however, is not more grand theory but knowledge of transactions drawn from field research. For some pertinent remarks on this point by an anthropologist see Crump (1981). For work on the psychology of money see Furnham and Lewis (1986).

2 The implications of that conclusion for sociology may be illuminated by comparing Smith (1973) and Cheal (1987a). In the one case the semiotics of consumption is seen as being legislated by corporations, and in the other it is seen as the unintended outcome of pragmatic decisions made by individuals acting within an environment of late capitalist consumerism.

3 *Ofrecijo* is one of several local names for this practice (Brandes 1973: 73).

4 Klymasz's investigations were concentrated in the Dauphin area of Manitoba, the Yorkton area of Saskatchewan, and the Vegreville area of Alberta.

5 In an open and pluralistic urban environment, like that of contemporary Winnipeg, many social meanings are likely to be problematic

and relative. That is particularly true for meanings derived from ethnic cultures, which can be taken for granted as unquestionable routines only in a context of residential and occupational segregation (see, for example, Suttles 1968). That does not mean that ethnic meaning systems must disappear in the absence of social separation. They may continue to exist so long as a number of culture carriers remain in contact with each other (Fischer 1975: 1325–6). It does mean, however, that few subcultural patterns of behavior will be regarded as the only possible ways to act (P. Berger and Luckmann 1966: 115; P. Berger 1967: 150–1). When group boundaries break down a variety of schemas become psychologically available as alternatives between which individuals can choose. Furthermore, the experience of choice as a fundamental condition of existence frequently leads to the realization that other options can be made available through acts of individual creation.

In isolated rural communities social forms drawn from ethnic cultures may be part of a coherent normative order. In cities, however, we are less likely to find such customs than we are to find reworked "traditions" which define how a social occasion is to be constructed, for those who happen to have an interest in doing so. These "recipes" are part of the individual's stock of knowledge, available for use on occasions to which they are deemed relevant. In this way individuals are able, within the limits of the negotiated expectations of significant others, to take up and adapt social forms derived from various groups as they construct lines of action to suit their purposes at hand. These practices make social life possible, and are therefore valued "traditions." At the same time their authentication is only conditional and provisional, and they cannot prevent innovative and unconventional interaction patterns from emerging.

Faced with this apparently chaotic situation, with its seemingly endless individual variations, it has sometimes been assumed that the principal characteristic of urban life is the absence of a framework of meanings (Durkheim 1964b: 297–301). Urban life may, however, be construed as a dialectical order of choices and means–end relations. One of the tasks of urban sociology is to identify the cultural ecology at work in such situations, as I have attempted to do here.

6 In the 1984 Winnipeg Area Study's random sample survey 90 per cent of those expressing an opinion (78 per cent of the total sample) stated that *presentation* weddings had become more common during the last ten years. That finding is particularly interesting in relation to the pluralistic ethnic composition of Winnipeg. In the 1984 survey the most popular self-designation of ethnic identity was simply Canadian. Those identifying themselves in this way comprised 38.5 per cent of the sample. Other notable self-identifications were: English, Scottish, or British 9.7 per cent; Ukrainian 7.2 per cent; French or French-Canadian 5.4 per cent; German 4 per cent. No other ethnic identity was cited by more than 3 per cent of the respondents.

7 The observation that opposed ritual preferences sometimes *provoke* tensions within families leads to a different conclusion about the place

of ritual in mass societies than that preferred by Caplow and his colleagues. They have claimed that the social uses of ritual lie in the fact that "ritual is concentrated on those aspects of a society that are at risk, so to speak, because of conflict or contradiction and loss of credibility." Their discussion continues as follows:

> If we think of society, or culture, as a system of variously interrelated ideas, rather than as a collection of interacting people, we can better understand that what is meant here is not a risk to individual relationships or political credibility but rather the risks created by tension between opposing fundamental cultural ideas. It is impossible for a system of cultural ideas to be free of contradictions, but the acceptability of such a system is diminished by a burden of obvious contradiction. Herein lies the risk. If the tension is so great that the members of the society become aware of it, they will reject as fallacious some or all of the ideas involved, with the result that the society becomes anomic. In an extreme case, its members would hold no common fundamental principles, no "self-evident truths," on which to base their behavior and their judgments. Such a situation clearly would be intolerable. We assume that rituals avert the threat to institutional survival by resolving the dilemmas created by conflicting values and by endowing the entire system with an aura of unimpeachable truth and virtue.
>
> (Caplow et al. 1982: 242–3)

This functionalist account of ritual (see also Eisenstadt 1956) is no longer tenable. Although interaction rituals are often used by individuals for purposes of *interpersonal* integration, they do not necessarily function to resolve strains in social systems, since ritual, too, is a locus of contradictions (Cheal 1987a). The change in ritual practices described in this chapter cannot be explained as a functional adaptation of the social system. Rather, it must be seen as the result of a dialectical process which sometimes places real strains upon relations between husbands and wives, and between parents and their children. Such strains are most typical of pluralistic societies such as Canada and the United States.

8 For an excellent critique of Mary Douglas's reliance upon boundary-marking models see Sahlins (1976: 117–20).

9 In Weber's terms symbolic gifts therefore belong to one or more of the following types of social action: value-rational action, that is, action that is determined by a conscious belief in the value "for its own sake" of some ethical, religious, etc. principle; affectual action, that is action that is determined by the actor's emotions or feeling states; traditional action, that is, action that is habitual (Weber 1968: 24–5).

10 It will be recalled from Chapter 6 that the hypothesis that symbolic gifts are of only nominal financial value was used to help explain variations in gift outlays between occasions. We see here that the same logic is used within an occasion, to set a low maximum value for what would otherwise be defined as a costly good.

8 The social future

1 For recent discussions of individualism see especially Macfarlane (1979) and Abercrombie, Hill, and Turner (1986).

2 The simplified description of Durkheim's argument presented here ignores the singular position of marriage within the modern institution of the family, which Durkheim came to refer to as the conjugal family (Durkheim 1978). See below (pp. 105ff.)

3 Durkheim believed that the cult of the individual was ultimately a destructive force, leading to the "dissolution of society":

> If it turns all wills towards the same end, this end is not social. It thus occupies a completely exceptional place in the collective conscience. It is still from society that it takes all its force, but it is not to society that it attaches us; it is to ourselves. Hence, it does not constitute a true social link.
>
> (Durkheim 1964a: 172)

In claiming that the cult of the individual has no part to play in the reproduction of social life he was certainly wrong. His mistake was to assume (in this passage, if not elsewhere) that the only social attachments are those to society, that is, to macrostructures. That argument overlooks the possibility of interpersonal attachments, and therefore the importance of microstructures (Cheal 1988b). It can be argued, as I have done elsewhere (Cheal 1988a), that any decline in the structuring of the life course at a macrolevel is likely to have been accompanied by its restructuring at microlevels. There is little evidence to suggest that the members of modern societies have lost interest in having predictable social futures. On the contrary, increased longevity is likely to have increased the salience of those relationships, such as kinship ties, that have the longest terms (Riley 1983).

4 We must be very clear about what exactly this statement means, and what it does not mean. It means that the possibilities for developing, and the consequences for everyday life of having, bonds of attachment, sentimentality, sociability, and economic cooperation are greater in conditions of high presence-availability than they are in conditions of low presence-availability. It does not mean that the nuclear family household is an adaptive system for meeting individuals' developmental needs. We shall see below that it is possible for a nuclear family relationship to have high levels of presence-availability and economic cooperation together with low levels of attachment and sentimentality, where one member feels that some, but not all, of her personal needs are being met.

One of the problems with the structural-functional theory of the family has been the tendency to assume that the elemental social bonds of presence-availability, attachment, sentimentality, sociability, and economic cooperation are all positive, and are positively combined, within the family (nuclear or extended). Eichler has pointed out that it is necessary to deconstruct this monolithic model of "the family" by conceiving of familial interactions as consisting of a number of theoretically independent dimensions of social life (Eichler 1981). It is that logic of analysis which has been followed here (although not her method, which is insufficiently general).

5 Durkheim's prediction that occupational organizations would replace families as the bases for social continuity was in fact a conditional statement. For that to come about, he said, the form of the occupational organization would first have to be reconstituted.

> By this we do not mean that it must necessarily be made obligatory, but the important thing is for it to be so constituted as to play a social role instead of expressing only various combinations of particular interests. This is not all. For the frame not to remain empty, all the germs of life of such a nature as to flourish there must find their places in it.
>
> (Durkheim 1951: 379)

In his view, occupational organizations would have to be transformed from political economies of interest advancement into moral economies of social reproduction before they could have a truly general function in social life. As we now know, that did not happen.

6 Durkheim's concept of the sacred has become so famous that it is often forgotten how he concluded that the sacred alone could not be a satisfactory criterion for religion. He summarized his position as follows:

> Thus we arrive at the following definition: *A religion is a unified system of beliefs and practices relative to sacred things, that is to say, things set apart and forbidden – beliefs and practices which unite into one single moral community called a Church, all those who adhere to them.* The second element which thus finds a place in our definition is no less essential than the first; for by showing that the idea of religion is inseparable from that of the Church, it makes it clear that religion should be an eminently collective thing.
>
> (Durkheim 1947: 47)

Goffman has been the most influential sociologist who appropriated Durkheim's concept of the sacred for his own use (see chapter 1, note 4), but who simultaneously ignored his concept of the moral community. That decision had important consequences for Goffman's own work, and through him upon the sociology of interaction rituals. The present study has therefore attempted to introduce into the sociology of interaction rituals that half of Durkheim's theory of religion which Goffman left out.

7 Turner's justly acclaimed *communitas* model of ritual (1969) is therefore a special case of the general theory outlined here. My intellectual debt to Turner's model has been described in detail elsewhere (Cheal 1988a).

8 Degradation ceremonies in initiation rites for brides in England (see Westwood 1984: 115–16) appear to have similar symbolic effects to

certain features of bridal showers in Canada in asserting the power of female communities over their members.

9 Conclusion

1 The rejection of Gregory's and Collins' energy flow models of society does not mean that we should stop investigating the flows of social objects between social actors. On the contrary, the justification for transactional sociology is precisely that there is much to be learned about social life from studying how positively valued objects move. However, there are two important reasons why a transactional sociology grounded in the theory of action is to be preferred to energy flow models. Firstly, the metaphorical use of concepts such as emotional charge obscures the fact that the objects which circulate are utilities and symbols, for which particular methods of analysis are required (see, for example, Cheal 1987a). Secondly, it is important to recognize (as I implied in an earlier comment on Collins – chapter 2, note 2) that "social energy" does not usually flow in an undirected process of contagion (see especially Collins 1981a). Socially valued objects normally flow along well-defined paths within identifiable systems of social organization. The process by which transaction paths are constructed is the process of institutionalization, as demonstrated in chapter 3. The consequence of that process is social closure, as described in this chapter.

2 Eichler has claimed that the connection between women's domestic labor and female love within the nuclear family is due to the economic dependence of non-employed housewives upon their husbands. Personal dependence has asymmetric consequences for affective relations, she has argued, so that, "For the dependent, the attitudes considered proper are a mixture of gratitude, awe, obedience, submissiveness, loyalty, and love" (Eichler 1973: 49).

3 Overing (1986) has suggested that the notion of separate spheres of public and private activities cannot capture the complexity of gender relations in primitive societies either. For relevant ethnographic materials on rituals among Aboriginal women in Australia see Bell (1983).

4 The comparative concepts of political economy and moral economy that have been used here have certain similarities to the concepts of system integration and social integration adopted by Habermas (1975: 4–5). In Habermas's usage social integration refers to life worlds which are symbolically organized, which may include ritualization. The differences between Habermas's views on ritual and those outlined in this study deserve a separate discussion.

5 On the concept of relational culture see Wood (1982).

References

Abercrombie, N., Hill, S., and Turner, B. (1986) *Sovereign Individuals of Capitalism*, London: Allen & Unwin.

Adorno, T. (1978) *Minima Moralia*, London: Verso.
(1981) *Prisms*, Cambridge, Mass.: MIT Press.

Aguilar, J. (1984) "Trust and exchange: expressive and instrumental dimensions of reciprocity in a peasant community," *Ethos* 12 (1): 3–29.

Alba, R. (1982) "Taking stock of network analysis," in S. Bacharach (ed.) *Research in the Sociology of Organizations*, vol. 1, Greenwich, CT: JAI Press.

American Council of Learned Societies (1969) *Surnames in the United States Census of 1790*, Baltimore: Genealogical Publishing Co.

Argyle, M. (1984) "The components of long-term relationships," in K. Lagerspetz and P. Niemi (eds) *Psychology in the 1990s*, Amsterdam: North-Holland.

Argyle, M. and Henderson, M. (1985) "The rules of relationships," in S. Duck and D. Perlman (eds) *Understanding Personal Relationships*, London: Sage.

Askham, J. (1984) *Identity and Stability in Marriage*, Cambridge: Cambridge University Press.

Balakrishnan, T. (1976) "Ethnic residential segregation in the metropolitan areas of Canada," *Canadian Journal of Sociology* 1 (4): 481–98.
(1982) "Changing patterns of ethnic residential segregation in the metropolitan areas of Canada," *Canadian Review of Sociology and Anthropology* 19 (1): 92–110.

Barker, D. (1972) "Young people and their homes: spoiling and 'keeping close' in a South Wales town," *Sociological Review* 20 (4): 569–90.
(1978) "A proper wedding," in M. Corbin (ed.) *The Couple*, Harmondsworth: Penguin.

Barnes, J. (1967) "Genealogies," in A. L. Epstein (ed.) *The Craft of Social Anthropology*, London: Tavistock.
(1969) "Networks and political process," in J. C. Mitchell (ed.) *Social Networks in Urban Situations*, Manchester: Manchester University Press.

Barrett, M. (1980) *Women's Oppression Today*, London: Verso.

Barrett, M. and McIntosh, M. (1982) *The Anti-social Family*, London: Verso.

Baudrillard, J. (1975) *The Mirror of Production*, St. Louis: Telos.
(1981) *For a Critique of the Political Economy of the Sign*, St. Louis: Telos.

Beechey, V. (1985) "Familial ideology," in V. Beechey and J. Donald (eds) *Subjectivity and Social Relations*, Milton Keynes: Open University Press.

Befu, H. (1967) "Gift-giving and social reciprocity in Japan," *France-Asie* 21 (188): 161–77.

(1968) "Gift-giving in a modernizing Japan," *Monumenta Nipponica* 23 (3–4): 445–6.

(1974) "Power in exchange: strategy of control and patterns of compliance in Japan," *Asian Profile* 2 (6): 601–22.

Belk, R. (1979) "Gift-giving behavior," in J. Sheth (ed.) *Research in Marketing*, vol. 2, Greenwich, CT: JAI Press.

Bell, C. (1968) "Mobility and the middle class extended family," *Sociology* 2 (2): 173–84.

(1971) "Occupational career, family cycle and extended family relations," *Human Relations* 24 (6): 463–75.

Bell, C. and Newby, H. (1976) "Husbands and wives: the dynamics of the deferential dialectic," in D. L. Barker and S. Allen (eds) *Dependence and Exploitation in Work and Marriage*, London: Longman.

Bell, D. (1983) *Daughters of the Dreaming*, Melbourne: McPhee Gribble/ Allen & Unwin.

Bleshaw, C. (1965) *Traditional Exchange and Modern Markets*, Englewood Cliffs: Prentice-Hall.

Benn, S. and Gaus, G. (1983) "The public and the private: concepts and action," in S. Benn and G. Gaus (eds) *Public and Private in Social Life*, London: Croom Helm.

Bennett, J. (1968) "Reciprocal economic exchanges among North American agricultural operators," *Southwestern Journal of Anthropology* 24 (3): 276–309.

Berg, E. (1987) "Feminist theory: moving sociology from the 'malestream,' " *Footnotes* 15 (3): 5, 11.

Berger, B. and Berger, P. (1983) *The War Over the Family*, Garden City: Doubleday.

Berger, C. and Bradac, J. (1982) *Language and Social Knowledge*, London: Edward Arnold.

Berger, P. (1967) *The Sacred Canopy*, New York: Doubleday.

Berger, P., Berger, B. and Kellner, H. (1973) *The Homeless Mind*, New York: Random House.

Berger, P. and Kellner, H. (1964) "Marriage and the construction of reality, *Diogenes* 46: 1–24.

Berger, P. and Luckmann, T. (1966) *The Social Construction of Reality*, New York: Doubleday.

Bernardes, J. (1985) " 'Family ideology': identification and exploration," *Sociological Review* 33 (2): 275–97.

Blau, P. (1964) *Exchange and Power in Social Life*, New York: Wiley.

Bloch, M. (1973) "The long term and the short term: the economic and political significance of the morality of kinship," in J. Goody (ed.) *The Character of Kinship*, London: Cambridge University Press.

Blood, R. and Wolfe, D. (1960) *Husbands and Wives*, New York: Free Press.

Blum, A. and McHugh, P. (1971) "The social ascription of motives," *American Sociological Review* 36 (1): 98–109.

Blumer, H. (1960) "Early industrialization and the laboring class," *Sociological Quarterly* 1 (1): 5–14.

—— (1969) *Symbolic Interactionism*, Englewood Cliffs: Prentice-Hall.

Bochner, A. (1984) "The functions of human communication in interpersonal bonding," in C. Arnold and J. W. Bowers (eds) *Handbook of Rhetorical and Communication Theory*, Boston: Allyn & Bacon.

Boholm, A. (1983) *Swedish Kinship*, Göteborg: Acta Universitatis Gothoburgensis.

Bott, E. (1957) *Family and Social Network*, London: Tavistock.

Botting, H. and Botting, G. (1984) *The Orwellian World of Jehovah's Witnesses*, Toronto: University of Toronto Press.

Bourdieu, P. (1977) *Outline of a Theory of Practice*, Cambridge: Cambridge University Press.

—— (1979) *Algeria 1960*, Cambridge: Cambridge University Press.

Brandes, S. (1973) "Wedding ritual and social structure in a Castilian peasant village," *Anthropological Quarterly* 46 (2): 65–74.

Bruegel, I. (1978) "What keeps the family going?" *International Socialism* 2 (1): 2–15.

Bulmer, M. (1986) *Neighbours: The Work of Philip Abrams*, Cambridge: Cambridge University Press.

Burstyn, V. (1985) "Masculine dominance and the state," in V. Burstyn and D. Smith *Women, Class, Family and the State*, Toronto: Garamond.

Cancian, F. (1985) "Gender politics: love and power in the private and public spheres," in A. Rossi (ed.) *Gender and the Life Course*, New York: Aldine.

—— (1986) "The feminization of love," *Signs* 11 (4): 692–709,

Cantor, M. (1979) "The informal support system of New York's inner city elderly," in D. Gelfand and A. Kutzik (eds) *Ethnicity and Aging*, New York: Springer.

Caplow, T. (1982) "Christmas gifts and kin networks," *American Sociological Review* 47 (3): 383–92.

—— (1984) "Rule enforcement without visible means: Christmas gift giving in Middletown," *American Journal of Sociology* 89 (6): 1306–23.

Caplow, T., Bahr, H., Chadwick, B., Hill, R. and Holmes Williamson, M. (1982) *Middletown Families*, Minneapolis: University of Minnesota Press.

Caron, A. and Ward, S. (1975) "Gift decisions by kids and parents," *Journal of Advertising Research* 15 (4): 15–20.

Cheal, D. (1975) "Political radicalism and religion: competitors for commitment," *Social Compass* 12 (2): 245–59.

Cheal, D. (1978a) "Religion and the social order," *Canadian Journal of Sociology* 3 (1): 61–9.

Cheal, D. (1978b) "Models of mass politics in Canada," *Canadian Review of Sociology and Anthropology* 15 (3): 325–38.

Cheal, D. (1979) "Hegemony, ideology and contradictory consciousness," *Sociological Quarterly* 20 (1): 109–17.

Cheal, D. (1980) "Rule-governed behaviour," *Philosophy of the Social Sciences* 10 (1): 39–49.

Cheal, D. (1981) "Ontario loyalism: a socio-religious ideology in decline," *Canadian Ethnic Studies* 13 (2): 40–51.

Cheal, D. (1983) "Intergenerational family transfers," *Journal of Marriage and the Family* 45 (4): 805–13.

Cheal, D. (1984) "Transactions and transformational models," in N. K. Denzin (ed.) *Studies in Symbolic Interaction*, vol. 5, Greenwich CT: JAI Press.

Cheal, D. (1986) "The social dimensions of gift behavior," *Journal of Social and Personal Relationships* 3 (4): 423–39.

Cheal, D. (1987a) " 'Showing them you love them': gift giving and the dialectic of intimacy," *Sociological Review* 35 (1): 150–69.

Cheal, D. (1987b) "The private and the public: the linkage role of religion revisited," *Review of Religious Research* 28 (3): 209–23.

Cheal, D. (1987c) "Intergenerational transfers," in A. Bryman, B. Bytheway, P. Allatt, and T. Keil (eds) *Rethinking the Life Cycle*, London: Macmillan.

Cheal, D. (1988a) "Relationships in time: ritual, social structure and the life course," in N. K. Denzin (ed.) *Studies in Symbolic Interaction*, vol. 9, Greenwich CT: JAI Press.

Cheal, D. (1988b) "Women together: bridal showers and gender membership," in B. J. Risman and P. Schwartz (eds) *Gender in Intimate Relations*, Belmont, CA: Wadsworth.

Cheal, D. (1988c) "Theories of serial flow in intergenerational transfers," *International Journal of Aging and Human Development* 26 (4): 181–93.

Chen, Y-P. and Chu, K-W. (1982) "Household expenditure patterns," *Journal of Family Issues* 3 (2): 233–50.

Chodorow, N. (1978) *The Reproduction of Mothering*, Berkeley: University of California Press.

Cicirelli, V. (1983a) "Adult children and their elderly parents," in T. Brubaker (ed.) *Family Relationships in Later Life*, Beverly Hills: Sage.

(1983b) "Adult children's attachment and helping behavior to elderly parents," *Journal of Marriage and the Family* 45 (4): 815–25.

Clarke, J., Hall, S., Jefferson, T., and Roberts, B. (1976) "Subcultures, cultures and class," in S. Hall and T. Jefferson (eds) *Resistance Through Rituals*, London: Hutchinson.

Cohen, A. (1985) *The Symbolic Construction of Community*, London: Tavistock.

Cohen, S. and Syme, S. L. (eds) (1985) *Social Support and Health*, Orlando: Academic Press.

Collier, J., Rosaldo, M., and Yanagisako, S. (1982) "Is there a family? New anthropological views," in B. Thorne and M. Yalom (eds) *Rethinking the Family*, New York: Longman.

Collins, R. (1975) *Conflict Sociology*, New York: Academic Press.

(1980) "Erving Goffman and the development of modern social theory," in J. Ditton (ed.) *The View from Goffman*, London: Macmillan.

(1981a) "On the microfoundations of macrosociology," *American Journal of Sociology* 86 (5): 984–1014.

(1981b) "Micro-translation as a theory-building strategy," in K. Knorr-Cetina and A. Cicourel (eds) *Advances in Social Theory and Methodology*. Boston: Routledge & Kegan Paul.

(1985) *Three Sociological Traditions*, New York: Oxford University Press.

Coulter, J. (1979) *The Social Construction of Mind*, Totowa, NJ: Rowman & Littlefield.

Cramer, J. (1977) "Christmas: an American paradox," *Humboldt Journal of Social Relations* 5 (1): 2–25.

Craven, P. and Wellman, B., (1973) "The network city," *Sociological Inquiry* 43 (3/4): 57–88.

Crump, T. (1981) *The Phenomenon of Money*, London: Routledge & Kegan Paul.

Csikszentmihalyi, M. and Rochberg-Halton, E. (1981) *The Meaning of Things*, London: Cambridge University Press.

Cutler, A., Hindess, B., Hirst, P., and Hussain, A. (1978) *Marx's "Capital" and Capitalism Today*, vol. 2, London: Routledge & Kegan Paul.

Darcovich, W. (1980) "The statistical compendium," in W. R. Petryshyn (ed.) *Changing Realities*, Edmonton: Canadian Institute of Ukrainian Studies.

Davids, L. (1980) "Family change in Canada, 1971–1976," *Journal of Marriage and the Family* 42 (1): 177–83.

Davis, J. (1972) "Gifts and the U.K. economy," *Man* n.s. 7 (3): 408–29.

Davis, K. (1948) *Human Society*, New York: Macmillan.

Delia, J., O'Keefe, B., and O'Keefe, D. (1982) "The constructivist approach to communication," in F. Dance (ed.) *Human Communication Theory*, New York: Harper & Row.

Denzin, N. (1986) "Postmodern social theory," *Sociological Theory* 4 (2): 194–204.

di Leonardo, M. (1984) *The Varieties of Ethnic Experience*, Ithaca: Cornell University Press.

Donzelot, J. (1979) *The Policing of Families*, New York: Pantheon.

Douglas, J. (1971) *American Social Order*, Free Press: New York.

Douglas, M. and Isherwood, B. (1979) *The World of Goods*, New York: Basic.

Driedger, L. (1980) "Urbanization of Ukrainians in Canada," in W. R. Petryshyn (ed.) *Changing Realities*, Edmonton: Canadian Institute of Ukrainian Studies.

Duck, S. and Perlman, D. (1985) "The thousand islands of personal relationships," in S. Duck and D. Perlman (eds) *Understanding Personal Relationships*, London: Sage.

Dulude, L. (1984) *Love, Marriage and Money. . . . An Analysis of Financial Relations Between the Spouses*, Ottawa: Canadian Advisory Council on the Status of Women.

Durkheim, E. (1947) *The Elementary Forms of the Religious Life*, Glencoe: Free Press.

    (1951) *Suicide*, New York: Free Press.

    (1953) *Sociology and Philosophy*, London: Cohen & West.

    (1964a) *The Division of Labor in Society*, New York: Free Press.

    (1964b) *The Rules of Sociological Method*, New York: Free Press.

    (1978) "The conjugal family," in M. Traugott (ed.) *Emile Durkheim on Institutional Analysis*, Chicago: University of Chicago Press.

Eichler, M. (1973) "Women as personal dependents," in M. Stephenson (ed.) *Women in Canada*, Toronto: New Press.

    (1980) *The Double Standard*, New York: St. Martin's Press.

    (1981) "The inadequacy of the monolithic model of the family," *Canadian Journal of Sociology* 6 (3): 367–88.

Eisenstadt, S. N. (1956) "Ritualized personal relations," *Man* 56 (96): 90–5.

Eisenstadt, S. N. and Roniger, L. (1984) *Patrons, Clients and Friends*, Cambridge: Cambridge University Press.

Ekeh, P. (1982) "Structuralism, the principle of elementarism, and the theory of civilization," in I. Rossi (ed.) *Structural Sociology*, New York: Columbia University Press.

Elder, G. (1984) "Families, kin, and the life course: a sociological perspective," in R. Parke (ed.) *Review of Child Development Research*, vol. 7, Chicago: University of Chicago Press.

Elliot, F. R. (1986) *The Family*, Atlantic Highlands, NJ: Humanities Press.

Emerson, R. (1976) "Social exchange theory," in A. Inkeles (ed.) *Annual Review of Sociology*, vol. 2, Palo Alto, CA: Annual Reviews Inc.

    (1981) "Social exchange theory," in M. Rosenberg and R. Turner (eds) *Social Psychology*, New York: Basic.

Epstein, A. L. (1981) *Urbanization and Kinship*, London: Academic Press.

Ewen, S. (1976) *Captains of Consciousness*, New York: McGraw-Hill.

Ewen, S. and Ewen, E. (1982) *Channels of Desire*, New York: McGraw-Hill.

Finch, J. (1987) "Research note: the vignette technique in survey research," *Sociology* 21 (1): 105–14.

Firth, R. (1967) "Themes in economic anthropology," in R. Firth (ed.) *Themes in Economic Anthropology*, London: Tavistock.

Fischer, C. (1975) "Toward a subcultural theory of urbanism," *American Journal of Sociology* 80 (6): 1319–41.

    (1981) "The public and private worlds of city life," *American Sociological Review* 46 (3): 306–16.

    (1982) *To Dwell Among Friends*, Chicago: University of Chicago Press.

Flandrin, J-L. (1979) *Families in Former Times*, Cambridge: Cambridge University Press.

Fortes, M. (1969) "Introduction," in J. Goody (ed.) *The Developmental Cycle in Domestic Groups*, London: Cambridge University Press.

Fox, B. (1980) *Hidden in the Household*, Toronto: The Women's Press.

Fraser, N. (1985) "What's critical about critical theory? The case of Habermas and gender," *New German Critique* 35: 97–131.

Furnham, A. and Lewis, A. (1986) *The Economic Mind*, Brighton: Wheatsheaf.

Gamarnikow, E. and Purvis, J. (1983) "Introduction," in E. Gamarnikow, D. Morgan, J. Purvis, and D. Taylorson (eds) *The Public and the Private*, London: Heinemann.

Gergen, K. (1985) "The social constructionist movement in modern psychology," *American Psychologist* 40 (3): 266–75.

Gerson, J. and Peiss, K. (1985) "Boundaries, negotiation, consciousness: reconceptualizing gender relations," *Social Problems* 32 (4): 317–31.

Gerth, H. and Wright Mills, C. (1953) *Character and Social Structure*, New York: Harcourt, Brace, and World.

Giddens, A. (1976) *New Rules of Sociological Method*, London: Hutchinson.

    (1979) *Central Problems in Social Theory*, London: Macmillan.

    (1982) *Profiles and Critiques in Social Theory*, Berkeley: University of California Press.

    (1985) "Time, space and regionalisation," in D. Gregory and J. Urry (eds) *Social Relations and Spatial Structures*, New York: St. Martin's Press.

Glaser, B. and Strauss, A. (1967) *The Discovery of Grounded Theory*, Chicago: Aldine.

    (1971) *Status Passage*, Chicago: Aldine-Atherton.

Glick, P. (1984) "American household structure in transition," *Family Planning Perspectives* 16 (5): 205–11.

Goffman, E. (1959) *The Presentation of Self in Everyday Life*, New York: Doubleday.

    (1963) *Behavior in Public Places*, New York: Free Press.

    (1967) *Interaction Ritual*, Garden City: Doubleday.

    (1971) *Relations in Public*, New York: Basic.

    (1974) *Frame Analysis*, New York: Harper & Row.

    (1977) "The arrangement between the sexes," *Theory and Society* 4 (3): 301–31.

    (1979) *Gender Advertisements*, New York: Harper & Row,

    (1983) "The interaction order," *American Sociological Review* 48 (1): 1–17.

Goody, J. (1983) *The Development of the Family and Marriage in Europe*, Cambridge: Cambridge University Press.

Gouldner, A. (1960) "The norm of reciprocity," *American Sociological Review* 25 (2): 161–78.

    (1973) *For Sociology*, London: Allen Lane.

Granovetter, M. (1973) "The strength of weak ties," *American Journal of Sociology* 78 (6): 1360–80.

    (1985) "Economic action and social structure: the problem of embeddedness," *American Journal of Sociology* 91 (3): 481–510.

Gregory, C. A. (1982) *Gifts and Commodities*, London: Academic Press.

Haas, D. and Deseran, F. (1981) "Trust and symbolic exchange," *Social Psychology Quarterly* 44 (1): 3–13.

Habermas, J. (1970) "Towards a theory of communicative competence," *Inquiry* 13 (4): 360–75.

    (1975) *Legitimation Crisis*, Boston: Beacon.

(1984) *The Theory of Communicative Action, Vol. 1 Reason and the Rationalization of Society*, Boston: Beacon.

Hansen, K. (1981) " 'Black' exchange and its system of social control," in D. Willer and B. Anderson (eds) *Networks, Exchange and Coercion*, New York: Elsevier.

Hareven, T. (1980) "The life course and aging in historical perspective," in K. Back (ed.) *Life Course*, Boulder: Westview Press.

Harré, R. (1986) "An outline of the social constructionist viewpoint," in R. Harré (ed.) *The Social Construction of Emotions*, Oxford: Blackwell.

Harris, C. C. (1983) *The Family and Industrial Society*, London: Allen & Unwin.

Hartmann, H. (1981) "The family as the locus of gender, class, and political struggle: the example of housework," *Signs* 6 (3): 366–94.

Hartsock, N. (1983a) "The feminist standpoint: developing the ground for a specifically feminist historical materialism," in S. Harding and M. B. Hintikka (eds) *Discovering Reality*, Dordrecht: Reidel.

(1983b) *Money, Sex, and Power*, New York: Longman.

(1985) "Exchange theory," in S. G. McNall (ed.) *Current Perspectives in Social Theory*, vol. 6, Greenwich, CT: JAI Press.

Hausen, K. (1984) "Mothers, sons, and the sale of symbols and goods: the 'German Mother's Day,' " in H. Medick and D. Sabean (eds) *Interest and Emotion*, Cambridge: Cambridge University Press.

Hekman, S. (1983) *Weber, the Ideal Type, and Contemporary Social Theory*, Notre Dame: University of Notre Dame Press.

Hesse-Biber, S. and Williamson, J. (1984) "Resource theory and power in families," *Family Process* 23 (2): 261–78.

Hobsbawm, E. (1983) "Introduction: inventing traditions," in. E. Hobsbawm and T. Ranger (eds) *The Invention of Tradition*, Cambridge: Cambridge University Press.

Hobsbawm, E. and Ranger, T. (eds) (1983) *The Invention of Tradition*, Cambridge: Cambridge University Press.

Hochschild, A. (1979) "Emotion work, feeling rules, and social structure," *American Journal of Sociology* 85 (3): 551–75.

(in press) "The economy of gratitude," in D. Franks and E. Doyle McCarthy (eds) *The Sociology of Emotions*, Greenwich, CT: JAI Press.

Holton, R. (1986) "Talcott Parsons and the theory of economy and society," in R. Holton and B. Turner (eds) *Talcott Parsons on Economy and Society*, London: Routledge & Kegan Paul.

Holy, L. and Stuchlik, M. (1983) *Actions, Norms and Representations*, Cambridge: Cambridge University Press.

Homans, G. (1961) *Social Behavior*, London: Routledge & Kegan Paul.

Humphries, J. (1977) "Class struggle and the persistence of the working-class family," *Cambridge Journal of Economics* 1 (3): 241–58.

Jayyusi, L. (1984) *Categorization and the Moral Order*, Boston: Routledge & Kegan Paul.

Johnson, C. (1974) "Gift giving and reciprocity among the Japanese Americans in Honolulu," *American Ethnologist* 1 (2): 295–308.

(1977) "Interdependence, reciprocity and indebtedness: an analysis of

Japanese American kinship relations," *Journal of Marriage and the Family* 39 (2): 351–63.

Josephides, L. (1985) *The Production of Inequality*, London: Tavistock.

Kaye, V. (1975) *Dictionary of Ukrainian Canadian Biography: Pioneer Settlers of Manitoba 1891–1900*, Toronto: Ukrainian Canadian Research Foundation.

Kellner, D. (1983) "Critical theory, commodities and the consumer society," *Theory, Culture and Society* 1 (3): 66–83.

Klymasz, R. (1970) "Ukrainian folklore in Canada," Ph.D. thesis submitted to Indiana University.

Kobrin, F. (1976) "The primary individual and the family," *Journal of Marriage and the Family* 38 (2): 233–9.

Kuhn, A. (1978) "Structures of patriarchy and capital in the family," in A. Kuhn and A. Wolpe (eds) *Feminism and Materialism*, London: Routledge & Kegan Paul.

Kuz, T. (1979) *Winnipeg: A Multivariate Analysis, 1951, 1961, and 1971*, Winnipeg: City of Winnipeg Development Plan Review.

Land, H. (1983) "Poverty and gender: the distribution of resources within the family," in M. Brown (ed.) *The Structure of Disadvantage*, London: Heinemann.

Lebra, T. (1969) "Reciprocity and the asymmetric principle," *Psychologia* 12 (3–4): 129–38.

—— (1976) *Japanese Patterns of Behavior*, Honolulu: University Press of Hawaii.

Lee, G. (1985) "Kinship and social support of the elderly," *Ageing and Society* 5 (1): 19–38.

Leiss, W. (1976) *The Limits to Satisfaction*, Toronto: University of Toronto Press.

Leonard, D. (1980) *Sex and Generation*, London: Tavistock.

Leonard, D. and Speakman, M. (1986) "Women in the family: companions or caretakers?" in V. Beechey and E. Whitelegg (eds) *Women in Britain Today*, Milton Keynes: Open University Press.

Lévi-Strauss, C. (1969) *The Elementary Structures of Kinship*, Boston: Beacon.

Linton, R. (1936) *The Study of Man*, New York: Appleton-Century.

Litwak, E. (1985) *Helping the Elderly*, New York: Guilford.

Litwak, E. and Szelenyi, I. (1969) "Primary group structures and their functions: kin, neighbors, and friends," *American Sociological Review* 34 (4): 465–81.

Long, N. (1958) "The local community as an ecology of games," *American Journal of Sociology* 64 (3): 251–61.

Lowenthal, M. (1975) "The social economy in urban working-class communities," in G. Gappert and H. Rose (eds) *The Social Economy of Cities*, Beverly Hills: Sage.

Lowes, B., Turner, J., and Wills, G. (1971) "Patterns of gift giving," in G. Wills (ed.) *Exploration in Marketing Thought*, Bradford: Bradford University Press.

Luckmann, B. (1978) "The small life-worlds of modern man," in T.

Luckmann (ed.) *Phenomenology and Sociology*, Harmondsworth: Penguin.

Luhmann, N. (1976) "Generalized media and the problem of contingency," in J. Loubser, R. Baum, A. Effrat, and V. M. Lidz (eds) *Explorations in General Theory in Social Science*, vol. 2, New York: Free Press.

(1979) *Trust and Power*, Chichester: Wiley.

(1982) *The Differentiation of Society*, New York: Columbia University Press.

Lukes, S. (1973) *Emile Durkheim*, London: Allen Lane.

Lüschen, G. (1972) "Family interaction with kin and the function of ritual," *Journal of Comparative Family Studies* 3 (1): 84–98.

Lüschen, G., Staikof, Z., Stolte Heiskanen, V., and Ward, C. (1972) "Family, ritual and secularization," *Social Compass* 19 (4): 519–36.

Lux, A. (1972) "Gift exchange and income redistribution between Yombe rural wage-earners and their kinsfolk in western Zaïre," *Africa* 42 (3): 173–91.

Luxton, M. (1980) *More Than a Labour of Love*, Toronto: Women's Press.

McConnel, C. and Deljavan, F. (1983) "Consumption patterns of the retired household," *Journal of Gerontology* 38 (4): 480–90.

McCracken, G. (1985) "Culture and consumption I: a theoretical account of the structure and content of the cultural meaning of consumer goods," *Consumer Studies Working Paper Series* 85–102, University of Guelph.

Macfarlane, A. (1979) *The Origins of English Individualism*, New York: Cambridge University Press.

Maffesoli, M. (1979) *La Conquête du Présent*, Paris: Presses Universitaires de France.

Marchak, P. (1985) "Canadian political economy," *Canadian Review of Sociology and Anthropology* 22 (5): 673–709.

Marx, K. and Engels, F. (1962) "Manifesto of the Communist Party," in K. Marx and F. Engels *Selected Works*, vol. 1, Moscow: Foreign Languages Publishing House.

Mauss, M. (1954) *The Gift*, Glencoe: Free Press.

Mehan, H. (1982) "Le constructivisme social en psychologie et en sociologie," *Sociologie et Sociétés* 14 (2): 77–96.

Meillassoux, C. (1981) *Maidens, Meal and Money*, Cambridge: Cambridge University Press.

Miles, A. (1985) "Economism and feminism: hidden in the household," in P. Armstrong, H. Armstrong, P. Connelly and A. Miles *Feminist Marxism or Marxist Feminism*, Toronto: Garamond.

Mitchell, J. C. (1983) "Case and situation analysis," *Sociological Review* 31 (2): 187–211.

Munn, N. (1973) "Symbolism in a ritual context," in J. Honigmann (ed.) *Handbook of Social and Cultural Anthropology*, Chicago: Rand McNally.

Murdock, G. (1947) "Bifurcate merging: a test of five theories," *American Anthropologist* 49 (1): 56–68.

Overing, J. (1986) "Men control women? The 'Catch 22' in the analysis of gender," *International Journal of Moral and Social Studies* 1 (2): 135–56.

Pahl, J. (1983) "The allocation of money and the structuring of inequality within marriage," *Sociological Review* 31 (2): 237–62.

—— (in press) *Money and Marriage*, London: Macmillan.

Parsons, T. (1949) *The Structure of Social Action*, Glencoe: Free Press.

—— (1951) *The Social System*, Glencoe: Free Press.

—— (1966) *Societies*, Englewood Cliffs: Prentice-Hall.

—— (1967) *Sociological Theory and Modern Society*, New York: Free Press.

—— (1977) *Social Systems and the Evolution of Action Theory*, New York: Free Press.

Parsons, T. and Bales, R. (1955) *Family, Socialization and Interaction Process*, Glencoe: Free Press.

Parsons, T. and Shils, E. (1962) "The social system," in T. Parsons and E. Shils (eds) *Toward a General Theory of Action*, New York: Harper & Row.

Pedraza-Bailey, S. (1982) "Talcott Parsons and structural Marxism: functionalist theories of society," in S. McNall (ed.) *Current Perspectives in Social Theory*, vol. 3, Greenwich, CT: JAI Press.

Peter, K. and Whitaker, I. (1981) "The acquisition of personal property among Hutterites and its social dimensions," *Anthropologica* 23 (2): 145–55.

Pitcher, G. (1964) *The Philosophy of Wittgenstein*, Englewood Cliffs, NJ: Prentice-Hall.

Plakans, A. (1984) *Kinship in the Past*, Oxford: Blackwell.

Polanyi, K. (1957) *The Great Transformation*, Boston: Beacon.

Reiss, I. (1965) "The universality of the family: a conceptual analysis," *Journal of Marriage and the Family* 27 (4): 443–53.

Reiter, R. (1975) "Men and women in the south of France: public and private domains," in R. Reiter (ed.) *Toward an Anthropology of Women*, New York: Monthly Review Press.

Richardson, R. J. and Wellman, B. (1985) "Structural analysis," *Canadian Review of Sociology and Anthropology* 22 (5): 771–93.

Riches, D. (1981) "The obligation to give," in L. Holy and M. Stuchlik (eds) *The Structure of Folk Models*, London: Academic Press.

Riley, M. (1983) "The family in an aging society: a matrix of latent relationships," *Journal of Family Issues* 4 (3): 439–54.

Ritzer, G. (1985) "The rise of micro-sociological theory," *Sociological Theory* 3 (1): 88–98.

Rogerson, A. (1969) *Millions Now Living Will Never Die*, London: Constable.

Rosenthal, C. (1985) "Kinkeeping in the familial division of labor," *Journal of Marriage and the Family* 47 (4): 965–74.

Sahlins, M. (1972) *Stone Age Economics*, Chicago: Aldine-Atherton.

—— (1976) *Culture and Practical Reason*, Chicago: University of Chicago Press.

Salaff, J. (1981) *Working Daughters of Hong Kong*, Cambridge: Cambridge University Press.

Sarason, I. and Sarason, B. (eds) (1985) *Social Support*, Dordrecht: Martinus Nijhoff.

Sarsby, J. (1983) *Romantic Love and Society*, Harmondsworth: Penguin.

Schwartz, B. (1967) "The social psychology of the gift," *American Journal of Sociology* 73 (1): 1–11.

Scott, J. (1976) *The Moral Economy of the Peasant*, New Haven: Yale University Press.

Shanas, E. (1980) "Older people and their families: the new pioneers," *Journal of Marriage and the Family* 42 (1): 9–15.

Shibutani, T. (1955) "Reference groups as perspectives," *American Journal of Sociology* 60 (6): 562–9.

Shurmer, P. (1971) "The gift game," *New Society* 18 (482): 1242–4.

Simmel, G. (1978) *The Philosophy of Money*, London: Routledge & Kegan Paul.

Smart, C. and Smart, B. (1978) *Women, Sexuality and Social Control*, London: Routledge & Kegan Paul.

Smelt, S. (1980) "Money's place in society," *British Journal of Sociology*, 31 (2): 204–23.

Smith, D. (1973) "Women, the family and corporate capitalism," in M. Stephenson (ed.) *Women in Canada*, Toronto: New Press.

Smith, J., Wallerstein, I., and Evers, H-D. (1984) *Households and the World-Economy*, Beverly Hills: Sage.

Smith-Rosenberg, C. (1975) "The female world of love and ritual," *Signs* 1 (1): 1–29.

Stacey, M. (1981) "The division of labour revisited or overcoming the two Adams," in P. Abrams, R. Deem, J. Finch, and P. Rock (eds) *Practice and Progress: British Sociology 1950–1980*, London: Allen & Unwin.

Stephens, R., Blau, Z. S., Oser, G., and Millar, M. (1978) "Aging, social support systems, and social policy," *Journal of Gerontological Social Work* 1 (1): 33–45.

Stokes, R. and Hewitt, J. (1976) "Aligning actions," *American Sociological Review* 41 (5): 838–49.

Strathern, A. (1979) "Gender, ideology and money in Mount Hagen," *Man* n.s. 14 (3): 530–48.

Strathern, M. (1981) *Kinship at the Core*, Cambridge: Cambridge University Press.

Stroup, H. (1945) *The Jehovah's Witnesses*, New York: Columbia University Press.

Sussman, M. (1970) "The urban kin network in the formulation of family theory," in R. Hill and R. König (eds) *Families in East and West*, The Hague: Mouton.

Suttles, G. (1968) *The Social Order of the Slum*, Chicago: University of Chicago Press.

Swanson, G. (1960) *The Birth of the Gods*, Ann Arbor: University of Michigan Press.

Thomason, B. (1982) *Making Sense of Reification*, Atlantic Highlands, NJ: Humanities Press.

Thompson, E. P. (1971) "The moral economy of the English crowd in the eighteenth century," *Past and Present* 50: 76–136.

Thorne, B. (1982) "Feminist rethinking of the family," in B. Thorne and M. Yalom (eds) *Rethinking the Family*, New York: Longman.

Tiryakian, E. (1985) "On the significance of de-differentiation," in S. N. Eisenstadt and H. J. Helle (eds) *Macro-Sociological Theory*, London: Sage.

Turnbull, C. (1972) *The Mountain People*, New York: Simon & Schuster.

Turner, B. (1986) "Parsons and his critics: on the ubiquity of functionalism," in R. Holton and B. Turner *Talcott Parsons on Economy and Society*, London: Routledge & Kegan Paul.

Turner, J. C. (1982) "Towards a cognitive redefinition of the social group," in H. Tajfel (ed.) *Social Identity and Intergroup Relations*, Cambridge: Cambridge University Press.

Turner, J. C. and Oakes, P. (1986) "The significance of the social identity concept for social psychology with reference to individualism, interactionism and social influence," *British Journal of Social Psychology* 25 (3): 237–52.

Turner, J. H. (1986) *The Structure of Sociological Theory*, 4th edn, Chicago: Dorsey.

Turner, V. (1969) *The Ritual Process*, Chicago: Aldine.

Unruh, D. (1983) *Invisible Lives*, Beverly Hills: Sage.

van Gennep, A. (1960) *The Rites of Passage*, Chicago: University of Chicago Press.

van Velsen, J. (1967) "The extended-case method and situational analysis," in A. L. Epstein (ed.) *The Craft of Social Anthropology*, London: Tavistock.

Veblen, T. (1918) *The Theory of the Leisure Class*, New York: Huebsch.

Wadel, C. (1979) "The hidden work of everyday life," in S. Wallman (ed.) *Social Anthropology of Work*, London: Academic Press.

Wargon, S. (1979) *Canadian Households and Families*, Ottawa: Statistics Canada.

Wearing, B. (1984) *The Ideology of Motherhood*, Sydney: Allen & Unwin.

Weber, M. (1947) *The Theory of Social and Economic Organization*, Glencoe: Free Press.

——— (1948) "The social psychology of the world religions," in H. H. Gerth and C. Wright Mills (eds) *From Max Weber*, London: Routledge & Kegan Paul.

——— (1949) *The Methodology of the Social Sciences*, New York: Free Press.

——— (1958) *The Protestant Ethic and the Spirit of Capitalism*, New York: Scribner.

——— (1965) *The Sociology of Religion*, London: Methuen.

——— (1968) *Economy and Society*, vol. 1, New York: Bedminster.

Webley, P., Lea, S., and Portalska, R. (1983) "The unacceptability of money as a gift," *Journal of Economic Psychology* 4 (3): 223–38.

Weigert, A. and Hastings, R. (1977) "Identity loss, family, and social change," *American Journal of Sociology* 82 (6): 1171–85.

Weigert, A. and Thomas, D. (1971) "Family as a conditional universal," *Journal of Marriage and the Family* 33 (1): 188–94.

Weir, T. (1978) *Atlas of Winnipeg*, Toronto: University of Toronto Press.

Wellman, B. (1979) "The community question: the intimate networks of East Yorkers," *American Journal of Sociology* 84 (5): 1201–31.

(1981) "Applying network analysis to the study of support," in B. H. Gottlieb (ed.) *Social Networks and Social Support*, Beverly Hills: Sage.

(1982) "Studying personal communities," in P. V. Marsden and N. Lin (eds) *Social Structure and Network Analysis*, Beverly Hills: Sage.

(1983) "Network analysis: some basic principles," in R. Collins (ed.) *Sociological Theory 1983*, San Francisco: Jossey-Bass.

Wellman, B., Craven, P., Whitaker, M., Stevens, H., Shorter, A., Du Toit, S., and Bakker, H. (1973) "Community ties and support systems: from intimacy to support," in L. S. Bourne, R. D. Mac-Kinnon, and J. W. Simmons (eds) *The Form of Cities in Central Canada*, Toronto: University of Toronto Press.

Wellman, B. and Hall, A. (1986) "Social networks and social support: implications for later life," in V. Marshall (ed.) *Later Life*, Beverly Hills: Sage.

Wenger, G. C. (1984) *The Supportive Network*, London: Allen & Unwin.

Westwood, S. (1984) *All Day Every Day*, London: Pluto Press.

Williams, R. G. A. (1981) "The art of migration: the preservation of kinship and friendship by Londoners during a history of movement," *Sociological Review* 29 (4): 621–47.

(1983) "Kinship and migration strategies among settled Londoners: two responses to population pressure," *British Journal of Sociology* 34 (3): 386–415.

Wilson, M. (1957) *Rituals of Kinship Among the Nyakyusa*, London: Oxford University Press.

Winch, P. (1958) *The Idea of a Social Science*, London: Routledge & Kegan Paul.

Wolff, K. (1950) *The Sociology of Georg Simmel*, New York: Free Press.

Wood, J. (1982) "Communication and relational culture," *Communication Quarterly* 30 (2): 75–83.

Yanagisako, S. (1979) "Family and household: the analysis of domestic groups," in Bernard Siegel (ed.) *Annual Review of Anthropology*, vol. 8. Palo Alto, CA: Annual Reviews Inc.

Yeatman, A. (1984) "Gender and the differentiation of social life into public and domestic domains," *Social Analysis* 15 (August): 32–49.

Zelizer, V. R. (1979) *Morals and Markets*, New York: Columbia University Press.

Name index

Subject index